The Jastorf Culture in Poland

Zenon Woźniak
Michał Grygiel
Henryk Machajewski
Andrzej Michałowski

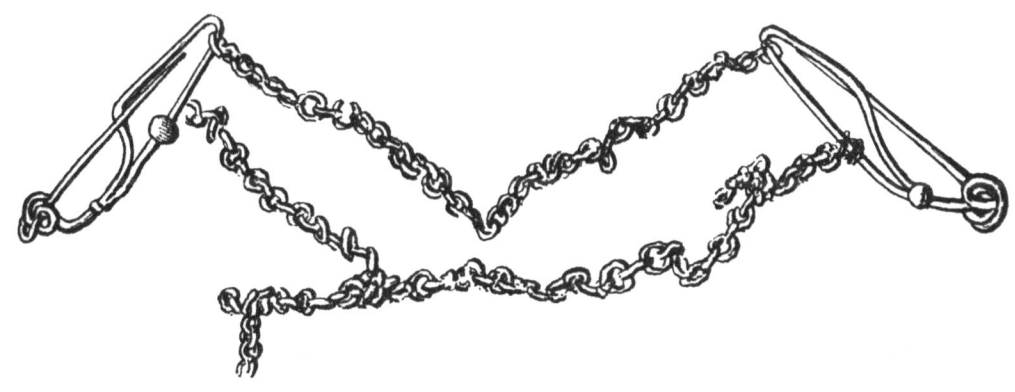

BAR International Series 2579
2013

Published in 2016 by
BAR Publishing, Oxford

BAR International Series 2579

The Jastorf Culture in Poland

ISBN 978 1 4073 1202 6

© The authors individually and the Publisher 2013

The authors' moral rights under the 1988 UK Copyright,
Designs and Patents Act are hereby expressly asserted.

All rights reserved. No part of this work may be copied, reproduced, stored,
sold, distributed, scanned, saved in any form of digital format or transmitted
in any form digitally, without the written permission of the Publisher.

BAR Publishing is the trading name of British Archaeological Reports (Oxford) Ltd.
British Archaeological Reports was first incorporated in 1974 to publish the BAR
Series, International and British. In 1992 Hadrian Books Ltd became part of the BAR
group. This volume was originally published by Archaeopress in conjunction with
British Archaeological Reports (Oxford) Ltd / Hadrian Books Ltd, the Series principal
publisher, in 2013. This present volume is published by BAR Publishing, 2016.

Printed in England

BAR
PUBLISHING

BAR titles are available from:

BAR Publishing
122 Banbury Rd, Oxford, OX2 7BP, UK
EMAIL   info@barpublishing.com
PHONE   +44 (0)1865 310431
FAX   +44 (0)1865 316916
www.barpublishing.com

Contents

Introduction 1
Andrzej Michałowski

Chapter 1
The Middle of the 1st Millennium. The Role of Celts and Jastorf Culture in Cultural and Ethnic
Changes in the Lands of Poland in the Latter Half of the 1st Millennium BC 5
Zenon Woźniak

Chapter 2
The Jastorf Culture on the Polish Lowland 23
Michał Grygiel

Chapter 3
The Jastorf Culture in Northwest Poland 47
Henryk Machajewski

Chapter
Jastorf Culture in Wielkopolska 61
Andrzej Michałowski

Conclusion 70
Henryk Machajewski

Catalogue of Jastorf culture sites from the Northwest Poland... 72
Henryk Machajewski and Andrzej Michałowski

Bibliography 84

List of Figures

Fig. 1 The Jastorf Culture after Seyer 1976, with additions. 3
Fig. 2. Map of the fibulae of Ha D3 type. 5
Fig. 3. Map of the fibulae dated back to LT A phase and fibulae of Kowalowice type. 6
Fig. 4. The Celtic finds in south-east Poland. 10
Fig. 5. The Celtic finds in the teritory of Moldavia. 10
Fig. 6. Significant sites and settlement zones of Jastorf culture in Central and South Poland. 13
Fig. 7. Main types of pottery linked with the older phase of Jastorf culture setlements in Brześć Kujawski, site 3 and 4 (after Grygiel 2004). 14
Fig. 8. Examples of pottery linked with the younger phase of Jastorf culture setlements in Brześć Kujawski, site 4 (after Grygiel 2004). 14
Fig. 9. Settlement and burial ground the Jastorf culture on Polish Lowland 24
Fig. 10. Finds the Jastorf culture on Polish Lowland 25
Fig. 11 Jastorf culture dish - a vase with a separate neck. 26
Fig. 12. Jastorf culture dish - a vase without a neck. 27
Fig. 13. Jastorf culture dish - goblet and cups of spherical or barrel belly and small, cone-shaped cups or goblet. 29
Fig. 14. Jastorf culture dish – bowls with outside deflected edge. 30
Fig. 15. Jastorf culture dish - bowl without the lip. 31
Fig. 16. Jastorf culture dish –pots 32
Fig. 17. Jastorf culture dish – storage pots. 34
Fig. 18. Celtic origin iron brooches found in Jastorf culture graves. 38
Fig. 19. Bronze finds with the Jastorf culture origin from Poland. 41
Fig. 20. Jastorf culture settlement in northwest Poland. 48
Fig. 21. Chronology of selected Jastorf culture sites in northwest Poland 50
Fig. 22. Group I of Jastorf culture ceramics in northwest Poland. 51
Fig. 23. Group II of Jastorf culture ceramics in northwest Poland 52
Fig. 24. Group III of Jastorf culture ceramics in northwest Poland. 53
Fig. 25. Distribution of Zachow type fibulae in northwest Poland. 54
Fig. 26. Distribution of neck rings with cylindrically thickened ends in northwest Poland. 55
Fig. 27. Distribution of winged pins with a perpendicular plate in northwest Poland. 56
Fig. 28. Distribution of fibulae with a pair of beads reminiscent of types A and B according to Kostrzewski (1919) in northwest Poland. 57
Fig. 29. Distribution of crown neck rings, following Kostrzewski's typology (1919), in northwest Polande. ... 59
Fig. 30. Individual stone-curbed graves 1., 2. Koninko (after Blume 1911); 3. Wierzenica 62
Fig. 31. The pre-Roman Iron Age pottery forms from Wierzenica (after Kostrzewski 1919-1920). 62
Fig. 32. Jastorf pins from Wielkopolska. 63
Fig. 33. Distribution of fibulae with pellet-decorated bow in Wielkopolska. 63
Fig. 34. Distribution of fibulae with a step-like bow in Wielkopolska. 64
Fig. 35. Crown-shaped torques (*Kronenhalsringe*) 64
Fig. 36. Kuźnica Żelichowska. Single-partite band belt buckles (after Gałezowska 1996). 65
Fig. 37. Chain pendant with two fibulae from Kostrzewski's type A from Rosko, site 7 65
Fig. 38. Equipment from grave 41 in Sokołowice (after Łuka 1953). 66
Fig. 40. Horse-headed buckles from Wielkopolska. 66
Fig. 39. Equipment from grave 1 in Biała (after Kostrzewski 1923). 66
Fig. 41. Hinged belt buckles from Wszedzień (after Michałowski 2005). 66
Fig. 42. Distribution of fire wolves in Wielkopolska. 67
Fig. 43. Distribution of clay spoons in Wielkopolska. 68
Fig. 44. Wszedzień: 1. Bornholm-type fibula; 2., 3. decorated fibulae with beads (after Michałowski 2008). ... 69

Introduction

Andrzej Michałowski

The middle of the 1st millennium BC was a major turning point in the history of Europe's interior. It was then that the might and domination of the Hallstatt culture faded away. Until then, the elites of this culture, controlling Alpine salt deposits, accumulated wealth by supplying salt to the civilizations of the Mediterranean. The Hallstatt elites set the tone for the whole of this cultural circle and were responsible for its domination in the foothills of the Alps and along the middle Danube. The more so as the Hallstatt culture was the first in the continent's interior to master the production of iron. Their descendants – historical Celts related to the La Tène culture (from the site of La Tène on Swiss Lake Neuchâtel) – by improving on the skills of their forefathers became masters of black metallurgy, which laid the foundations for their greatness. The revolution of the 5th century BC, having abolished tribal aristocracy settling the area between the Alps and the Danube, moved the centres of power to the homes of new elites located on the Marne and Mosel rivers, and in Bohemia.

The time when Celts dominated and the Iron Age civilization flourished in Europe is referred to as the La Tène period. In principle, it corresponded to the second half of the 1st millennium BC. The rise of the La Tène civilization coincided with the golden age of Greek colonies and, consequently, with the zenith of their trade with the 'barbarian' hinterland. The Greeks, whose civilization had already entered the period of written history, left us a written record of the world they lived in. In it, a prominent place was occupied by Celts, emerging from the mists of time. In ancient records, Celts are recognized by their lifestyle, political institutions and appearance. The language they spoke did not interest contemporary chroniclers as for the Greeks it was a matter of little importance. For it was commonly known that all non-Greek peoples spoke simply a barbarian language. The result was that under the name of Celts, known to the Greeks, other peoples of 'barbarian' Europe could well have been meant.

In some areas, in Europe's interior and in the north of the continent, where the Nordic Bronze Age dominated as late as the turn of the 6th century BC and whose traditions went back deep into the Bronze Age, in parallel with the transformations taking place in the Celtic world, cultures harking back to the traditions of the Hallstatt period thrived. In consequence, the times corresponding to the Celt domination in the south of the European *Barbaricum* (i.e. the La Tène period), here were called the Pre-Roman period, which kept its own dynamics of development and civilization changes despite being correlated with La Tène phases (Hachmann 1961).

On the substrate of these transformations, changes in the Jastorf culture occurred. This culture, as a result of revived southern influence, encompassed that part of Europe which lies between the Weser River, south Jutland, the lower Elbe and Oder rivers, in the zone where the impact of the Iron Age civilization could be felt. In effect, a new style developed, visible in pottery, metal dress elements and funerary rites, resembling the traditions of the Hallstatt world but at the same time making north Germany culturally different (Schwantes 1950:119-130).

Initially, the name of Jastorf culture referred exclusively to the lands on the lower Elbe, in the environs of Uelzen and Lüneburg. For it was there that in 1897 Gustav Schwantes excavated an urn cemetery in the village of Jastorf, Uelzen district, Lower Saxony. The investigations, carried out with his brother Carl, of the cemeteries in Jastorf, Ripdorf and Seedorf, allowed Schwantes to draft a preliminary scheme of the development of local communities in the Pre-Roman period (Schwantes 1904, 1911), while the names of these sites became eponyms for the chronological phases he had distinguished.

The first horizon was called the Wessenstested phase by Schwantes who considered it the beginning of the Early Iron Age and correlated it with the VI period of the Bronze Age according to Montelius. As its markers, he used forms of graves and grave goods discovered at a cemetery in Bromberge near Wessenstedt (Meyer 1897). The burials at the cemetery had been placed under flat barrows or were flat urn graves with or without a stone lining. Among the grave goods were ceramic vessels with tall necks, bearing an ornament typical of the late Lusatian culture – horizontal circular grooves, zigzags, furrows, and sequences of impressed pits. Metal goods included chiefly swan's neck pins (among them specimens made of iron), various rings and knives.

The second horizon was concurrent with the Jastorf phase which Schwantes treated as an effect of the adaptation of Hallstatt culture elements by local communities. Relying on the observations he had made on the cemetery in Jastorf (Schwantes 1904), he claimed that the horizon was exclusively characterized by flat urn graves with a heavy stone lining. The urns themselves could have been covered by special flat stones. The variability of micro-morphological division of ceramic vessels found in Jastorf graves persuaded Schwantes to break up the Jastorf phase into three successive styles (a-c). This division has been used until today (Müller 2000: 47) and is used in this study. Style Jastorf 'a' is characterized by single-shape vessels with an inverted lip. Style Jastorf 'b' is distinguished by two-shape vessels with a strongly marked and everted rim.

Among them are blackened and carefully burnished urns of the *Todendorf*-type. Style Jastorf 'c', in turn, is set apart by clearly shortened necks and a noticeable division of the upper parts of vessels into three shapes. This distinct division of the ceramic material made Schwantes, while designing his categories, give up the strict assigning of metal objects to the styles he distinguished. This is particularly true for styles 'a' and 'b'. As typical of both styles, tongue buckles (*Zungengürtelhaken*) are considered as well as bent-stem pins (*Kropfnadeln*), plate fibulae (*Platenfibeln*), drum fibulae (*Paukenfibeln*), and band fibulae (*Bandfibeln*). The main distinguishing traits of style Jastorf 'c', in turn, are buckles with a perpendicular fastening plate (*Haftarmgürtelhaken*), belt rings as well as Holstein pins (*Holsteiner Nadeln*).

The third, Ripdorf horizon was defined by Schwantes as an effect of mixing La Tène influence with the local post-Hallstatt sub-stratum. The data for its description, Schwantes found on the cemetery in Ripsdorf (Schwantes 1958). This horizon shows clear affinities with style Jastorf 'c'. Specifically, Holstein pins and belt buckles continue to be found in it. What sets it apart from Jastorf 'c', however, is the strongly noticeable presence of La Tène influence, visible especially in the fibulae of early and middle La Tène designs. In pottery, tall profiled pots, typical of the Jastorf stage, are replaced with vase-shaped vessels and bowls.

The last, fourth horizon was called Seedorf by Schwantes after the Schweizerhof cemetery explored there (Schwantes 1909). What makes it special is a further decline of traditional Jastorf forms under a strong La Tène impact. At that time, cemeteries began to feature urn graves without any stone structures or ceramic add-ons. Urns, often *situlate* in shape, are not covered with lids. The pottery of this phase has frequently faceted rims and sometimes bears an ornament of lines and dots. Metal inventories are dominated by belt buckles and late La Tène fibulae. Graves begin to feature weapons too.

With time, the term Jastorf culture became synonymous with the changes that constituted cultural transformations, taking place at the end of the Hallstatt and in the La Tène periods in central and northern Europe. The term Jastorf civilization (Schwantes 1950) contributed towards a far-reaching integration of the way central European *Barbaricum* was perceived. Thereby the concept of Jastorf culture became much broader and encompassed areas neighbouring on its original homeland, i.e. the lands located between the Weser River, southern Jutland, and the lower Elbe and Oder rivers (Fig. 1). The Jastorf group (referred to also as the Lower Elbe group – *Unterelbe-Gruppe* - Seyer 1976: 191, 192), thereby became one of the local groups of the formation so defined. Apart from it, the formation's zone of compact settlement comprises a further eight territorial units:

- North, Middle and South Jutland groups living on the Jutland Peninsula. The South Jutland group stands apart here by the presence of barrow cemeteries. The South and Middle Jutland vessel pottery typically features bowl rim ornaments and pots with a handle placed inside. There also appears a custom of making holes in the bottoms and walls of already fired vessels. A common element is also clay figurines – *Feuerböcke*. Among metal goods, distinctive forms include local varieties of Holstein pins and fibulae as well as triangular belt buckles (Becker 1969; Martens 1992a). In the north of Jutland, there develops a group featuring a special variety of ceramic forms, known as the so-called Kraghede group (Martens 1994a; 1997, 1998).

- The Warnow-Oder group (*Wa-rnow-Odermündungs-Gruppe*) covers areas located between Schweriner See and the mouth of the Oder River, and east of the lower course of this river (West Pomerania[1]). The leading forms of this group include Pomerania fibulae (*Pommerische Fibeln*), *Rautennadel, Kreuzkopfnadeln*, classical forms of winged pins (*Flügenadeln*), and three-piece belt buckles. A distinctive trait of pottery is particularly tall, funnel shaped necks in pot- and vase-shaped vessels (Keiling 1968).

- The Lakeland group (*Seengruppe*) occupies the Mecklenburg Lakeland, south of Plauersee, Tollensesee and Lake Müritz. The markers of this group include *Flügenadeln* with perpendicular plates, *Sanduhrkropfnadeln*, Zach-ow-type fibulae, and late La Tène-design fibulae with H-shaped enamel inlays (*Spätlatènefiebeln mit Emaileeinlagen in H-Form*). As far as pottery is concerned, single-handle pots with a bow-like rim are typical here (Keiling 1969).

- The Middle Elbe-Havel group (*Mit-telelbe-Havel-Gruppe*) occupies the territory of present-day Branden-burg between the middle Elbe and Havel rivers. Forms typical of the group are those drawing on Hallstatt traditions such as band, shield and sail earrings (*Bandohringe, Schildohringe, Segelohringe*), fibulae with chains (*Posamenteriefiebeln*), bronze drum fibulae (*Doppelpaukenfiebel*), iron band fibulae (*Bandfibeln*), iron pins with a bronze biconical head, shield pins (*Schieldnadeln*), late La Tène-design fibulae with a step-like bow (*Fibel von Spätlatènschema mit stufenformigem Bügel*), and *Ringplattengürtelhaken*. Among the ceramic materials, a common find is a clay spoon (Seyer 1982).

- The Elbe-Saale group (*Elbe-Saale-Gruppe*) had its settlements located primarily on the Black Elster, Elbe, Mulde and Saale rivers. This area felt the

---

[1] The territory of this group, lying east of the Oder River within the borders of present-day Poland, was named the Oder group by Wołągiewicz (1970).

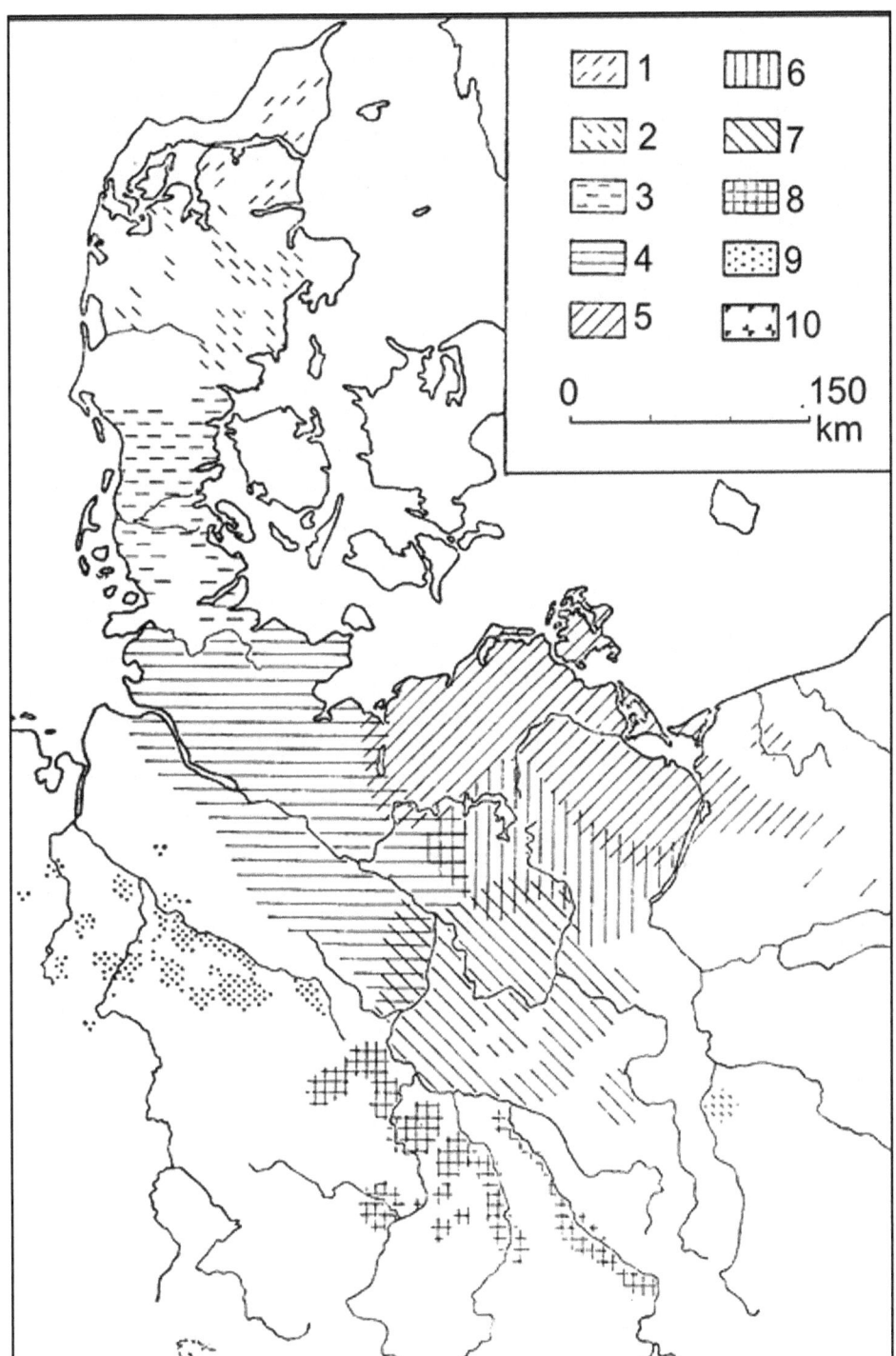

Fig. 1 The Jastorf Culture after Seyer 1976, with additions.
Legend: 1. North Jutland group; 2. Middle Jutland group; 3. South Jutland group; 4. Jastorf group; 5. Warnow-Oder group; 6. Lakeland group; 7. Middle Elbe-Havel group; 8. Elbe-Saale group; 9. Harpsted-Nienburg group; 10. Gubin group.

strong impact of the Celtic world, coming chiefly from southern Thuringia whose centre was the *oppidum* in Steinsburg. Doubtless because of that, besides goods typical of the whole Jastorf culture, distinctive forms of this group include spur belt buckles (*Sporengürtelhaken*), buckles with animal heads, coral inlaid buckles (*Korallenfiebeln*), tutulus pins (*Tutulusnadeln*), and chain belts. In ceramic materials, there appear wheel-turned vessels, bearing an ornament of horizontal grooves, and Braubach-type bowls (R. Müller 1985).

- The Gubin group (*Gubbiner Gruppe*) occupies two small, compact areas separated by a settlement vacuum. The first is located on both banks of the Lusatian Neisse River, extending from where it empties into the Oder River to the lower course of the Lubsza and Wodra rivers. The other spans both banks of the Oder, north of the Dalków Hills (*Wzgórza Dalkowskie*). Its materials include sail earrings, necklaces with bowl ends, buckles with raised edges, middle La Tène-design fibulae, both with globes and those of type A according to Kostrzewski (Domański 1975).

Besides the assemblages listed here, within the broad Jastorf circle the Harpsted-Nienburg group is also included, which took shape in the northwest of the German Geest, between the Lower Elbe and Ems, but displayed great geographical dif-ferences. Its eastern branch, known as the Nienburger group (*Nienburger Gruppe*), strongly gravitates towards the Jastorf culture from its location on the Weser and Aller rivers. Among its typical forms are Jastorf tongue buckles (*Zungegürtelhaken*), bent-stem pins (*Kropfnadeln*), sail earrings (*Segel-ohrringe*), and local disc earrings (*Schei-benohrringe*). Characteristic ceramic artefacts include Nienburg cups, pots with a corrugated rim of the Harpstedt type, Launingen vessels, and lids with a pair of openings on the rim (Gensen 1963; Tackenberg 1934; Zoller 1963). On the peripheries of the Jastorf world, one may refer to the Danish Isles and southern Sweden, where forms showing affinities with the cultural circle in question occur (Becker 1969: 271-80).

In spite of territorial differences and certain local variation noticeable in the communities making up these regional settlement clusters, it is abundantly clear that they underwent the same transformations, keeping not only an analogous artefact style but also a common system of values. The latter is seen, for one thing, in a similar cremation funerary rite. They are rightly treated, therefore, as a component part of a larger cultural province broadly referred to as the Jastorf circle. Its adaptation to the central European civilization milieu must have been a very attractive proposal also for other communities, occupying adjoining territories. This model must have been initially disseminated through bilateral contacts (trade, political and family relations) but already in the older Pre-Roman period it started to be spread as a result of mass population movements. Whole population groups originating from Jastorf-culture-settled areas expanded in various directions. As early as the 3rd century BC, we observe the founding of Jastorf cemeteries on the Unstrut River. Expanding southwards and entering Thuringia, until then settled by Celts (Seyer 1976: 194), Jastorf populations come into direct contact with the Celtic cultural circle. The greatest upheaval, however, was the migration of Germanic tribes called the Bastarnae and the Scirii in written records. They moved to locations on the middle Seret, Prut and Dniester rivers (Babeş 1993).

The rise of the Poieneşti-Lukaševka culture in the second quarter of the 2nd century BC is related to the eastward expansion of the Jastorf culture. Owing to recent excavations, the expansion is ever more traceable in the territory of modern Poland. Particularly important in this connection, Wielkopolska, with the Noteć and Warta rivers flowing east – west, was a natural route for population groups moving east. This can perfectly explain why migrating Jastorf culture populations appeared in these very areas and why no such activity is observed in Central Pomerania, which is crossed by rivers flowing north – south, despite its close proximity to the Oder group of the Jastorf culture (Wołągiewicz 1979: 36). The Warta-Noteć route could have been attractive also because of a lower population density than that observed along the Oder River at the end of the older Pre-Roman period. In the latter area, an obstacle to migration might have been presented by the Celtic settlement in Lower Silesia. From the related populations of the Decline Pomerania culture, if only because of mutual contacts, the migrants could expect if not goodwill then at least neutrality. The neutrality of those who controlled the lands crossed by the migrants therefore was a matter they surely planned before departing. This is a basic precaution in the case of the passage of settlement groups, which are not made up of warriors only as is the case with war or looting expeditions (Michałowski, forthcoming). To be able to see the dynamics of the transformations, it is certainly necessary to determine chronological relations and successions holding between the cultural situation in Wielkopolska and Kujawy, and similar developments, taking place in the east of Poland, in the environs of Kraków (Woźniak & Poleska 1999), in the areas settled by the so-called Czerniczyn group (Czopek 1991a, 1992a, 1992b), and in Mazovia and the Lublin province, whence the materials of the provenance under discussion also come. The observed intensity of the Jastorf culture settlement activity makes some researchers suggest distinguishing a new group of this culture in part of modern Poland's territory. It is quite possible that such a group developed here beginning with the early older Pre-Roman period (Dąbrowska & Woźniak 2005: 92).

This study is thus an attempt to sum up the research carried out so far and our current knowledge on Jastorf culture populations in northwest Poland with a special focus on the distinctive traits of the Jastorf settlement in two regions: Pomerania and Wielkopolska. It aims to depict a particular qualitative breakthrough that was witnessed in Polish research into this cultural formation in the late 20th and early 21st centuries. We must be aware of course that materials of Jastorf provenance studied so far, found in the lands of present-day Poland, especially those which have been included in this study, certainly do not exhaust the list of assemblages that illustrate the issues discussed here (Dąbrowska & Woźniak 2005:92). The findings presented in this study, and above all the pool of sources, are aimed at providing a basis for discussing the cultural situation in northwest Poland in the early younger Pre-Roman period. In our opinion, the sources form a significant stepping stone for the necessary review of the current findings as to the moment when the cultural picture of the central European *Barbaricum* was taking shape in the last few centuries BC.

Chapter 1

The Middle of the 1st Millennium
The Role of Celts and Jastorf Culture in Cultural and Ethnic Changes in the Lands of Poland in the Latter Half of the 1st Millennium BC

Zenon Woźniak

The Bronze Age and the beginning of the Iron Age in the lands of present-day Poland were characterized by continuous Lusatian culture settlement and steadfast cultural traditions, as well as a permanent domination of external contacts via routes running from the south toward the north, over those extending east – west. For the majority of (present-day usunąć) Polish territory, in the Ha C and early Ha D periods, the relationships with the East Hallstatt circle were crucial. In recent years, however, attention has been drawn to a strong southeast impact or even to the likelihood of the influx of people from today's western Ukraine onto (chyba błąd) part of the Polish territory in the Early Iron Age (R. Grygiel 1995; Czopek 2007, Kłosińska 2007; Gawlik 2010).

The latter half of the 1st millennium BC, however, witnessed fundamental changes that were ushered in by the rise of Pomeranian culture in Pomerania, which sometime later, in the course of period HaD3, spread to cover most of the Polish territory that had been occupied by the Lusatian culture (except for the area forming the core of Tarnobrzeg group) and spilled into west Polissya and Volhynia, reaching as far as west Podolia (Czopek 1992a: 100, Fig. 29). The chronology of this expansion can be determined with some precision because the early versions of fibulae with an ornamented foot – *Fusszierfibeln* (Fig. 2) – are known chiefly from Lusatian culture assemblages, while their younger versions are encountered mainly in Pomeranian culture ones (Gedl 1991: 77-82, 121; 2004: 103-124; Parzinger 1993; Woźniak 1995: 202, 208, Fig. 1; 4:a-c.f; 2010, 44-59, Fig. 1-3, maps 1-2; 2011, 13, Fig. 1-2, Map 1).

It follows that this process began in early phase Ha D3 and basically ended in the beginnings of phase LT A or in the early 5th century BC.[2] The fibulae testify to the close contacts between Lusatian culture populations and areas occupied by the West Hallstatt culture, believed to be the chief archaeological representative of the Celts. The contacts, continued by the populations of the Pomeranian culture and doubtless greatly facilitated by the settlement centre at Kleine Gleichberge bei Römhild in south Thuringia, replaced traditional relations with the south via the so-called amber route, i.e. across the Moravian Gate, which lost its importance due to Scythian invasions

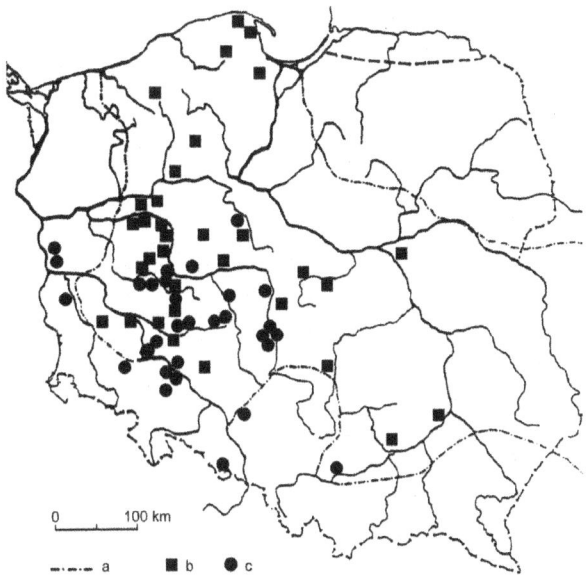

Fig. 2. Map of the fibulae of Ha D3 type.
Legend: a. the range of Pomerania culture; b. Pomeranian culture fibulae; c. Lusatian culture fibulae

(Bukowski 1978; Gedl 1985: 38-43; 1991: 121). Curiously enough, "Pome-ranian blacksmiths", who were active in the new areas – in south Wielkopolska and Silesia – gradually started making iron fibulae instead of bronze ones. In the middle section of LT A, these ornaments were made solely from iron (Kowalowice fibulae known also as *Altmarkische-* or *Bandfibeln*, specimens of Piekary Wielkie type and those with a "stylized duck head").

The contacts of Pomeranian culture populations with the La Tène culture are borne out by La Tène-style artefacts, belonging to phase LT A (imports, in part local products), which are known from 'Pomeranian' assemblages. The latter are the most numerous in Silesia but are found also in Wielkopolska, Małopolska, central Poland and in rare cases in Pomerania (Woźniak 1995: 202, 209, Fig. 2; 4:e; 5:g,h; 2010: 62-74, Fig. 4-7, maps 3, 4). Among them, a group of open-work artefacts merits attention. They exhibit an early Celtic art style and ere found in Pomerania culture assemblages in Silesia and Pomerania (Fig. 3), which can be linked in principle, to the middle section of phase LT A. These are iron belt buckles of the Hochscheid–Linz type found in Bobrowice, Żagań district, Bojano, Wejherowo district, Gogolewo, Tczew district, Wrocław Księże

---
[2] The absolute dates given here are based on the findings by Trachsel (2004).

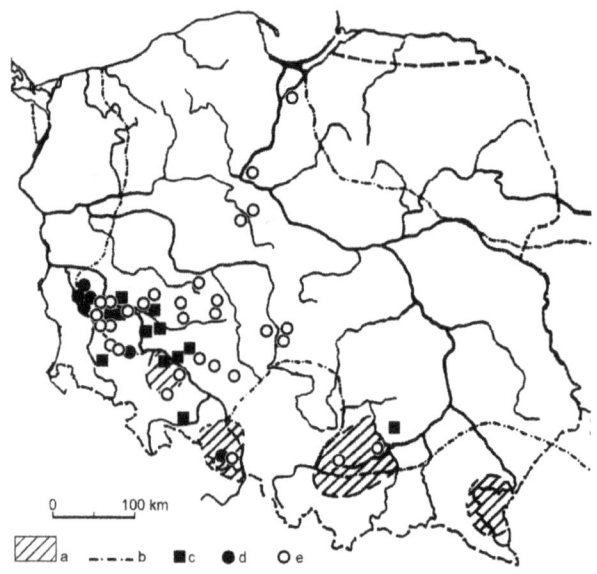

FIG. 3. MAP OF THE FIBULAE DATED BACK TO LT A PHASE AND FIBULAE OF KOWALOWICE TYPE.
LEGENDS: A CELTIC SETTLEMENT ZONES; B. THE RANGE OF POMERANIAN CULTURE TERRITORY; C. ZOOMORPHIC FIBULAE; D. FIBULAE OF PIEKARY WIELKIE; E. FIBULAE OF KOWALOWICE TYPE

Wielkie, and five highly ornamented iron fibulae of the Piekary Wielkie type from the vicinity of Zielona Góra (Woźniak 1995: 203, 209, Fig. 2; 4:h; 2010: 66-68, 92, Fig. 5: 5-8, Map 3; Megaw 2005) as well as some Kowalowice fibulae of type III according to Lorentzen (1992-1993: 64-71) – in particular specimens from Ulesie, Legnica district, and Jezierzyce Małe, Dzierżoniów district, (Woźniak 2010: 62, 90, Fig. 4:1-2).[3]

The fibulae of Piekary Wielkie type are unique relics and can be considered products of a local workshop active in Lower Silesia in which Kowalowice fibulae could have been made as well (*Bandfibeln* of type III according to Lorentzen), featuring open-work plates and the motif of trefoil palmette, popular in Celtic art. Curiously enough, it is from Neufeld an der Leitha, Burgerland, and Loretto, Lower Austria, (Jerem 1996: 101, Fig. 7:1, 10:5) that very similar fibulae are known (although made from bronze). Possibly, it was from the Middle Danube region that a stimulus came to take up the production of ornaments consistent with the fashion prevailing in the Celtic lands by 'Pomeranian' blacksmiths from Lower Silesia.[4] The youngest group of fibulae following the Late Hallstatt design, (strongly twisted spring on the axle, crossbow chord) is made up of iron fibulae with stylized "duck" or "naïve deformed head" on a foot (varieties 16 and 23 of zoomorphic fibulae in Binding's systematics [1993]), which (except for 1 specimen) come from Silesia (Woźniak 2010: 72-74, 93, Fig. 6:3, 5-8, Map 4:a). They must have been manufactured in Silesia, because all of them are made of iron (likewise Kowalowice fibulae) and not of bronze, as similar specimens known from the Celtic world are.

Few artefacts found in Poland's (present-day usunąć) territory represent the style of late phase LT A. These are above all imported bronze fibulae with a stylized head of a long-billed bird on a foot (variety 17 of zoomorphic fibulae in Binding's systematics (1993)) and an iron specimen of the rare Dorn type from Płoski, Góra Śląska district, (Woźniak 2010: 74, Fig. 6:4, 9-11, 13, Map 4:b). In addition, they stand out because of their different design: absence of an axle, and a front chord and a short spring. These artefacts provide evidence of contacts between Celts (from Bohemia) and Pomeranian culture populations from Lower Silesia and Wielkopolska not later than the 3rd quarter of the 5th century BC.

In late phase LT A, contacts were established between the region of Kietrz in Upper Silesia and Małopolska, on the one part, and the Middle Danube region on the other. Imports from this region include figural fibulae from Kietrz, Kraków Tyniec and the environs of Kraków (Woźniak 2010: 71, 93, Fig. 6: 12, Map 4d), and Speikern-type fibulae (Woźniak 2010: 72, 93, Fig. 6:2, Map 3:d; Dehn & Stöllner 1996: 3-16, 46). Another import from this region, a wheel-turned bowl of the Stupava type was found in a fragment in a Pomeranian culture settlement in Jakuszowice, Kazimierza Wielka district (Woźniak 1996a, Fig. 3:1; 2010: 77, 92, Fig. 7: 4; Tankó 2005). Doubtless of the same provenance, a bronze Marzabotto-type fibula with a wire bow from the environs of Przemyśl (Woźniak 2010: 75, 93, Fig. 6:10) had a design characteristic of forms dated to the end of phase LT A. The fibulae of this type represent one of the basic forms of 'the western circle of the early La Tène culture' (Dehn & Stöllner 1996: 15-24), but are also found, albeit less often, in Austria, Czech Republic or even southwest Slovakia and western Hungary. Trachsel (2004, 88) dates south-German specimens of this type to late LT A. In the Czech Republic, they are encountered in the youngest graves from phase LT A and in 'the assemblages of the pre-Duchcov horizon of flat Celtic cemeteries' or in phase LT B1a (Holodňak & Waldhauser 1984: 36-42). Analogously, i.e. to the second half of the 5th century BC, the specimen from the Przemyśl environs should be dated.

More fundamental changes took place in the lands of modern Poland in the late 5th and early 4th centuries BC. It was then that the first group of Celtic settlers arrived in (present-day usunąć) Poland and the spread of Jastorf culture began. Also at the same time, a clear demographic regression is observable, with some regions of southern Poland being completely depopulated, which is seen in the results of palynological analyses (Godłowski 1985: 27-29,

---

[3] Contrary to the opinion of Lorentzen (1992-1993, 71) and the previous views of this author (Woźniak 1979: 143-146; 2007: 391), wrongly suggesting that some Kowalowice fibulae could be linked even to phase LT B1, they should be dated in principle to the middle section of phase LT A (Woźniak 2010: 67-69).

[4] It is worth mentioning that the Lower Silesian settlement centre 'exported' type III Kowalowice fibulae (displaying elements of the La Tène style and drawing inspirations from the Middle Danube region) to the southeast zone of the Jastorf culture (Lorentzen 1992-1993, Tab. 8: 5, 8, 9; Woźniak 2010:62-66). On the other hand, lands occupied by the Pomeranian culture were reached by single specimens of type II *Bandfibeln*, coming from the same areas of the Jastorf culture (Lorentzen 1992-1993: 68-72; Woźniak 2010: 66, Fig. 4:13).

38, 47, 59; Kurnatowski 1983; 1992; Dzięgielewski 2010). Curiously enough, in the course of phase LT B, despite the existence of Celtic settlement enclaves in Lower and Upper Silesia, there are no finds of Celtic artefacts from the majority of Polish lands, in particular from areas lying north of these enclaves. It is reasonable to believe that in those times contacts along the traditional 'amber route' were severed. The few imports from east Poland and adjacent areas are exceptions.[5] They form a loose chain, the final link of which seems to be a settlement in Rembielin, Przasnysz district, (Waluś 1991) where a considerable number of artefacts of Celtic provenance were found. It can be only presumed that an outpost trading in Sambia amber was located there and was frequented by Celtic merchants from the northeast Carpathian Basin (Woźniak 1995: 206; 2010: 79, 84, Map 5).

Towards the end of phase LT A (shortly before 400 BC), a historic expansion of the Celts in the eastern direction took place, leaving behind flat inhumation burials in Bohemia (Holodňak & Waldhauser 1984; Drda & Rybová 1998), Moravia (Meduna 1965; Čižmář 1970) and in the borderland of Austria, Slovakia and Hungary (Pieta 2010: 18-22). The migration is commonly identified with the expedition mentioned by Livy (Titus Livius, *Ab urbe condita* V 34) to the Hercynian Forest (*Hercynia silva*)[6], commanded by Segovesus, a nephew of Ambigatus, 'king' of the Bituriges from central Gaul. The expedition was to be contemporaneous with the invasion of Italy by Bellovesus. The invasion's climax was the battle at Allia and the capturing of Rome in the summer of 387 BC (Birkhan 1997: 85-150; Woźniak 2004a).

Archaeological sources help trace the spreading of Celtic settlement across the Carpathian Basin in phase LT B. The Celts overran southwest Slovakia and the whole of Hungary, and even reached Transylvania (Bujna 1982; 1994; Szabó 1992: 22; 1997; Teleagă 2008; Zirra 1991; 1997; Woźniak 2004b: 140). In contrast the great invasion of Macedonia, Greece and Thrace by the Celts in 279 BC is known mainly from written records (Birkhan 1997: 130-140).[7] The final stage of Celtic conquest of the Carpathian Basin took place after part of the Celts retreated from Greece in 277 BC. The traces of this stage include cemeteries and settlements founded in east Slovakia and part of Trans-Carpathian Ukraine in the period straddling phases LT B2 and LT C1 (Miroššayová & Tomášová 2004; Szabó 1992; Ščukin & Eremenko 1991; Pieta 2010: 22-

32). Their location enabled them to radiate their influence from there to Małopolska and western Ukraine.

The Celts settled four regions in the south of Poland (see Fig. 3). Their first group came from Bohemia and made their home in a small area in the vicinity of Wrocław, between the Oder River and the Sudeten Foothills. Single assemblages from this area, likewise the oldest graves in flat Celtic cemeteries in Bohemia and Moravia, may date back even to phase LT B1 (Woźniak 1970: 41-46; 1979). Hence, these early arrivals may be treated as an offshoot of the Celtic wave that overran Bohemia. Thus, it seems justified to consider Livy's laconic mention of Segovesus's expedition to the Hercynian Forest, mentioned above, as the first written record of an event that occurred in Poland (Woźniak 2004a: 141).

La Tène culture materials found in Lower Silesia show close affinities with those known from Bohemia. We know from this region ? of? several Celtic settlements and over 20 cemeteries where discoveries are made mostly of inhumation graves from phase LT B and less numerous cremation graves from phases LT B2 and LT C1 (Kamiński & Kosicki 1992; Kosicki 1996; Woźniak 1970: 40-84; 1979; 1992). A somewhat longer existence of Celtic settlement (until LT C2?) seems to be suggested, however, by settlement finds (Pazda 1992; Kosicki 1996). A settlement hiatus cannot be excluded, however, separating the youngest Celtic materials from this area and the earliest Przeworsk culture ones (Godłowski 1985, 20-24; Dąbrowska 1988, 106-111). In the opinion of this author, there are reasons to believe that the mysterious prehistoric stone sculptures from around Mt. Ślęża (lying on the edge of the area settled by Celts) are the work of Celtic 'stonecutters' (Woźniak 2004c). An obvious consequence of accepting this hypothesis is accepting that a "sacred space" (*nemeton*) existed in the Ślęża Massif where "Lower Silesian" Celts celebrated their religious rituals. However, this hypothesis is still questioned (Gediga 2002).

Doubtless somewhat later, in phase LT B1b, Celts from Moravia expanded to settle Głubczyce Upland – a region of Upper Silesia situated at the mouth of the Moravian Gate. Single graves were discovered there and one large bi-ritual cemetery in Kietrz (Gedl 1978). Several settlements were investigated (Bednarek 1996; Woźniak 1970: 85-104; 1979a; 1992; 1996a), including an upland settlement in Nowa Cerekwia, Głubczyce district, (Czerska 1976). Made in recent years on this site, new discoveries of over 250 Celtic coins (most belong to the Roseldorf–Němčice type) and numerous other metal relics (Bednarek 2009; Rudnicki et al. 2009, 116 and information by courtesy of M. Rudnicki) show that an important craft and trade centre was active there from the 3rd to the 2nd century BC. Coins were also minted at the centre which was connected to the famous Celtic emporium in Němčice, Moravia (Čižmář & Kolníková 2006; Kolníková 2006).

Obviously, the settlement in Nowa Cerekwia exerted during this period an impact far beyond its immediate vicinity.

---

[5] As the only exception can be treated the foot of a bronze fibula with a richly relief-ornamented globe from Lutomiersk – Koziówki (Muzolf 2012) as it was certainly a specimen of the early La Tène design, co pozwala zaliczyć fibulę which would justify assigning it to phase LT B2 (Wozniak 2011, 31: Fig. 7:12).

[6] Julius Ceasar (*Gallic War*, VI 24-25) applies this name to a vast area lying north of the Danube and east of the Rhine as far as the territories of the Daci and the Anartes or as far as southwest Slovakia. A similar interpretation may be given to the mention by Tacitus (*Germania* 28, 30). (Kolendo 2004: 16; Woźniak 2007a: 300, footnote 16.

[7] Recent archaeological discoveries have supplied interesting data on the mysterious Celtic state with its capital at Tylis (Bouzek 2005; Emilov 2005).

There is no doubt that its inhabitants mediated contacts with the Celtic enclave in west Małopolska. However, the rise of such a vibrant and rich cultural centre in Upper Silesia was only possible owing to the contacts with Przeworsk culture populations, as well those of the Jastorf culture no doubt, which are evidenced by a fragment of a crown neck ring (*Kronenhalsring*; information courtesy of M. Rudnicki). It can be argued that it was merchants from Nowa Cerekwia (and Němčice, travelling via Nowa Cerekwia) who triggered the process of La Tène model and art acquisition (Latenization) that reached a zenith in Poland's territory in the younger Pre-Roman period. The process was visible not only in the influx of many Celtic imports (Biborski & Kaczanowski 2010; Bochnak 2005: 154-164; 2006; 2011; Bockius 1996; Dąbrowska 1988: 105-150; 199; 2008: 103-190; Dąbrowska & Woźniak 2005, Fig. 2; Karwowski 1997; Łuczkiewicz 1997; 2006: 173-223, 359-361; Wielowiejski 1986; 1991) but also in adjustment to Celtic fashions, for instance, in the manufacture of fibulae. For it was thanks to the Celtic impact that the populations of the Przeworsk and Oksywie cultures began using many new and improved implements such rotary querns, crude scythes, scissors and iron anvils (Woźniak 1981; 1983; 1988; Żygadło 2002: 174 and *passim*). Weapons used by warrior were for the most part imported from the Celtic world (Bochnak 2005: 156-161; 2006; Dąbrowska 1988: 134-138; 2008, 40-56; Łuczkiewicz 1997; 2006: 173-223, 359-361). Even the manner of suspending swords from the waist was taken over from the Celts, which is shown by metal clasps and rings (Bochnak 2005: 56-60, 159), as well as the use of spurs (Bochnak 2004a; 2005, 134-136; Łuczkiewicz 2006: 146-150). It can be safely assumed that warriors in the lands of (present-day usunąć) Poland used the same types of warfare (Bochnak 2004a; 2005: 23-32, 137-175; Kontny 1998; Łuczkiewicz 2006: 225-258), and doub-tless were organized in similar social structures – *Männerbünde* and *Gefolg-schaften* (Woźniak 1988: 241; Łuczkiewicz & Schönfelder 2009; Dobesch 1996).

The youngest Celtic relics from Upper Silesia may be dated to the period straddling phases LT C and LT D (Woźniak 1979a; 1981; 1992; Bednarek 1996) or to the 3rd quarter of the 2nd century BC. Since then, for about 100 years, there had been no traces of settlement in southern Upper Silesia (Godłowski 1985: 24-28, 46). A similar date is put on the fall of the Moravian emporium at Němčice and the centres at Smolenice and Plavecké Pohradie in the range of Malé Karpaty (Little Carpathians, western Slovakia). These developments – raczej occurrences are associated with (Čižmář & Kolníková 2006: 269; Pieta 2010: 85) the historical expedition of the Cimbri (prior to 120 BC) from Himmerland, Jutland, south across the lands of the Boii, towards the lands of the Scordisci and Noricum (Dobesch 1982; Birkhan 1997, 126-129; Kaul & Martens 1995: 151-154, Fig. 1; Bockius 1990). It is very likely that the decline of the Celtic settlement in this part of Silesia was also a result of this occurrence (Woźniak 1992: 14; 2007a, 301).

Hailing (Coming?) also from Moravia (and Upper Silesia?), another group of Celtic settlers overran the loess areas of west Małopolska, stretching along both banks of the Vistula River, towards the end of phase LT B2. To the oldest (of LT B2 and LT C1) phase of the Celtic settlement, one can assign here several cremation graves (and possibly the remains of one inhumation burial: Woźniak 1981, Tab. XXXVI 1-2) and a number of settlements. These features yielded mainly materials analogous to those known from Moravia and Upper Silesia (Woźniak 1992: 14; 1996a; Poleska 2006: 255; Meduna 1980: 33-35, 142-145, 150, Abb. 19, 20) but also included objects from the Carpathian Basin. These materials were first called simply "Celtic culture materials" (Woźniak 1970: 105, 142; 1981: 255-259) to distinguish them from later assemblages classified as the Tyniec group and characterized by the materials of the classic La Tène culture and the Przeworsk culture occurring along one another (Woźniak 1981: 255-262; 1986: 16).[8] Later, for practical reasons, they came to be called the older (I) phase of the Tyniec group (Woźniak 1992: 14).

According to the state of research prior to the discoveries made at the construction of the A4 motorway, it was justified to distinguish phase II of the Tyniec group (correlated basically with phase LT C2), containing mixed materials, representing the La Tène and early Przeworsk cultures (Rudnicki 1996; Kubicha 1997: 305; Poleska 2006: 132-136, 256). Discoveries in recent years have greatly expanded our artefact collections, especially those dating to phase LT C. Several newly exposed settlements yielded exclusively 'pure' La Tène culture materials which were dated, interestingly enough, not only to phase LT C1 but also to phase LT C2 (Okoński 2004; Chmielewski et al. 2006; Dzięgielewska 2006; Jarosz & Rodak 2006; Grygiel & Pikulski 2006; Grygiel, Pikulski & Trojan 2009: 207-213; Dzięgielewski, Purowski 2011). By contrast, no new features have been found that would contain materials, showing traits of the Tyniec group, phase II. It must be stressed that the 'purely Celtic' settlement, most thoroughly investigated on site 17 in Podłęże (Dzięgielewska 2006; Dzięgielewski, Purowski 2011), unquestionably ceased to exist only towards the end of LT C2 or on breakthrough LT C2 and LT D1, i.e. simultane-ously with the collapse of the Celtic settlement in Upper Silesia. This seems to suggest that west Małopolska too was affected by the 'disturbance' caused by the migration of the Cimbri (Woźniak 1992: 14; 2007b: 301; Dulęba 2009: 27). A question arises whether an analogous situation prevailed throughout that part of Małopolska that had been settled by the Celts earlier (?) as some researchers believe (Dulęba 2009; Grygiel, Pikulski & Trojan 2009: 214-221). The new discove-ries clearly have not yielded compact assemblages of La Tène artefacts characteristic of phase LT D1. Hence, there are more and more arguments in favour of the older hypotheses (Woźniak 1986, 17) about part of west Małopolska being occupied by Przeworsk culture populations at that time, which (even

---

[8] The introduction of the concept of the Tyniec group instead of the earlier term 'Celtic-Przeworsk mixed group' (Woźniak 1970: 105), resulted from the discussions held by the editorial board of *Prehistory of Polish Lands*, vol. V (Woźniak 1981: 255).

to a broader extent) is claimed by the researchers quoted above.

Another change occurred in west Małopolska towards the end of phase LT D1 when a new wave of settlers arrived in the vicinity of Kraków from beyond the Carpathians. They originated the 'classic Tyniec group' (or its phase III), which lasted until phase B1a of the Roman period. The newcomers included potters producing excellent painted pottery, which closely corresponds to the wares made in workshops from around Bratislava and in the Zemplín centre in east Slovakia, as well as dolia (Woźniak 1990; 1996a; 2000; Cumberpatch 1993; Poleska 2000; 2006: 35-123, 127-144). To the newcomers, we owe hand-moulded vessels of the types known from the Púchov and Dacian cultures (Pieta 1982: 86-122; Pieta & Zachar 1993; Březinová 2009; Čambal et al. 2009). In addition, many vessels were used that belong to the Przeworsk culture type from phases A2/A3 and A3. At this time, external contacts were reoriented brought about by the fall of *oppida* in Bohemia and Moravia and the decline of Celtic settlement in Upper Silesia. The major trade route from the Polish lands south since then ran not across Upper Silesia and through the Moravian Gate in the direction of Němčice or the *oppidum* in Staré Hradisko but from west Małopolska, across the lands of the Púchov culture, to the *oppida* in Bratislava and Devín (Pieta & Zachar 1993), then next in to Aquileia (Dąbrowska 1988: 123-133; 1996: 131; Woźniak 1996b; 2004a: 56).

Along this route, there came to west Małopolska and next to east Poland, late Celtic imports (and fashion) and those from the East Alpine region, including, for instance, disc fibulae (variant J after? Kostrzewski 1919a: 31-32, fig. 16) and others of types A65, A18, A236, A238, Gurina, Jezerine, Langton Down (Dąbrowska 1988:125; 1996; 2008:29-33, 104-109, 189-191; Harasim 2011; Okulicz-Kozaryn & Nowakowski 1996; Poleska 2006:148-154), as well as single glass vessels (Poleska 2006, 144). What merits special attention is fragments of painted plates from Kraków Krzesławice – possibly local imitations of early *terra sigillata* (Poleska 2006: 45, Fig. 8: 10, 11). By contrast, as a surprise come, known from Mazovia, fragments of hand-moulded (most likely produced locally) painted wares, which imitate Celtic original patterns (Dąbrowska 2008: 74). In this phase, strong Celtic impact is observed (including Noricum and Balkan) as far as the weapons of Przeworsk culture warriors is concerned. Some of them, in particular some double-edge swords (e.g. specimens with stamps, scabbards decorated with *opus interrasile* plates and bronze elements) as well as a coat of mail from Opalenie, Tczew district, (Kostrzewski 1919a:139) may be considered imports brought along a version of the amber route, running across the territory of the Tyniec group and Púchov culture (Bochnak 2004a; 2004b; 2005: 161-164; Böhme – Schönberger 2002; Czarnecka 2002; Dąbrowska 1996: 131-138; 2008: 44, 54, 105-109; Dulęba 2006). Of course, the most spectacular relic of foreign origin is an East Celtic helmet from Siemiechów (Jażdżewska 1986; 1992, Pl. 387; 1994; Bochnak 2005:132; Kaczanowski 1992, 172; Łuczkiewicz 2006), which may be interpreted as the spoils of war.[9]

Next to the distribution of late Celtic imports in the lands of Poland (their concentration on the Vistula River), another argument in favour of the hypothesis about the vital role of the Tyniec group (including Kraków environs) as an intermediary in the amber trade concerns amber finds (being very rare) discovered in Tyniec group settlements in Kraków Krzesławice (Poleska & Tobota 1987: 21-23, 38-41) and Kraków Tyniec (Lenczyk 1956: 36). The fact that the inhabitants of west Małopolska had a substantial share in long-distance trade is confirmed by the increase in the number of finds of Celtic gold coins and especially by documented minting activity (Woźniak 1977; 1984; Kaczanowski 1996; Rudnicki 2003; 2005; Rudnicki et al. 2009; Byrska-Fudali, Przybyła, Rudnicki 2009). This shows that once a rich "wordlings" elite lived in this area, the members of which possessed large numbers of gold coins of high purity, they brought minter(s) and profited from minting coins of lower purity.

The youngest assemblages displa-ying traits of the Tyniec group can be dated to phase B1a of the Roman period or similarly to the so-called "catastrophe disaster horizon" in the oecumene of the Púchov culture (Pieta 1982: 32, 39-45, 162; 1986). Later materials found in the areas on the left bank of the Vistula River show characteristics of the Przeworsk culture, whereas settlements lying on the right bank of the river yielded artefact assemblages that display affinities with those belonging to the late Púchov culture in Slovakia (Pieta 1986; Woźniak 1986, 19; Godłowski 1995; Madyda-Legutko 1995; 1996; 2004; Lasota & Pawlikowski 2009).

The fourth region of modern Poland where traces of Celtic settlement were exposed in basins? of the upper and middle San and Wisłoka rivers in the Carpathian Foothills. The amount of materials known from this region continues to be small although it continues to grow (Fig. 4). No grave assemblages have been found while the scope of investigations on the few known settlements remains narrow, resulting in few pottery series and single artefacts made of other materials (Ginalski & Muzyczuk 1999; Madyda-Legutko 1996; Olędzki 2004; Parczewski 1978; 2000; Parczewski & Pohorska-Kleja 1995; Poradyło 1997; Przybyła 2004; 2009; Woźniak 2004a: 49-52).[10] Nevertheless, there are enough artefacts to formulate a hypothesis that this rather vast area was settled by groups of Celtic populations (Madyda-Legutko 1996; 2004; Woźniak 1992: 16; 2004b; 2007a: 394, Fig. 3). Surprising as they are, the discoveries at a stronghold in Trepcza,

---

[9] The question of the role of wars as a "channel" of importing items of weaponry in this age is discussed in detail by Łuczkiewicz (2006: 218-223).

[10] What merits special attention is the finding in this region of a Celtic gold coin in Trepcza, two Geto-Dacian silver coins in Medyka and another one in Przemyśl Zasanie (Mikołajczyk 1982: 13-15, Tab. IV 2,V 2); information on the finds of Greek coins, except for a specimen from Mrukowa, is unclear (Mielczarek 1988: 135, 144-146, 152; Madyda-Legutko 1995: 13).

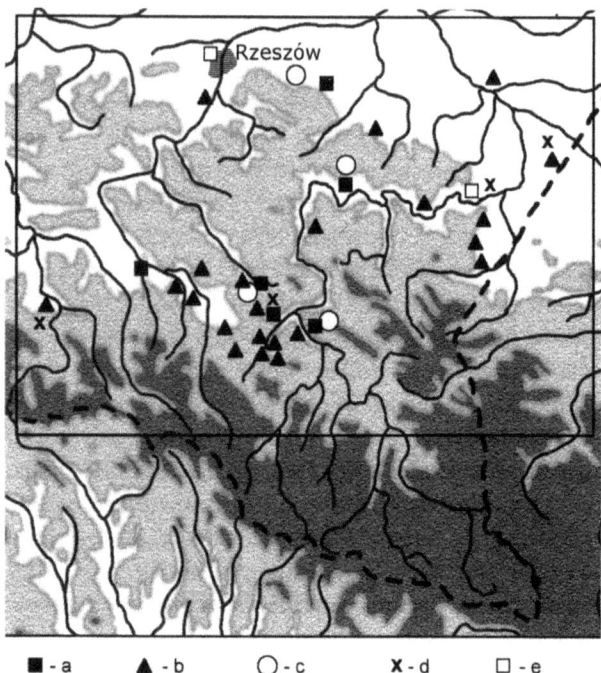

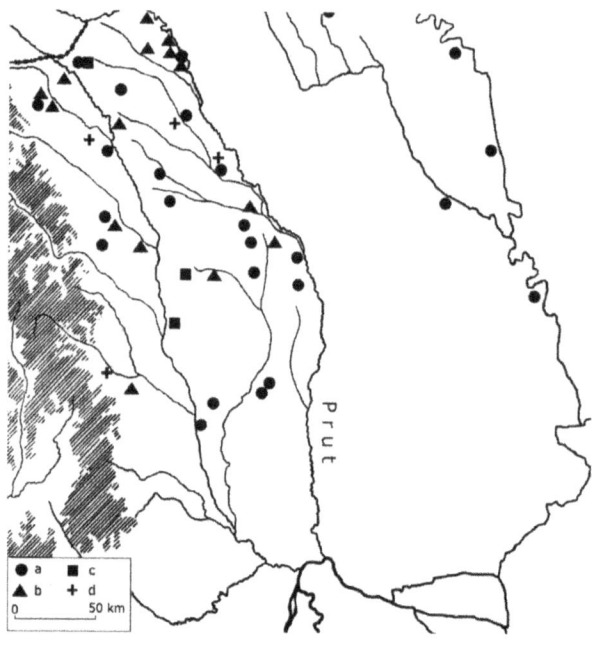

■ - a   ▲ - b   ○ - c   X - d   □ - e

FIG. 4. THE CELTIC FINDS IN SOUTH-EAST POLAND.
LEGENDS: A SETTLEMENT; B. LOOSE POTTERY FINDS; C. COINS;
D. GLASS FINDS; E. METAL FINDS

FIG. 5. THE CELTIC FINDS IN THE TERITORY OF MOLDAVIA.
LEGENDS: A SETTLEMENT; B. LOOSE FINDS; C. HOARDS;
D. GRAVES.

district Sanok, which suggest that defences connected to the Celts could have existed there, should be treated with the utmost caution (Karwowski & Ginalski 2002). A known artefact assemblage shows clearly that the origins of the settlement were not related to west Małopolska but that the settlers came from beyond the Carpathians, from east Slovakia or Trans-Carpathian Ukraine (Woźniak 1974: 139; 2004a; Madyda-Legutko 1996: 40; Poradyło 1997: 86; Olędzki 2004). Almost all materials known to date display characteristics which allow researchers to date them to phase LT C (Karwowski 2004b), although a few potsherds, including in particular single fragments of painted wares from Lipnik (Przybyła 2004; 2009) and Medyka, site 62, (Poradyło 1997: 74, 78, Fig. 7:1) confirm that the settlement continued to early phase LT D. This is a surprising concurrence with the chronology of an *oppidum* in Mukačevo-Lovačka (Ščukin & Eremenko 1991; Kobal 1995/1996; Dzembas 1995). Thus, it can be presumed that both regions were closely related. Also, the fall of settlement in both regions was most likely brought about by the same causes. Where the east frontier of this zone of the Celtic settlement lay remains an open question. At the Przemyśl Gate, sites containing graphite ware finds continue as far as the state border, hence it seem obvious that one can expect similar discoveries in the adjacent regions of Ukraine as field research intensifies, especially surface surveys. Possibly, the terraine across the whole area between the San River and Bovšiv, near Halič, where a settlement with Celtic materials dating to phase LT C and known for a long time is located, (Krušelnickaja 1964), conceals traces of dispersed settlement from those times, but there is still no evidence to support this supposition.

In north Moldavia too, a rather small and dispersed group of Celtic relics was discovered (Fig. 5), including single graves, metal artefacts and pottery ("grey" and graphite), which span a long period from developed phase LT B1 to LT C1 (Woźniak 1974: 139-165; 2007a, 395, Fig. 4; Teodor 1988; Babeş 1993: 52, 71, 90, 103, 125-127; Rustoiu 1993), but do not form compact assemblages.[11] Most (older relics) are contemporaneous with the strongholds of the Stînceşti type that functioned here in the 4th-3rd centuries (Babeş 1993: 21). These artefacts testify to the intense involvement of the Celts, most likely from Transylvania, in contacts with the people inhabiting this area. It is not certain, however, if they can be considered traces of a compact group of Celts settling here in the period before the arrival of the Bastarnae. They can be also considered an archaeological indication of a Celtic component in the population of the union of the Bastarnae. The presence of such a component seems to be suggested by written records (Łowmiański 1963: 200; Woźniak 1974: 21-23; Babeş 1993, 168-180; Mačinskij 1973; Shchukin 1989: 63). Younger relics (including most of graphite ware finds) are found in the assemblages of the Poieneşti-Lukaševka culture and represent chiefly imports from the eastern Carpathian Basin. A small number of Celtic imports are also known from the regions of Ukraine lying further east and northeast but they do not form any clear clusters (Woźniak 1974, 139-159, 193-195, Map 3;

---

[11] An astounding contrast can be observed between north Moldavia and the Republic of Moldova whence only single Celtic imports come: a bronze figurine form Lukaševka, Orgeyev district, and bronze fibulae from Mala Sacharna, Reziny district, Parkany, Tiraspol district (Woźniak 1974, 194, Fig. 13:6,7, 14:3; Tkaciuk 1994, Fig. 8: 20), Rudi, Donduşeni district, and Kalfa near Bender (Čebotarenko, Ščerbakova & Ščukin 1987, Fig. 1).

Mačinskij 1973; Kasparova 1981; Shchukin 1989: 63-64, 234-236, I:ll. 20:B).

A short outline of certain and presumed Celtic settlements in the outskirts (periphery?) of the Celtic world in central Europe was necessary as they had formed a base for the Celtic impact on their northern and north-eastern neighbours. A result of this impact, "Latènisation" affected vast areas of central Europe in the younger Pre-Roman period and consisted in adopting many elements of the higher civilization of the Celts, from fashion to social structure, by their closer and more distant neighbours (Godłowski 1977: 111-120; Woźniak 1983: 76-78; 1988; Dąbrowska 1988: 105-150; 2008: 101-109; Dąbrowska & Woźniak 2005: 93). "Latènisation" had a particularly strong impact on the Przeworsk culture[12] and a weaker one on the Oksywie culture (Wołągiewicz 1979; 1981; Maciałowicz 2011; Bokiniec 2001).

It is fitting to remind the reader here of the fact mentioned earlier that Celtic imports did not reach most of the Pomeranian culture oecumene in phases LT B1 and LT B2. Few (mainly from Pomerania culture graves) are known from areas east of the Vistula River, which can be interpreted as the traces of a route along which Celts living on the upper Tisza River maintained enigmatic contacts doubtless with the sphere of the Western Baltic Kurgans culture (Woźniak 1974: 140-144, 193-195, Fig. 13; 1995: 203, Fig. 3; 2010: 79, Fig. 8, Map 5). Its point of destination could have lain at the presumed Sambian amber-trading outpost discovered in Rembielin, Przasnysz district, (Waluś 1991; Okulicz-Kozaryn & Nowakowski 1996). On the other hand, these finds testify to the Pomeranian culture settlement continuing there at least to the end of phase of LT B1; by this very fact they suggest that the settlement could have collapsed in the other areas occupied by the Pomeranian culture already towards the end?? of phase LT A. Hence, a doubt is cast on the hypotheses suggesting that Pomeranian culture populations continued to settle all the areas they inhabited earlier until this time.

Out of various theories which could explain why the contacts with the South (Celts) were severed in the late 5th century BC (Woźniak 2010; 2011), the most probable seems the one blaming contact (nie podoba mi się) re-orientation and migrations from the northwest or the impact of the Jastorf culture and the influx of this culture's populations from Poland. It has been mentioned earlier that in the areas occupied once by the Jastorf culture, there occur many fibulae (*Bandfibeln*) resembling Kowalowice ones (*Kaulwitzer-fibeln*), known from the assemblages of the Pomeranian culture (Lorentzen 1992-1993: 64-71; Woźniak 2010: 59-66, Fig. 3, Map 3). This proves beyond any doubt that there existed contacts between the Middle Elbe-Havel group of the Jastorf culture and the populations of the Pomeranian culture in Lower Silesia and Wielkopolska (specimens typical of one zone are encountered in the other – see footnote 4). Such contacts paved the way for the future expansion of Jastorf culture populations east of the Oder River.

It has been known for a long time that the right-bank part of West Pomerania east of Oder River as far as the Rega and Pasłęka interfluve was included in the bounds of the Jastorf culture (Warnow-Oder group) in the beginning of the older Pre-Roman Iron Age. Later, but still before the Ripdorf phase, the Gubin group of this culture took shape, which was genetically related to the Middle Elbe-Havel group. The Gubin group spread to lands extending on both banks of the lower Nysa Łużycka River (Neisse River) and the adjacent areas of Lower Silesia of which some had been settled earlier by Pomeranian culture populations (Wołągiewicz 1963; 1979; Domański 1981; Wołągiewicz 1981b: 192; Domański 1975; 1996). From the other Polish regions, we have also known for a long time of a rather small number of other metal relics, types characteristic of the Jastorf culture, partly preceding the Ripdorf phase. At the earliest, already over one hundred years ago, notice was taken of the occurrence of bronze necklaces – so called crown neck rings (*Kronenhalsring*) – in the lands of Poland and western Ukraine. They were linked to similar artefacts found in northeast Germany and Jutland (Demetrykiewicz 1900; Kostrzewski 1919a: 75-79; 1926; Woźniak 1977: 272, 276, Fig. 4; Dąbrowska 1988:180-183, Map 22; Maciałowicz 2011: 89-104, Fig. 7-14). The number of such finds grew after the Second World War,[13] owing to specimens from Moldavia and the region of Ukraine lying on the Dnieper (Popko 1965; Babeş & Untaru 1969; Babeş 1993: 107-108, 232, Fig. 28; Shchukin et al. 1993).[14] "Classical" Jastorf-forms are also brooches type Zachow (Prochowicz 2011). In addition, there are also ear-rings (*Segelohrringe*), differently types of pins (*Spatenkopf-, Holsteiner-*[15] *Kropf- und Scheibennadeln, Flügelnadeln*), triangle and tongue-form belt buckle (Wołągiewicz 1979: 36, 67, Fig. 14; Woźniak 1977: 271, Fig. 2; Woźniak & Poleska 1999; Dąbrowska

---

[12] It should be noted in this context that the term 'Latènisation' is sometimes wrongly used in the literature in another meaning, namely it is applied to the spreading of the custom of faceting vessel rims, and several other pottery style traits (chiefly of tableware), characteristic of the style of pottery from the younger Pre-Roman Iron Age period. This pottery style, evidently, was not inspired by the Celtic patterns. Suffice it to remember that La Tène vessels, unlike the so-called 'latènised' wares of the Przeworsk and Jastorf cultures, did not have handles, hence they could not inspire the spreading of narrowed handles or faceted (ridged?) rims typical of this style.

[13] In recent years, a fragment of a necklace of this type has been found in a settlement in Nowa Cerekwia – an important Celtic centre in Upper Silesia (information by courtesy of M. Rudnicki, M.A.) and further in the emporium Němčice na Morawach (information by courtesy of M. Rudnicki, M.A.), and in Radovesice, okr. Teplice in North Bohemia (Budinský, Waldhauser 2004).

[14] A surprising find of a fragment of a graphite *situla*, having a late-type rim, was made while exploring a settlement located close to the place where both crown neck rings had been found, within the *khutor* of Greblya, Mena district, Chernihiv province. The settlement yielded also hand-moulded pottery in the type of the Zarubintsy culture and an iron belt buckle tongue – form? (Shchukin, Val'kova & Shevchenko 1993: 53, Fig. 16: 1, 2). The closest region to Greblja where graphite wares were certainly produced was Transylvania. For it does not seem that they were made in north Moldavia (Rustoiu 1993). In any case, the vessel travelled several hundred kilometres.

[15] The list is expanded by a recently discovered pin from Tomasze, Ostrołęka district, (Prochowicz 2006a: 385, Fig. 1a).

& Woźniak 2005: 87-93, Fig. 1; Dąbrowska 2008: 95-99, 191; Maciałowicz 2011, 80, Fig. 1-2; Müller 1985, 49, 52, 55, 84-86). We do not know the context of many of them; some originated with the assemblages of the Pomeranian culture, while the youngest (including *Flügelnadeln*)[16] can be linked already to the younger Pre-Roman period.

These Jastorf-type artefacts (except for artefacts from Pomerania) were interpreted as a presumed trace of the trek of the Bastarnae (and the Scirae) from the Jastorf culture oecumene to Black Sea zone (Woźniak 1977: 272; Dąbrowska 1988, 187, 194-196, Map 23; Peschel 1992; Babeş 1993: 154-162). The discoveries of many Poieneşti–Lukaševka culture sites in north Moldavia and the Republic of Moldova bear out this interpretation (Vulpe 1953; 1955; Fedorov 1960; Babeş 1993; Tkaciuk 1994, 228-247, Fig. 7; Hânceanu 2008) because this culture is unquestionably part of the Jastorf cultural circle. What's more, it shows affinities with various zones of this circle. Perceptible traits indicate its connections to the Przeworsk and – possibly – Pomeranian cultures (Dąbrowska 1988, 175; Babeş 1993, 69, 159). However, numerous new discoveries justify a fundamental change of views on Jastorf culture materials from central Poland.

The first signal of the occurrence of atypical pottery from the Pre-Roman period in eastern Poland came in the wake of the investigations of a settlement in Werbkowice Kotorów, Hrubieszów district, (Dąbrowska, Liana 1963). This, in turn, drew attention to similar materials from the well-known settlement in Brześć Kujawski, Włocławek district, excavated by Jażdżewski (Jażdżewski 1939, tabl. VIII-XIII; Dąbrowska 1988: 196) prior to WWII. In the 1980s, in the southeast Lublin province, adjacent to the Hrubieszów district, many sites were exposed yielding similar pottery, including three graves from Czerniczyn, Hrubieszów district, (Czopek 1991a: 94) and one in Chełm Bieławin (Dzieńkowski & Gołub 1999: Fig. 2: 12), which where referred to as the Czerniczyn group, first associating them with the early Zarubintsy[17] and then Jastorf cultures (Czopek 1991a; 1999; Kokowski 1986: 185-187; Mazurek 1995a; 2001; Mazurek & Mazurek 1997a; Prochowicz 2006a).[18] Unfortunately, these are mainly finds resulting from surface surveys or making small test pits, with finds of metal objects being very rare, which are necessary for precisely establishing a chronology. Most sites yielded pottery of the type known from Werbkowice-Kotorowo that can be dated to phases A1-A2 of the younger Pre-Roman period as the assemblages often contain some Przeworsk culture pottery, showing traits of an early style. These materials show affinities with the pottery of the Jastorf circle, mostly from Denmark, and that of Poieneşti–Lukaševka culture (Dąbrowska 1994; 2001; Grygiel 2004, 38-45). It is also possible to distinguish a group of slightly older finds without the addition of Przeworsk elements. Such a group would comprise above all some materials from a settlement in Wytyczno (Mazurek & Mazurek 1996; Mazurek 2001). This shows that the emergence of Jastorf settlement in eastern Poland (usuwam: only slightly) preceded the emergence of pottery displaying early Przeworsk style, while the Czerniczyn group was originally believed to comprise the materials in the type of the youngest assemblages of the Pomeranian culture (Czopek 1991a; 1992a: 119-131; Grygiel 2004: 48).

Reasons for a major revision of views on the cultural situation in the lands of (present-day usunąć) Poland in the older Pre-Roman period and the role the Jastorf culture played in the then transformations were given by discoveries made in the course of rescue investigations on the route of the Yamal gas pipeline and A2 motorway in north Wielkopolska. From this area, no compact assemblages showing Jastorf connections had been known earlier. Now, we know of over twenty settlements with Jastorf-type pottery in this region (including Kujawy) (Machajewski 2004, Fig. 1; Machajewski & Pietrzak 2004) and single graves –altogether about thirty sites (Fig. 6). Information on these sites was presented in a number of papers at a conference in Poznań in 2002; most of them were published as conference proceedings (Machajewski 2004). In Mazovia as well, a substantial growth in the number of sites with Jastorf materials was observed (about 25 sites): settlements, single graves and minor finds (Dąbrowska & Woźniak 2005: 87-93, Fig. 1; Dąbrowska 2008: 95-98, Fig. 11, 28, 29, Map 6). However, these data justify formulating a hypothesis about Jastorf culture settlement existing in this region (probably filling a "settlement gap" between the settlement of the Pomeranian culture and that of Przeworsk culture) although it is hard to precisely establish its chronological brackets due to the nature of the available sources (Dąbrowska & Woźniak 2005: 92).

The discoveries mentioned above inspired M. Grygiel to thoroughly re-analyze abundant Jastorf-type materials from sites 3, 4 and 5 in Brześć Kujawski (Grygiel 2004) and interestingly outline the question of Jastorf settlement in Poland (leaving out, however, Pomerania and the Gubin group). Unfortunately, the materials from these sites lack any metal relics. Hence, the chronology of the sites can be established only by comparing vessel forms and ornaments with pottery from other areas of the Jastorf circle known for many southern imports or for which dendrochronological dates are available. Such areas include Jutland and the south zone of the classic Jastorf culture, on the one

---

[16] The list is expanded by a recently discovered specimen at a Celtic settlement from phase LT C, site 17 in Podłęże, Wieliczka district (information courtesy of K. Dzięgielewski, M.A.) and other two (without a context) on site 11 in Kamieńczyk, Wyszków district (Dąbrowska 2008: 142, Fig. 11: 1) and Szynych, Grudziądz district (Maciałowicz 2011: 80, Fig. 1).

[17] Similarities between Zarubintsy culture pottery and that of Werbkowice--Wytyczno type made it difficult to classify properly the latter. However, a detailed study of the unquestionably Zarubintsy materials found in Poland has shown that they belong to the late phase of this culture from the Roman period (Kasparowa 1992: 300; Andrzejowski 1999; Dąbrowska 2004).

[18] On archaeological maps, the east range of the Werbkowice type materials is marked by the Bug River. This, no doubt, is an apparent limit, following from an insufficient collaboration between the Polish and Ukrainian researchers. This claim is borne out by the identification of the materials of this kind in the collections of the State Archaeological Museum in Warsaw. The materials come from the village of Krečov, Volodymyr-Volynsky district, located on the right bank of the Bug River (Dąbrowska 1994: 73). It can be expected that the collections of Ukrainian museums hold more of such finds from west Volhynia.

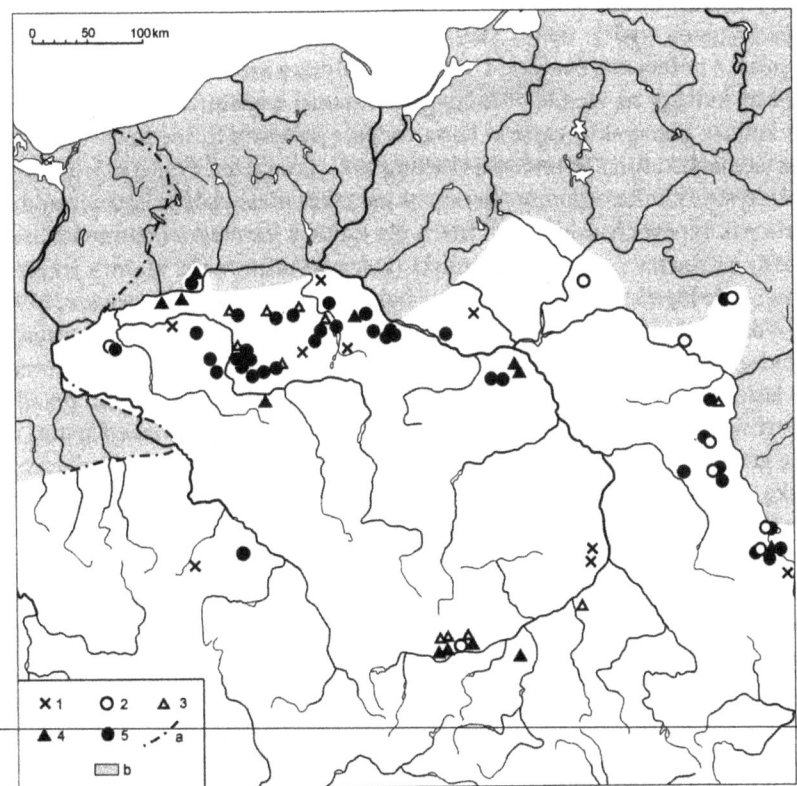

Fig. 6. Significant sites and settlement zones of Jastorf culture in Central and South Poland.
Legends: 1. crown-shaped necklaces; 2. fire dogs; 3. clay spoons; 4. Jastorf culture graves; 5. settlement with Jastorf culture pottery; a. eastern range of the territory of Gubin and Warnow-Oder grups of Jastorf culture; b. area outseide the scope of this work.

hand, and the zone of (oecumene usunąć) the Poieneşti–Lukaševka culture, on the other (and for a later period).

Grygiel divided ceramic materials from Brześć Kujawski into two phases: an older one, representing finds from all sites, and a younger one comprising finds from site 4 only (Grygiel 2004: 15-36; Dąbrowska 1988: 196; 1994: 73; 2008: 95-99; Dąbrowska & Woźniak 2005: 87-93). The older phase is characterized by the domination of vessel forms in the style of the Jastorf phase (Fig. 7) and the presence of only few specimens with rims faceted on the inside. There are clear similarities, in the first place, to the materials from Jutland – which was already pointed out by Dąbrowska (1988: 196-199) with respect to the finds from Werbkowice-Kotorowo – but affini-ties with forms typical of the southern zone of the Jastorf culture are encountered as well. As a surprise come finds of frag-ments of hand-moulded painted wares from Brześć Kujawski, typical of Holstein, which show connections to the Rhine pottery of this kind from the 5th century BC (Grygiel 2004: 29). This implies an unexpectedly early dating. This phase may be correlated essentially with the period straddling phases Jastorf b and Ripdorf and the older section of phase Ripdorf (phase Ib/IIa according to Seyer 1982: 13-22) and, indirectly, accord-ing to the systematics of the La Tène culture, with phases LT B2 and early LT C1 (Grygiel 2004: 24-29).

The younger phase materials from a settlement on site 4 (Fig. 8) in Brześć Kujawski show a distinctly local character. They are dominated by vessels with thickened rims faceted on the inside, with narrowed handles, rough-cast in a different manner and bands of incised ornaments. All these traits are typical of the pottery style of the Ripdorf phase. They can be dated to the period corresponding to developed phase LT C1 (Grygiel 2004: 29-35). Grygiel includes in the Jastorf culture and links to the younger section of this phase the following nearby settlements: Kobielice, Aleksandrów Kujawski district, and Osłonki, Radziejów Kujawski district (Grygiel 2004: 32-35, Fig. 9-11). Next to vessels analogous to those from the Brześć Kujawski younger phase, site 4, these settlements yielded also specimens with rims faceted on the outside, which is characteristic of the Przeworsk culture. The passage from the older to younger phase reflects the rhythm of changes, taking place throughout the area of the Jastorf circle.

The Jastorf culture settlements in Brześć Kujawski are a territorial link between the sites in Mazovia and Wielkopolska. The finds from all these regions have identical chronologies and external connections (Machajewski & Pietrzak 2004). In Wielkopolska, we know of the settlements which yielded finds belonging to the older phase (Pławce, Otorowo, Wojnowo: Makiewicz

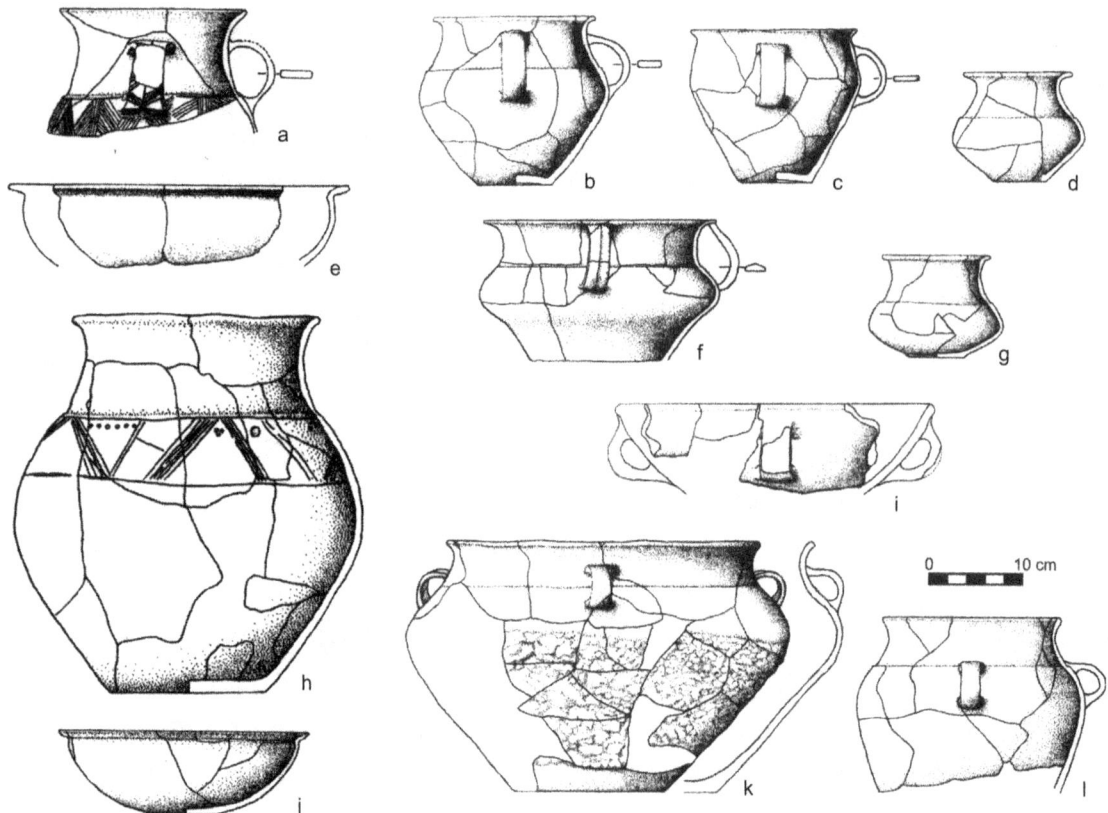

FIG. 7. MAIN TYPES OF POTTERY LINKED WITH THE OLDER PHASE OF JASTORF CULTURE SETLEMENTS IN BRZEŚĆ KUJAWSKI, SITE 3 AND 4 (AFTER GRYGIEL 2004).

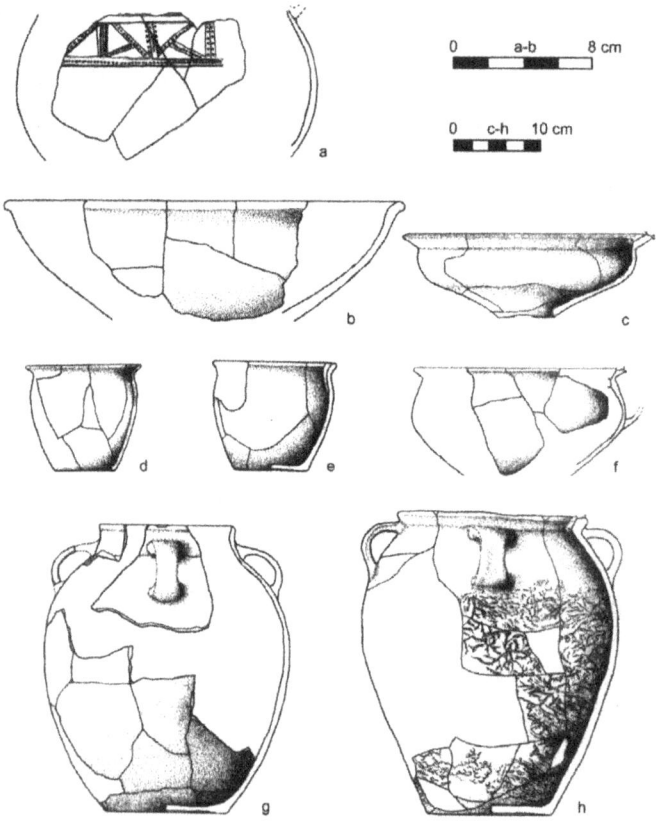

FIG. 8. EXAMPLES OF POTTERY LINKED WITH THE YOUNGER PHASE OF JASTORF CULTURE SETLEMENTS IN BRZEŚĆ KUJAWSKI, SITE 4 (AFTER GRYGIEL 2004).

2004; Kasprowicz 2004; Żychliński 2004), but the sites that yielded materials corresponding to the younger phase of Brześć Kujawski – displaying Ripdorf style traits – are more numerous (Wapniarnia, Więckowice: Machajewski 2003; Brzostowicz & Machajewski 2003). It is also to the younger phase that few graves, known from this area, are related (Biała site 1, Drawsko site 1, Rosko and Kuźnica Żelichowska, Czarnków–Trzcianka district, Nowe Miasto, Środa district, Zarębowo, Aleksandrów Kuj. district: Grygiel 2004: 51-57; Gałęzowska 1996, 56-62, Fig. 2; Machajewski & Walkiewicz 1993; Machajewski & Pietrzak 2004, 99; Machajewski, Maciejewski & Niedzwiecki 2004; Dernoga & Gajda 2004; Tetzlaff 1967: 284, 289, 296, Fig. 23, 24, 34).

As mentioned earlier, in recent years discoveries have been made in Mazovia too, concentrated in the environs of Warsaw and on the lower Bug River, of a considerable number of sites with Jastorf materials whose style resembled that of finds from Brześć Kujawski and north Wielkopolska (Dąbrowska 2008: 95, 191). These are predominantly settlement materials. Some of them: Izdebno Kościelne, Grodzisk Maz. district, site 1 (Kołacz 1995), Wykowo, Płock district, site 1, Haćki, Bielsk Podlaski district, site IC (Dąbrowska 2008: 95, 139, Fig. 28:1, 29:1) can be included in the older horizon of the settlements from Brześć Kujawski. However, single graves (Stare Koczargi and Stare Babice, West Warsaw district, Wilcza Wólka, Piaseczno district) and most of the other finds from the settlements can be correlated with the younger horizon (Andrzejowska & Andrzejowski 1997: 85-99; Dąbrowska 1994; 2001; 2008: 172, 183, Fig. 5:1-4; Dąbrowska & Woźniak 2005: 88; Grabarek 2011; Grygiel 2004: 37).

The existence of compact and relatively permanent Jastorf-type settlement in north Wielkopolska makes us revise the cultural attribution of Jastorf relics known from this region (Woźniak 1977, 271, Fig. 2; Wołągiewicz 1979, 36, 67, Fig. 14) and which have been until now considered imports included in the assemblages of the Pomeranian and Przeworsk cultures.[19] Many of them, however, were unattached finds, chance finds of uncertain context or came form destroyed cemeteries. Possibly most should be linked to the Jastorf settlement (except for the oldest – found in unquestionable Pomeranian assemblages dated to the decline of LT A and the beginnings of the older Pre-Roman period – and the youngest that can be referred to phase A2 of the younger Pre-Roman period). However, at that time, the 'Bastarnae trail must have been travelled in both directions. In the lands occupied by the Przeworsk culture, imports from 'old Jastorf lands' continue to occur, while in Jutland and in the lands occupied by the Jastorf culture a clear impact of the Przeworsk culture is observable (Dąbrowska 1988: 156-175; Martens 1994a). Likewise, a clear Przeworsk impact is observed to have affected the Poieneşti–Lukaševka culture (Dąbrowska 1988: 175-192; Babeş 1993: 114, 159), and some finds made on Polish territory may be considered a manifestation of this culture's influence – the archaeological trace of the Bastarnae.

In the first place, one can mention here ornamented iron bracelets, (mostly) with pipe-like bows and overlapping ends, seven (?)of which are known from graves nos. 47, 113, 186, 197, 214, 225 and from the layer in Błonie, Sandomierz district (Mycielska & Woźniak 1988: 42, 70, 97, 103, 106, 116, Tab. XXVI B:2, XCVIII B:10, CLXIV A:3, CLXX D:4, CLXXXI B:3, CLXXXVIII B:2; CXCIX 17). Another bracelet of this type comes from grave 212 in Kamieńczyk, Wyszków district, and one (grave 117) or two (fragment from grave 78) more were found in Karczewiec, Węgrów district (Dąbrowska 1973: 429, 454, Tab. XVIII 19, XXX 23; 2008, 34, Fig. 10: 1, 6; 2004a). Analogous ornaments, mostly made of iron, although there are bronze specimens as well, are found in the oecumene of the Poieneşti–Lukaševka culture; in particularly large numbers they occur on a cemetery in Boroseşti (Babeş 1993: 106, Taf. 2: 9:c, 13:k; 3: 16:c; 32; 201, 261b; 37: 519:c and next). Local craftsmen, however, were not to be credited with design of these ornaments. They imitated Celtic blacksmiths active nearby whence we know of the specimens that have an earlier chronology (Babeş 1993: 106; Dąbrowska 2005: 83-87). Probably, other evidence of the contacts between the Bastarnae and the inhabitants of (what is now usunąć?) southeast Poland include the finds of Geto-Dacian tetradrachmae of the Huşi-Vovreşti type (Woźniak & Poleska 1999, 386), minted in the oecumene of the Poieneşti-Lukaševka culture in central Moldavia (Preda 1974: 111, 144). These are five (three?) specimens from a Celtic settlement in Pełczyska, Pińczów district (Rudnicki 2003: 16-22, Fig. 9), possibly two from Medyka, Przemyśl district, and one from a feature of the Brześć-Werbkowice group in Hrebenne, Hrubieszów district, and possibly a specimen from Kruhel Mały, Przemyśl district (Florkiewicz 2009: 105-107, 112, 114, Fig. 2, Tab. I 3-9). A possible proof of the contacts between the Bastarnae (the population of the Poieneşti–Lukaševka culture?) and the unexpectedly distant mouth of the Elbe River (via Poland?) is the find of a fibula of the Zarubintsy type made in Holte, (Land) District Hadeln (Tackenberg 1963a).[20]

A probable trace of reverse contacts along the "Bastarnae trail", an 'altar' from Janikowo, Inowrocław district, (Makiewicz 1976: 122, 125, Fig. 2-23; 1977) points to connections with religious customs prevailing in the Mediterranean. However, similar features are known from Dacian settlements and those of the Poieneşti–Lukaševka culture in Romania. It can be reasonably believed that influences from this direction inspired the Kujawy 'temple founders' as well as Danish ones (Makiewicz 1976; 1977; Dąbrowska 1988, 183). A similar distribution (Jutland

---

[19] For example, a recently discovered fibula from Sowinki near Poznań (Makiewicz & Łaszkiewicz 2001) should be associated with the settlement of the younger phase of the Jastorf culture; previously it would have been considered an import in the Przeworsk culture.

[20] After all, this is more probable than considering this relic an 'import' from the northwest Balkans, where fibulae of this type occur too but more rarely.

and northern Germany, Poland and the territory of the Poienești–Lukaševka culture) is shared by the finds of fire dogs (*Feuerböcke*) or rather their fragments. In Poland, they were found on nine sites (Dąbrowska & Woźniak 2005, 89, Fig. 1:2) of which seven lie east of the middle Vistula (Dąbrowska 1988: 186-188, Fig. 15; 2008: 95, Fig. 11: 3; Mazurek 1995, Fig. 16:e), one on the lower Warta River (Nowa Wieś, Międzyrzecz district) and one in Małopolska (Kraków Wyciąże: Poleska & Woźniak 1999: 384, 388, Fig. 3 p, r). Most almost certainly belong to type II specimens according to Babeș (1993: 76-79, Fig. 22) and were discovered on Jastorf culture settlements. As exceptions type I 1 specimens according to Babeș (*loco cit.*) were found in two Przeworsk culture graves in Drohiczyn Kozarówka on the Bug River and two others from Kraków Wyciąż (from the layer). These *Feuerböcke* strongly differ from similar fire dogs from Thracian lands, therefore, it cannot be excluded that the emergence of the fire dogs from Poland and that of the Poienești–Lukaševka culture was inspired by archetypes from the 'native lands' of the Jastorf culture.

Another group of artefacts characteristic of the Jastorf circle within Poland's territory is made up of clay spoons. They occur also in the oecumene of the Poienești–Lukaševka culture (Babeș 1993: 76, Taf. 20:2-6; 21:43; 23:30, 26:49; 31:6) and in the 'home lands' of the Jastorf culture, including the Gubin group, having been subsequently researched processed by Michałowski (2004). Surprisingly, non clay spoons were found in thoroughly excavated settlements such as Brześć Kujawski and Werbkowice-Kotorów. These are usually found within settlements (often multi-cultural ones), mostly in cultural layers. The finds of spoons are known from six settlements in Wielkopolska (Michałowski 2004: 150-155, Fig. 1; Sobucki & Woźniak 2004: 207, 208, 212, Fig. 7:9; 11 and Żegotki, Mogilno district: Dąbrowska & Woźniak 2005: Fig. 1: 3). The most certain attribution to the Jastorf culture is that of spoons from site 226, Poznań Nowe Miasto, and site 23, Wojnowo, Poznań district. An isolated site in eastern Poland, Dobryń Mały, Biała Podlaska district, site VIII, feature 9, yielded three spoons (included one with a faceted handle), accompanied by Jastorf and Przeworsk pottery (Michałowski 2004: 150, Fig. 3:5, 13; 4:2). More spoons were found on four sites in Małopolska: Kraków Mogiła, Kraków Pleszów, Kraków Wyciąże and Otałęż, Mielec district (Michałowski 2004, 151; Woźniak & Poleska 1999, 385-388, Fig. 2:i-o). However, the specimen from Otałęż can hardly be linked to the Pre-Roman period as no other relics from this period were found at the settlement. The two spoons from Kraków Mogiła come from the features of the Tyniec group (from phase LT D2). Interestingly, the specimen from hut C 45/1951, with a faceted handle and rims, and a blackened, polished surface, displays Przeworsk characteristics from that time and should unquestionably be dated the same as the hut; the other spoons from this site may have shared the same chronology.

Another important group of relics is that made up of bronze crown neck rings (*Kronenhalsringe*), the early forms of which appeared first in Denmark and northern Germany. It is from this region that most such finds come (Kostrzewski 1919a: 73-78, Fig. 56-59; 1926; Pasternak 1944; Keiling 1970: 208, Abb 2; Woźniak 1977: 272, 276-278; Dąbrowska 1988: 181-183; Shchukin et al. 1993; Maciałowicz & Nowakowska 2006; Maciałowicz 2011: 89-104, Fig. 7-14). Unfortunately, these finds as a rule lack any context, which prevents researchers from precisely determining their age. Early specimens from Poland, included in type I according to Kostrzewski's systematics,[21] are known only from Pomerania (Chocielewko and Kopaniewo, Lębork district, Czarnów, Słubice district, Karnice, Łobez district, Kruszyna, Słupsk district, Długie and Ognica, Stargard Szczeciński district, Redło, Goleniów district, Szczecin Pogodno, Piekło, Sztum district (Kostrzewski 1919a: 73-75, 277, Fig. 56; 1966:93; Bohnsack 1938: 35-37; Eggers & Stary 2001: 47, ryc. 144, 6, 8; Maciałowicz 2011: 89-104, Fig. 8-10, 12, 13) and Piasutno, Szczytno district, from the oecumene of the West Baltic Kurgan culture (Kostrzewski 1926; 1966, 93; Okulicz 1973, 287, Fig. 132; Maciałowicz 2011: 90, Fig. 7).[22] Interestingly enough, większość z nich were found on the territory of the Oder group of the Jastorf culture and i te came unquestionably from graves (Czarnów, Długie, Ognica, Szczecin) lub znalezisk luźnych (2 pozostałe). Out of crown neck rings found farther east, the specimens from Kopaniewo, Kruszyna and Piekło were discovered in a aqueous environment, while those from Chocielewko and possibly from Piasutno mogły należeć were part of grave inventories (Maciałowicz 2011: 90-96, 100-104; Fig. 14). Type I specimens have close counterparts primarily in Jutland, on Danish islands, Schleswig - Holstein and on Rugia. Unfortunately, there are no reliable data to determine their chronology. Maciałowicz (2011: 96-102, Fig. 12) in his extensive study suggests wide chronological brackets (może limits): from LT B2 for simple forms to LT C2 for 'developed' ones. This means in respect of East and Middle Pomerania that at least some may be associated with other Jastorf elements (Maciałowicz 2011: 104-112) that arrived here from the west: from the territory of the Oder group of the Jastorf culture but also from other areas, especially from Jutland.

Slightly younger (typologically), type II specimens were found in Milczek, Chodzież district, (Kostrzewski 1919a: 75, Fig. 57; type B according to Babeș 1993: 107, Fig. 28B) and Rydzewo, Drawsko Pomorskie district in West Pomerania (Bohnsack 1938: 36; Eggers & Stary 2001: 54, tabl. 165:3)[23]. The first may be linked to the Jastorf

---

[21] Babeș (1993: 107-108, 232, Fig. 28) distinguished six types of crown neck rings (A-F) that in most cases agree with Kostrzewski's proposals. A slightly changed version of Kostrzewski's typology was presented also by Shchukin *et al.* (1993: 45-47, Fig. 15) who distinguished types I, II, IIIa, IIIb, IV and V.

[22] Possibly, one more specimen of type I should be added here - mentioned by Kostrzewski (1919b: 227, Beil. 34) who gave only a name of the locality (?) – Neumark – without giving a district name. Does this refer to an unspecified locality in New March (e.g. Czarnów) or maybe to the Nowy Targ, Sztum district?

[23] Eggers & Stary (2001, 170) in the village index taken into account only the one locality Rützow (now Rusowo, district Kołobrzeg), and missed the other Rützow in district Schievelbein, that is today Rydzewo, district

settlement in north Wielkopolska but there are no data to date it more precisely. The discovery of another crown neck ring of this type in a settlement of the Poieneşti–Lukaševka culture in Davideni, Piatra Neamţ district, in Moldavia (Babeş & Untaru 1969; Babeş 1993: 107, 197, Fig. 28B, Taf. 24: 3) suggests a later chronology – unquestionably LT C2. Intermediate characteristics between type II and type III are displayed by the oldest crown neck ring from Kazyonnoe, Leski I, in the drainage basin of the lower Desna, east of Chernihiv (Popko 1965: 181, Fig. 2: 2; Shchukin et al., 1993: 45, Fig. 11). This is a concentration of crown neck ring finds located on the edge of the Zarubintsy culture settlement zone(?).

Yet another group consists of type III crown neck rings according to Kostrzewski (and type E according to Babeş 1993, 108, Fig. 28:25). Similar specimens are known also from the 'home zone' of these artefacts. The former were found in Ćmachowo, Szamotuły district, (from a grave, Demetrykiewicz 1900: 76), Wybranowo, Inowrocław district[24], Świdnica, Lower Silesia (Kostrzewski 1919a, 76, 277, Fig. 58; possibly from a grave, Demetrykiewicz 1900, 78) and from the Bug River in Vilkovo (Ulwówek), near Sokal, western Ukraine (Pasternak 1944: Fig. 1:3) – not far from Werbkowice-Kotorowo. To this group belongs also another crown neck ring from the territory of the Poieneşti–Lukaševka culture, namely from Ţibucani, Piatra Neamţ district (Babeş & Untaru 1969: 289, Abb. 3; Babeş 1993: 108:217, Fig. 28E, Taf. 24: 12) and two others from the territory of the Zarubintsy culture: from Valok, Leski, and Greblya situated closer to Chernihiv (Popko 1965, 181; Fig. 2: 2; Shchukin et al. 1993: 46, Fig. 3-4; 13).[25] These crown neck rings should be doubtless correlated with the younger phase of Brześć Kujawski (late Ripdorf, LT C). The next ring found in a Celtic settlement in Nowa Cerekwia, district Głubczyce, Upper Silesia, (information courtesy of M. Rudnicki), and another one in Němčice on the Moravia (information by courtesy of M. Rudnicki, M.A.) and from Radovesice in northern Bohemia (information by courtesy of M. Grygiel, M.A.) may belong to this same type too.

Yet another group is made up of crown-shaped necklaces defined by Kostrzewski (1919a, 78) as intermediate forms between type III and type IV. Specimens from Kluczewo, Płock district, and former Lochstädt, Primorsk district, Sambia, belong here. They do not have exact matches in Germany or Denmark, therefore, it can be assumed that they were products of a (single?) workshop operating in Poland (Maciałowicz & Nowakowska 2006). A similar intermediate position is occupied by two specimens of *Kronenhalsringe* from Leski (hamlets of Kazyonnoe and Makhon'koe) and Dashev, Lypovets (Lipowiec) district, east of Vinnitsa, Ukraine (Shchukin et al. 1993: 46n.,

Fig. 6, 9, 12; Pasternak 1944: 106, Fig. 1:4), a crown neck ring from an isolated grave in Dwikozy, Sandomierz district, (Woźniak 1994, Fig. 9:c) and quite possibly a ring fragment, partially melted by the heat of the pyre, from grave 151 of the Przeworsk culture in Błonie, Sandomierz district, (Mycielska & Woźniak 1988: 83, Tab. CXXXVI 3). Grave 151 from Błonie may be dated to phase A2 of the younger Pre-Roman period (Woźniak 1994: 130) correlated with phase LT D1. The pottery from the grave in Dwikozy is not typical.

The youngest group of crown-shaped necklaces, type IV in systematics by Kostrzewski (1919a: 76, Abb. 59) is made up of five specimens: from a grave in Staw, Września district, Wielkopolska, Izdebno Kościelne, pow. Grodzisk (ze studni: Waluś, Domaradzka, Brzóska 2010) na Mazowszu, Zalissia (Zalesie), Borschiv (Borszczów) district, western Ukraine, Greblya and Leski (Makhonkovo) in the environs of Chernihiv (Demetrykiewicz 1900: 71, Fig. 1-2; Pasternak 1944, Fig.1: 8; Dąbrowska 1988: 181-183; Shchukin 1993: 46, Fig, 5, 10). Hence, they should be placed in the period corresponding to phase LT D1. These specimens do not have counterparts in the home regions of Germany and Denmark. Hence, they must have been manufactured at a workshop(s) operating in the area they were found in. Keeping in mind that in the period in question in these regions, bronze objects made by local craftsmen are rare, the hypothesis that they were made by newcomers from other regions seems to be more likely. These artefacts testify to permanent contacts, as late as phase LT D1, between the populations of the Przeworsk culture and the distant southeast peripheries of the Zarubintsy culture and, quite possibly, the territory of the Poieneşti–Lukaševka culture.

Crown-shaped necklaces were of course valuable objects as a lot of bronze, which was a much sought-after raw material, was needed to make them. Besides, they played an important ritual role. The fact that a vast majority of over 100 known crown neck rings are cult objects deposited in water or swamps indicates that they were not just common ornaments but objects having a specific function closely related to religious rituals in the broad sense of this term.[26] They are also an argument in favour of the hypothesis about the existence of strong ties in the sphere of 'religious life', connecting societies that settled vast expanses of land – from the drainage basins of the Desna and middle Prut rivers as far as Jutland. All five crown neck rings found on the territory of the Warnow-Oder group in all likelihood were part of grave inventories. Out of 16 other rings found in Poland's other regions as many as 5 or 6 (Chocielewko, Lębork district, Ćmachowo, Szamotuły district, Błonie and Dwikozy, Sandomierz district, Staw, Września district and possibly Piasutno, Szczytno

---

Drawsko (where was discovered crown-shaped necklace). This can cause a problem, which came Rützow this find.
[24] In Synogać, Konin district, Kujawy, in a peat bog, another crown ring of unknown type was discovered (Zielonka 1970:156).
[25] The three last-mentioned crown neck rings according to Shchukin et al. (1993: 46) belong to sub-type IIIa.

[26] The area where the custom of depositing crown neck rings in water or swamps was observed (it should be noted that today's swamps must have been small lakes two thousand years ago) as offerings for deities may be considered a reflection of a community of sorts with respect to rituals, customs or social structure.

district[27]), Świdnica come from graves.[28] It is worth noting that three of them (Błonie, Dwikozy, Staw) are specimens of late types – associated with the Przeworsk culture or a period directly preceding its rise. On some of the rest, we have unequivocal information that they were found in water (Kopaniewo, Lębork district, Kluczewo, Płock district, Izdebno Kościelne, Grodzisk district, Kruszyna, Słupsk district, Piekło, Sztum district and Synogać, Konin district - a specimen of an indeterminate type: Zielonka 1970, 156), while on other *Kronenhalsringe* from the area under discussion no information is available on the circumstances they were found in. Interestingly enough, the crown neck ring from Vilkovo (Ulwówek) near Sokal, western Ukraine, (Pasternak 1944), close to the Polish border, was found on the river bed of the Bug River as well.

Hence, there is a striking contrast between the situation in Poland and a majority of the other lands occupied by the Jastorf culture. For it is only in north Germany that we are faced with exceptional cases of finding a crown neck ring in a grave (e.g. grave no. 27 in Friedrichshof, Güstrow *Kreis*, Mecklenburg: Keiling 1970: 210, Fig. 1:g, Taf. 25:b). On the rest of the Jastorf territory – in Germany, Denmark and Sweden – and on the opposite end – on the territory of the Zarubintsy culture – there was a "ban" on placing crown neck rings in graves with the dead.[29] What surprises in this context is the concentration of crown-shaped necklaces finds (and swamp ones, too) – altogether seven specimens – of various chronologies (including late ones) in the (drainage-usunąć) basin of the lower Desna river, Ukraine. This concentration of artefacts is evidence of the longevity of the custom of offering them to deities in the same area. The comparison in this context makes one hypothesize that Jastorf culture societies settling central Poland originally observed a custom of offering crown neck rings to water deities and that the custom 'was abolished' when the Przeworsk culture was taking shape (under the influence of the Warnow-Oder group?).

The review of research into the Jastorf settlement in the lands of (modern usunąć) Poland justifies making several claims (może statement lub affirmation) of a more general nature. First, it must be stressed that Jastorf materials from north Wielkopolska, Kujawy, part of Mazovia, east Lublin province, and part of Podlassia have a lot in common but, at the same time, there is a striking contrast between these materials and the finds from the other areas of the Jastorf circle. The major difference is the fact that in the area under discussion a dozen graves were discovered, mostly single ones, while it was settlements that were investigated in the first place, which yielded mostly pottery. However, it is common knowledge that the Jastorf culture features large burial grounds are(?). This is true both for the 'home areas' of the Jastorf culture and the peripheral groups of the Jastorf circle: Gubin, Kobyly, Oder, and the Poienești-Lukaševka culture. Meanwhile, in the majority of Jastorf circle territories, except for Jutland and the Poienești-Lukaševka culture, until recently settlements have been poorly investigated.

These fundamental differences in the composition of the source base make it difficult to correlate materials from the territory of Poland with general chronology systems as, of necessity, chronologies may rely chiefly on tableware. Besides, this practice violates the principles of research methodology because tableware usually differed from pottery deposited in graves. Therefore, the degree of probability of their comparative analysis results must be reduced. Hence, one has to take into account the possibility that the scale of similarity between the pottery from Brześć Kujawski and Werbkowice, and that from Jutland has been overestimated in the literature. For the estimates may have been influenced by the fact that from Jutland and Holstein we know of a rich series of pottery from settlements (mostly table-ware), while from the "home territories" of the Jastorf culture there is a good knowledge of pottery types used for sepulchral purposes. In effect, we may overestimate the role of the Jutland connection and, in consequence, are willing to accept the hypothesis of massive migrations of Jutland inhabitants and not from Jastorf territories lying closer to Poland.

It would appear that the state of field research is advanced enough in Poland to justify finding, in the opinion of this author, the scarcity of Jastorf graves, in comparison to the number of known settlements, a proven fact. Of course, it cannot be excluded that some meagrely furnished Jastorf graves may have been wrongly classified as belonging to other cultures by their discoverers (e.g. to the Pomeranian culture) as the knowledge of the characteristics of Jastorf culture pottery among Polish archaeologists who do not specialize in the Pre-Roman period is insufficient. Hence, this author is in favour of the most plausible hypothesis that the inhabitants of such settlements as Brześć Kujawski and Werbkowice did not observe the funerary rituals prevailing in other territories of the Jastorf culture circle. Thus it is highly improbable that Jastorf graves were more exposed to destruction by erosion, caused either by human activity (e.g. deep ploughing) or natural causes, because on the lowlands this is not as prevalent as on the uplands and in the mountains.[30] Of course, there are no grounds for making any conjectures concerning funerary rites practised by the majority of inhabitants of such settlements as Brześć Kujawski or Werbkowice.[31]

---

[27] It was probably a secondary grave in the mound of an older barrow: Okulicz 1973: 287.

[28] Uzasadnienie opinii, że zabytek ten pochodził z grobu (Demetrykiewicz 1900: 78) nie w pełni przekonuje. It was suggested that the specimen found in Świdnica came from a grave, but this is doubtful.

[29] Both crown neck rings from the territory of the Poienești-Lukaševka culture do not come from graves but not from the aqueous environment either. However, it is not known whether to this culture can be attributed a crown neck ring found on the lower Zbruch River, in Zalissia (Zalesie) it must have been a cult offering too.

[30] In mountainous and upland areas, we encounter extensive erosion destroying both summits and slopes of hills, while in river valleys we are faced with lateral erosion and riverbed changes.

[31] It seems to be most probable that these could have been shallow pit graves with meagre grave goods. It is worth remembering that slightly later in the majority of Celtic territories, we find no cemeteries.

The study of Jastorf materials from the areas under discussion (chiefly pottery from settlements) exposed their numerous similarities to finds from Jutland but also revealed their affinities with the classic Jastorf culture. Hence, the materials of the Brześć Kujawski - Werbkowice type make up a set different from any other set known from all the Jastorf culture groups; it is additionally set apart by different funerary rites. Thus, this author believes it was right to argue (Dąbrowska & Woźniak 2005: 88, 92) for considering the set a local group of the Jastorf culture and further, takes the liberty here to argue unequivocally for categorising this local group as the Brześć Kujawski-Werbkowice. Initially, the group occupied north Wielkopolska and Kujawy and only later did its territory extend southeast, taking the shape of a crescent (Dąbrowska & Woźniak 2005, Fig. 1; Woźniak 2007a, Fig. 6). This distribution of the settlement of the Brześć Kujawski-Werbkowice group suggests that its settlements could have controlled the route, running along the Noteć, Vistula and Bug rivers, joining the north zone of the Jastorf culture with the Black Sea area. It could have been the route that the Bastarnae followed (later) in their migrations. Interestingly enough, their trek towards the Black Sea is usually traced in this very manner and called the 'Bastarnae trail" (Dąbrowska 1994). Travelling along this route, the Bastarnae (and possibly the Scirae) reached the Black Sea coast and destabilized the political situation on the lower Danube and on the northwest Black Sea coast, which put them on the pages of written history in the late 3rd century BC.

What else makes one wonder is the south range limit of the settlements of the Brześć Kujawski-Werbkowice group in Wielko-polska (Machajewski 2004, Fig. 1) because as a rule they do not cross the section of the middle Warta River flowing east – west (on its left bank, there are only two settlements in Nowe Miasto nad Wartą, Środa Wlkp. district).[32] Not far south of this section of the middle Warta, there ran the range limit of the high incidence of Kowalowice fibulae in Pomeranian culture grave inventories. The Kowalowice fibulae show similarities with the style of La Tène culture fibulae of middle phase LT A (Woźniak 2010: 59-69, Fig. 4, Map 3; 2011, Fig. 3).[33] Only two specimens (Szarlej, Inowrocław district, Unisław, Chełmno district) were found along the still functioning amber route', leading towards the Baltic coast. In its environs, we know of open-work fibulae of the Hochscheid–Linz type from Bojano, Wejherowo district and Gogolewo, Tczew district (Megaw 2005), which have a similar chronology. Kowalowice fibulae were the work of local craftsmen, hence it cannot be ruled out that they continued to be made for some time after fashion changed in the Celtic world, i.e. in the late section of LT A. In the decline phase of LT A, the territory settled by Pomeranian culture populations considerably contra-cted. As such, it could receive fewer "Celtic" imports displaying a new style or local products inspired by it. South Wielkopolska found itself outside of the La Tène impact (Woźniak 2010, 69, Fig. 6, Map 4; 2011, Fig. 5, Map 4), while only a single find of a bronze fibula from around Skulsk, Konin district (information courtesy of Prof. T. Makiewicz), shows that Old La Tène influences reached the region north of the middle Warta River. This means that already before the end of the 5th century BC, the traditional 'amber route' stopped functioning. Hence, the question arises whether the settlement by Pomeranian culture populations continued here in isolation or whether the demographic crisis affected north Wielkopolska and allowed in strangers who wanted to settle there.

A separate problem is posed by Jastorf culture relics from south Poland – chiefly from west Małopolska. Unlike in the case of north Wielkopolska, Mazovia and east Lublin province, they rather cannot be considered traces of a longer sojourn of Jastorf culture carriers in the environs of (present-day usunąć) Kraków. For most Jastorf relics occur in the clear context of Celtic materials in Małopolska. We know even of single graves of this culture from this region. On a partially investigated cemetery in Łętowice, Tarnów district, next to a Jastorf cenotaph no. 7a, there is Celtic grave 13 (Szpunar 1988: 185, 187, 191, Fig. 6:f, g, 8:j, k) and later graves attributed to the Przeworsk culture. In Kraków Pleszów, site 17, Jastorf grave no. 1187/1975 was discovered within the cemetery of the Pomeranian culture and perhaps other single damaged graves were exposed in settlements in Kraków Wyciąże and Kraków Mogiła (Woźniak & Poleska 1999: 381, Fig. 2; Poleska 2006: 26). Only in respect of the first two graves, can a dating be suggested to a period close to the beginnings of the Celtic settlement in west Małopolska.

We also know of other relics of Jastorf types (pins, buckles, 'fire wolves' (dogs?), clay spoons, single vessels) found within settlements, belonging chiefly to phase LT C, but also to phase LT D2 (Woźniak & Poleska 1999), that have already been discussed earlier. The artefacts from LT D2 may be evidence of late contacts with the territory of the Poienești-Lukaševka culture along the 'reversed Bastarnae (route) trail'. The fact that the precise chronology of earlier artefacts cannot be determined (the context of most of them is unknown) makes their interpretation difficult.

It is a well-known fact that initially it was believed that especially close ties had existed between the Poienești-Lukaševka culture and the Gubin group of the Jastorf culture. For this? reason, the trail of the Bastarnae's migration to the Black Sea was marked out across south Poland, including west Małopolska. Early, middle La Tène Jastorf finds from Małopolska (graves and finds) make up a set that gives the impression of traces of quite a quick

---

[32] I assume that the absence of any traces of the Jastorf settlement south of this section of the Warta River is not simply a result of the fact that excavations were not conducted there on a similar scale to those carried out north of the river.

[33] Recently, (Woźniak 2010: 60-69; 2011: 18-24) I have radically changed my view on the relative and absolute chronology of these fibulae. I reject my own (Woźniak 1979: 143-146) and Lorentzen's (1992: 68-72) proposals to date them even to phase LT B1. The adjustment to their dating is made larger by an overall change of absolute dates (down) of the Hallstatt and La Tène periods that took place towards the end of the 20th century.

passage. These finds remind us of traces of a slightly later migration south by the Cimbri. It is worth remembering here that two crown neck rings come from Silesia (Świdnica, Nowa Cerekwia – see above) and that from Lower Silesia we know of single shards of the Jastorf type (eg. Stary Zamek site. 6, hole 1, 2, 2a, 3, ,5; see Pescheck 1939, 104-105, 149-150, Taf. 8:7-10; Tackenberg 1930, 277, Fig. 16-18, 21-23; Pazda 1992, 104, Fig. 11:b,c, Tab. II:2; Domański, Lodowski 1984), although they were not properly recognized. So it can be supposition that there existed another, southern trail for migration of Jastorf culture populations (the Bastarnae) to the Black Sea. Attention should be drawn to the fact that the migration took place some time before 200 BC, i.e. around the late phase LT C1 and early LT C2 (Łowmiański 1963: 196-209; Babeš 1993: 168-180). Approximately at the same time, the enclave of Celtic settlement in Lower Silesia came to an end, leaving a settlement vacuum there for some time (ca. 50-60 years), until the Przeworsk culture settlement emerged in early phase A2 of the younger Pre-Roman Iron Age. A tempting hypothesis holds that Celts decided to migrate from Lower Silesia together with the groups of Jastorf culture populations (doubtless taking the south route across Małopolska) and joined the union of the Bastarnae. The claim that the Bastarnae were a people of a mixed ethnic composition – consisting of Germans and Celts – is based on the commentaries of Polybius (XXV 6) and Plutarch (*Vita Aemilii Pauli* 9, 6), referring to them as Celts, and especially on a reference by Livy (XL 57) who wrote outright that they knew the language of the Celts (Woźniak 1974: 22-24).[34] Of course, the Bastarnae also could have been joined by the groups of Celts from Transylvania, who penetrated Moldavia some time earlier (see above).

The section of prehistory of the Polish territory discussed here was, as this study attempted to show, a period of strife, human population shifts and demographic crises. The study of those times is made more difficult by the meagre amount of sources. It seems, however, that in recent years much progress has been achieved in this respect. Yet, it is still difficult to give an informed answer to the question about the dating of the youngest materials of the Pomeranian culture and the fate of its carriers. Now, it can be confidently claimed that the lands of (present-day-usunąć) Poland witnessed the arrival of substantial groups of people from the Jastorf circle territory. In the rise of the local Brześć Kujawski-Werbkowice group, a major role was played by arrivals from Jutland, although in the settlement process, people from other areas belonging to this circle participated as well. The peculiarity of the Brześć Kujawski-Werbkowice group is best seen in the specific funerary rite observed by most of its populations. It is very likely that these populations absorbed the groups of descendants of Pomeranian culture. In areas left unsettled by the newcomers (e.g. in central Poland), there must have striven for survival some groups of descendants of Pomeranian culture populations, lacking any organization and having no contact with the outer world.

The major trail of the Bastarnae continued most probably along the Noteć, middle Vistula and Bug rivers. Since the Poienești–Lukaševka culture shows traits making it closer to other groups of the Jastorf culture than to the Brześć Kujawski-Werbkowice group, it seems that in the trek towards the Black Sea, the dominant group was that of migrants hailing from lands lying farther northwest, although members of the Brześć Kujawski-Werbkowice group participated in it too (they could have even been the organizers of the first migration). The south trail (route) (via Małopolska), if it was used at all, played a secondary role. Groups of newcomers from the distant west reached the Ukrainian territory under the Zarubintsy culture. This is evidenced by the traces of Jastorf influence in settlements forms and funerary rites (Kasparova 1981; 1992; Shchukin 1989: 60-77; Maksymov 1999; Pačkova 1999; 2002), and also in religion as shown by the finds of crown neck rings from Dašev, Greblya and Liski (Popko 1965; Shchukin, Val'kova & Shevchenko 1992). More evidence is provided by the find of a "fire dog" in a settlement of the Zarubintsy culture, site 3, Litvinoviči, Sumy district, near the Seym River, Trans-Dnieper Ukraine (Oblomskij & Terpilovskij 1994: 162, Fig. 8:2).[35]

It seems, however, that a substantial part of Brześć Kujawski-Werbkowice populations did not move and were included in the populations of the rising Przeworsk culture because there is absolutely no evidence hinting at a possibility of the influx of new arrivals. It is reasonable to believe therefore that the populations of the Brześć Kujawski-Werbkowice group which stayed behind also integrated then with the descendants of Pomeranian culture populations. In earlier discussions later Jastorf relics were treated as possible traces of contacts along the Bastarnae trail (route?) but in the opposite direction. However, some may be considered a 'contribution' made into the emerging Przeworsk culture by that portion of the population of the Brześć Kujawski-Werbkowice group which stayed in Poland's territory. A good example is offered by bowls with broad "hanging handles". They are known from the sites of the "classic" Jastorf and Poienești-Lukaševka cultures, and several settlements of the Brześć Kujawski-Werbkowice group (Brześć Kuj., Izdebno Kościelne, Poznań Nowe Miasto, Wojnowo, Wytyczno), as well as Przeworsk culture settlements and cemeteries: Biejków, Białobrzegi district, Błonie, Janikowo, Inowrocław district, Oblin, Garwolin district, Suchodół, Sochaczew district, Tomasze, Ostrołęka district, and Warszawa Wilanów: Maciałowicz 2004). There is some similarity between these bowls and so-called Dacian bowls but it seems to be most plausible to consider their younger

---

[34] In this context, a reference is made to Olbia's decree for Protogenes from which we know of the threat to Olbia posed by the Galatians and Scirae (Woźniak 1974: 21-23).

[35] The mysterious finds from Liski and Greblya, Chernihiv environs, co-uld be associated more easily, in my opinion, with the materials of the Brześć Kujawski-Werbkowice group than with the Poienești–Lukaševka culture.

(Przeworsk) specimens a manifestation of continuation of local traditions by Przeworsk culture populations. The question of late crown neck ring find in the Przeworsk context (Błonie) should be analogously considered.

In the centre of Polish territory, with the beginning of the middle La Tène period, a fundamental change took place in comparison to the situation prevailing in phase LT B. Beginning with phase LT C1, a great influx of Celtic relics is observed into the regions they did not reach earlier (Dąbrowska 1988:127; 1996; 2004:215; Dąbrowska & Woźniak 2005; Kokowski 1991a; Łuczkiewicz 1998; Karwowski 1997, Abb. 1; Tomaszewska 1997; Bochnak 2005: 156-158, 209, 212). Their arrival marks the start of intensive Latènisation of these regions and the relics often do not have any context (e.g. a sword from Warszawa Żerań). This influx slightly precedes the rise of the developed Przeworsk culture.

One of the important factors that contributed to the strengthening of the Celtic impact on the centre of (modern-usunąć) Poland's territory was, no doubt, the founding by Celts of a rich trading centre in Nowa Cerekwia, Upper Silesia, which had ties to an important emporium in Němčice, Moravia (see above). A certain role in the spreading of Latènisation was played also by settlements in west Małopolska. North of the Celtic enclaves in Poland, there must have developed conditions conducive to long-distance trade, i.e. the rise of structures guaranteeing safety. The Celtic impact rapidly brought about radical changes not only in the 'superficial' manifestations of culture, as for instance fashion (shapes of fibulae, etc.), but also in other spheres such as better implements and weapons, including types of warfare, as well as funerary rites (pit graves, richer grave goods), and last but not least: changes of social structures (see above). After the fall of Němčice and Nowa Cerekwia, the centre of trade with the north moved to the *oppidum* in Stare Hradisko and in phase LT D2 – to the Tyniec group, especially settlements in the vicinity of Kraków. To the significance of these ties testifies the rise (foundation?) of an outpost (factory) near Kalisz where coins were minted (Rudnicki *et al.* 2009).

Around the transition from phase LT C1 and LT C2, the adaptation of strong La Tène impulses made the emerging Przeworsk culture the most "latènised" one outside of the Celtic world. It was also one of the most belligerent communities as shown by invasions by 'Przeworsk warriors' evidenced by well-known finds dated to the younger Pre-Roman period. These were discovered in the (drainage) basins of the upper Dniester, Slovakia and Moravia, as well as in particularly large numbers in central Germany and even as far as the Main River (see Hachmann 1956/1957; Dąbrowska 1988: 156n.; Peschel 1978; Seidel M. 1996). It follows from the earlier discussion that this author believes the following (skorygować 5 słów) hypothesis about the composition of the Przeworsk culture populations to be justified. Namely, they were composed of some members of the Brześć Kujawski-Werbkowice group of the Jastorf culture, disorganized descendants of Pomeranian culture populations and doubtless the groups of Celts who did not abandon Celtic settlement enclaves in south Poland. The last-mentioned may have played a significant role, which is indicated by their Celtic tribal name – the Lugii (Kolendo 1998).

It is difficult to delineate the region in which the Przeworsk culture developed. A hypothesis prevails that the core home region covered a vast area, comprising the north part of Lower Silesia, Wielkopolska with Kujawy, central Poland, south Mazovia, and the environs of Warszawa and Radom (Godłowski 1985: 16-29; Dąbrowska 1988: 69-73, maps 3 & 4; Dąbrowska & Woźniak 2005, 88, Fig. 2). Generally, this opinion seems to be right although it was formulated prior to the new discoveries in Nowa Cerekwia, which unexpectedly revealed the high rank of this settlement and, by the same token, its great significance for the Latènisation of the lands of (present-day-usunąć) Poland. As wrong, one should now consider the over-estimation of the role of the Celtic enclave in central Silesia and the north part of Lower Silesia in this process.[36] Apparently, the area where the culture developed is marked by the grave finds, the cultural attribution of which is unclear (e.g. Warszawa Żerań, Zarębowo, Aleksandrów Kujawski district, Dwikozy, district Sandomierz).

However, impulses stimulating Latènisation reached the territory of (present-day-usunąć) Poland not only from the south, directly from the Celts. In East Pomerania an important channel of dissemination of the La Tène fashion and the Celts' civilization achievements, next to a strong impact from the south – from the Przeworsk culture – was the influence of the Jastorf culture, which stayed in contact with Celtic centres lying farther west. The Jastorf influence came chiefly from the nearby Oder group but also from the north, by sea, from Gotland and Bornholm (Wołągiewicz 1981b; Kaul & Martens 1995: 130; Bokiniec 2001; Dąbrowska & Woźniak 2005: 93; Maciałowicz 2011). Owing to these influences, in the assemblages of the Oksywie culture, we often encounter such types of Jastorf artefacts as butt-end neck rings (*Halsringe mit verdicktem Kolbenende*), iron fibulae with a bronze slip on the bow (*mit einer Bronzehülse*) and *stufenförmigen Fibeln* (Bokiniec 2001; Maciałowicz 2011), which are very rare in the territories of the Przeworsk culture. The Oksywie culture took shape somewhat later than the Przeworsk culture and they differ from one another much more than it was believed earlier (Strobin 2011: 70-78, 82). It should be stressed that the greatest share in the population of the Oksywie culture was probably made up of the descendants of Pomeranian culture (Dąbrowska & Woźniak 2005: 94), next to arrivals from the west (from the Oder group), north (from Scandinavia) and also from the south – Przeworsk culture peoples. This varied population must have made the Oksywie culture heterogeneous, which gave rise to arguments about the attribution of materials from the

---

[36] Hence, I retract my previous comments on this question (Woźniak 2007a: 406).

younger Pre-Roman period from the Land of Chełmno either to the Oksywie or Przeworsk culture.

Finally, this study shall take the liberty to formulate a few research objectives concerning the questions discussed here. It is urgently needed to verify the context in which 'Jastorf imports' were found, as well as Celtic ones characteristic of phase LT C1, in the Polish territory. It is also necessary to review the cemeteries of the Pomeranian culture yielding late materials as well as materials from Przeworsk culture cemeteries with early assemblages because they may contain single graves of the Jastorf type. I am convinced that by tightening collaboration between Polish archaeologists working on the Pre-Roman period in southeast Poland and their Ukrainian counterparts active in Volhynia and east Galicia, it will be possible to find the real (course? of the chyba limit?) eastern frontier of the Celtic settlement enclave in the region of Rzeszów. I hope that the changed approaches to the cultural questions concerning the Polish territory in the older and in the early younger Pre-Roman periods offered here will encourage scholars to make a common effort in order to explain an even more important and also more difficult problem: the occurrence of Werbkowice type materials in Volhynia and east Galicia. This will offer a chance to verify our views on the origins of western elements observable in the Zarubintsy culture.

Chapter 2

The Jastorf Culture on the Polish Lowland

Michał Grygiel

The cultural situation prevailing in Poland in the age straddling the older and younger Pre-Roman Iron Age is still poorly recognized. It is generally assumed that in this period important changes took place within the Pomerania-Cloche culture, which occupied a considerable portion of the Polish Lowland and continued Early Iron Age traditions. It is further assumed that the changes were triggered by the strong impact of the La Tène culture and resulted in significant modifications in the spiritual and material culture of the then societies, inhabiting vast areas north of the zone covered by dense Celtic settlement.

As a result, in the early younger Pre-Roman period, the Pomerania-Cloche culture was replaced by, among others, the Przeworsk culture, showing strong La Tène traits. In the Polish literature on the subject, a still dominating view holds that the latter of the two cultures was a direct continuation of the former. The most important cause of the cultural change was believed for a long time to have been the Celtic impact. Only recently has the Jastorf culture been indicated as a possible contributor to the process. Its appearance on the lands of present-day Poland could have destabilized the social and economic conditions that had existed there since the older Pre-Roman period (Godłowski 1985: 137-138; Dąbrowska 1988: 226-229; 1994; Kaczanowski & Kozłowski 1998: 215-216). Possibly, the Jastorf factor greatly influenced the cultural picture that took shape on the vast expanses of the Polish lands in the early younger Pre-Roman period. An argument in favour of this view is the presence of dispersed but relatively numerous Jastorf culture finds on the Lowland, east of the culture's compact range and beyond the limits of the Oder and Gubin groups (Dąbrowska 1994, Fig. 8; Grygiel 2004; Dąbrowska & Woźniak 2005, Fig. 1; Woźniak 2007a: 398-406, Fig. 6). These are not only single unattached Jastorf artefacts or such artefacts found in another cultural context, but also and above all settlements, extremely significant for the questions at hand as they yielded long series of pottery characteristic of the Jastorf culture and single burials linked to it.

The traces of the Jastorf culture settlement on the Lowland are dispersed and do not form any clear clusters. This may be a result, in part, of the state of research. One of the obstacles it encountered was the difficulty in identifying Jastorf settlements as in many cases all that we have is sparse surface material. Relying on it, one cannot be absolutely certain about either cultural attribution or character of individual sites. It is for this reason that the lists of Jastorf culture settlements given in this paper include only those we know more about. These comments are also true, to some extent, for the lists of sepulchral sites and unattached finds associated with the Jastorf culture (Figs. 9, 10).

Beyond the native area of the Jastorf culture, its materials were identified the earliest, already in the 1950s, on the Prut, Seret and middle Dniester rivers. The materials were later included in the Poienești-Lukaševka culture that was associated with the Germanic tribe of the Bastarnae, known from written records (Vulpe 1955; Hachmann 1957; 1961, 117-120; 1970, 305-307; Tackenberg 1963a; Babeș 1973; 1988; 1993). On the early stage of research, however, no 'bridging' materials could be shown from central and east Poland, which would join the home ground of the Jastorf culture to the territory of the Poienești-Lukaševka culture.

The first publication that attempted to distinguish such finds, Woźniak (1977a), dealt only with a selected source category, namely Jastorf metal artefacts known from Poland. A milestone in the investigations of the Jastorf culture on the Lowland, the scholarly output of Dąbrowska (1988: 102-104, 196-199; 1994), was the first to discuss in detail settlement sites yielding Jastorf culture materials. Dąbrowska commented in the first place on finds, known already much earlier, from settlements in Brześć Kujawski, district Włocławek (Kujawy) and Werbkowice-Kotorów, ditrict Hrubieszów (east Lublin province) (Jażdżewski 1939; Piętka-Dąbrowska & Liana 1962; Dąbrowska & Liana 1963).

Moreover, Dąbrowska deserves special credit for analyzing and systematizing the materials of the so-called Czerniczyn group (Lublin province) from the point of view of their cultural attribution. In the first place, she exposed their links to the Jastorf culture (Dąbrowska 1988: 196-200; 1994, 71-73; 2001: 26-28). Earlier the Czerniczyn group had been associated with the Zarubintsy culture whose sites supposedly occurred in parts of the Lublin province, north of the Hrubieszów Basin. Attention was also drawn to the fact that among the finds assigned to the Czerniczyn group, Przeworsk culture artefacts were found (Czopek 1981; Kokowski 1983: 4-5). Later, the group was believed to have been a cultural unit combining the elements of the Pomerania-Cloche and Jastorf cultures, expanding its relatively narrow territorial range (Czopek 1985; 1991a; 1991b; 1992a; Kokowski 1986: 185; 1991a: 177, 180; Mazurek 1995a). Recently, Dąbrowska has observed that there are no grounds to treat the Czerniczyn group as a separate taxonomic unit in the cultural division of Poland's territory. She claims it to be only a set of unconnected materials of various cultural provenance, including, among others, Jastorf finds (Dąbrowska 2001: 26-27; Grygiel 2004: 14-15).

The occurrence of Jastorf finds east of the culture's home ground was explained, as already mentioned, by

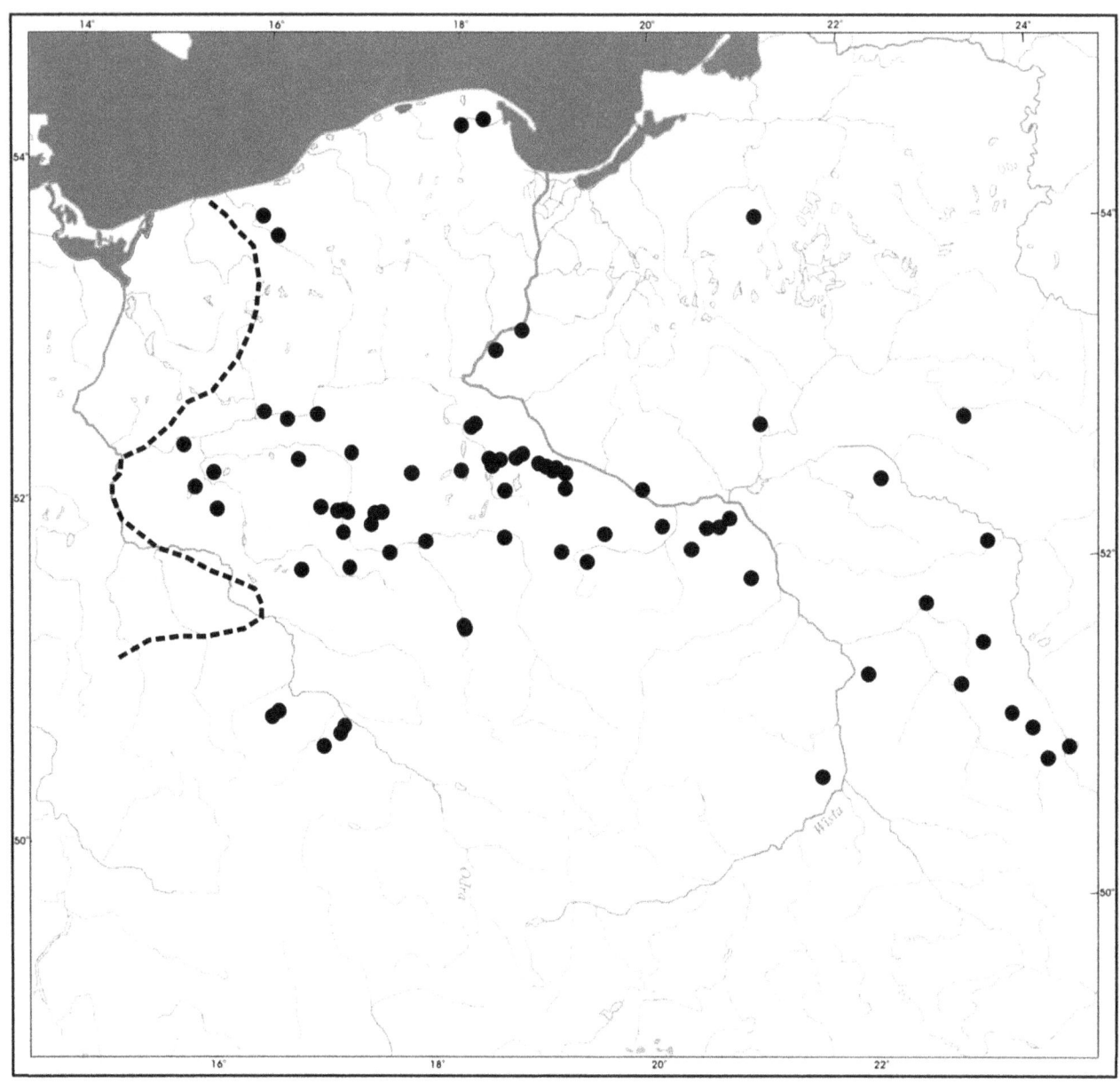

FIG. 9. SETTLEMENT AND BURIAL GROUND THE JASTORF CULTURE ON POLISH LOWLAND (DASHED LINES INDICATE THE EASTERN RANGE OF THE TERRITORY OF GUBIN AND WARNOW-ODER GRUPS OF JASTORF CULTURE).

the migration of the historically recorded Germanic tribes of the Bastarnae and Scirii in the direction of the Black Sea coast. It is widely believed that their itinerary crossed the territory of modern Poland (Woźniak 1977a; 1988: 240-242; 2007:398; Pačkowa & Romanovskaja 1983; Godłowski 1977: 199-203; 1985: 137-138; 1992; Peschel 1992: 121-122; Dąbrowska 1988: 175-192, 226-227; 1994; Shchukin, Val'kova & Schevchenko 1992; Babeş 1993: 154-162; Domański 1996, 1999; Kaczanowski & Kozłowski 1998:216; Poleska & Woźniak 1999; Dąbrowska & Woźniak 2005).[37] As evidence of these events, , relatively numerous artefacts especially characteristic of the Jastorf culture were taken, such as crown-shaped necklaces and clay figurines known as fire wolves. For the most part these are unattached finds, frequently without any cultural context, which, according to some, supposedly testify to a relatively quick migration of the Germanic tribes across the drainage basins of the Oder and Vistula rivers (Woźniak 1988: s. 240-242). On the strength of this assumption it was believed that the migration had not left behind any permanent traces, such as settlement remains or sepulchral features, and had been but a short episode.

This view had a strong impact on most discussions of the Pre-Roman period in the territory of modern Poland by guiding the interpretations of cultural changes taking place then in central Europe. The interpretations did not take at all into account the Jastorf factor. Numerous recent discoveries of Jastorf culture settlements and single burials, made in Wielkopolska, Land of Lubusz, south-eastern part of Lower Silesia, central Poland, Kujawy, Mazovia, Podlassia and the east Lublin province, as well

---

[37] For questions of ethnic interpretation see Łowmiański 1963: 198-200; Venskus 1976; Babeş 1993: 168-174

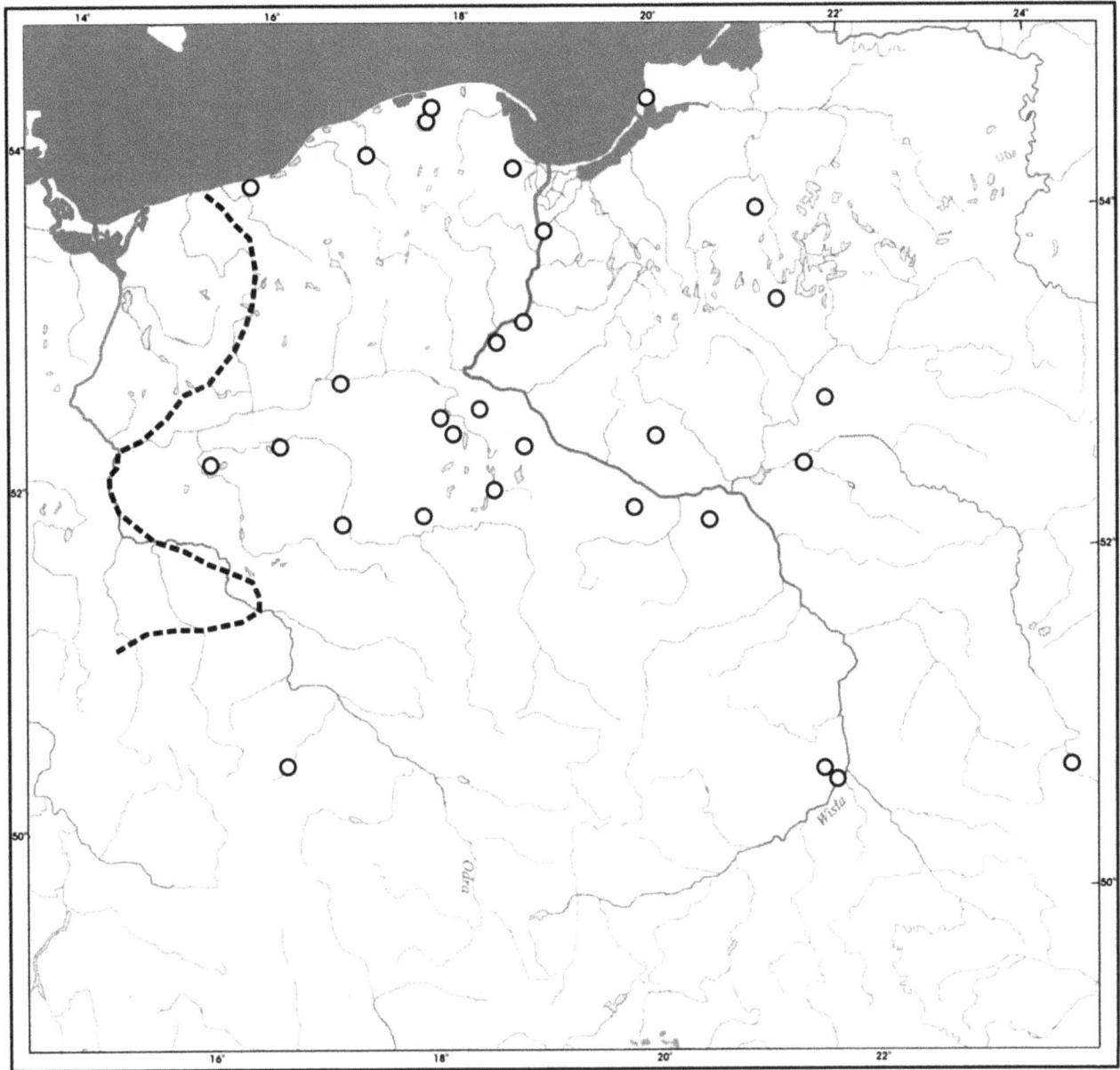

Fig. 10. Finds the Jastorf culture on Polish Lowland (dashed lines indicate the eastern range of the territory of Gubin and Warnow-Oder grups of Jastorf culture).

as single discoveries made on the Gdańsk Seaboard, in the drainage basin of the Parsęta River, in the Land of Chełmno, in the Sandomierz Land and in the northeast of Poland - Fig. 9 (see Grygiel 2012, list 28), significantly alter the picture of the cultural situation in these areas. Consequently, the relation-ships of the Jastorf culture with other cultural units flourishing on the Lowland in the Pre-Roman period are modified as well. One of the most important questions concerning these relationships is the determination of the chronological position of Lowland Jastorf culture materials.

Important data for establishing the chronology of Lowland Jastorf culture materials are obtained by comparing pottery, being the most numerous among them, with finds from other Jastorf settlement zones (Dąbrowska 1994; Grygiel 2004; Woźniak 2007a; Machajewski 2010: 202-213). The compa-rison is based on the chronological systems of the native Jastorf culture. These, however, may be only roughly correlated with the periodization of the La Tène culture (Grygiel 2004: 18-19). Moreover, it must be noted that only a small portion of Lowland Jastorf pottery can be dated in this way. The is so because most of these materials come from settlements and not all find analogies in precisely dated pottery forms from other parts of the Jastorf culture territory, which in turn come chiefly from burial grounds.

Another limitation is the poor state of preservation of Lowland Jastorf culture pottery. To be precise, dominating settlement finds are greatly comminuted, which in many instances prevents vessel forms from being reconstructed.

The characteristic forms of Lowland Jastorf culture pottery include thin-walled vase-like vessels of various sizes. They have a bi- or tripartite structure and carefully

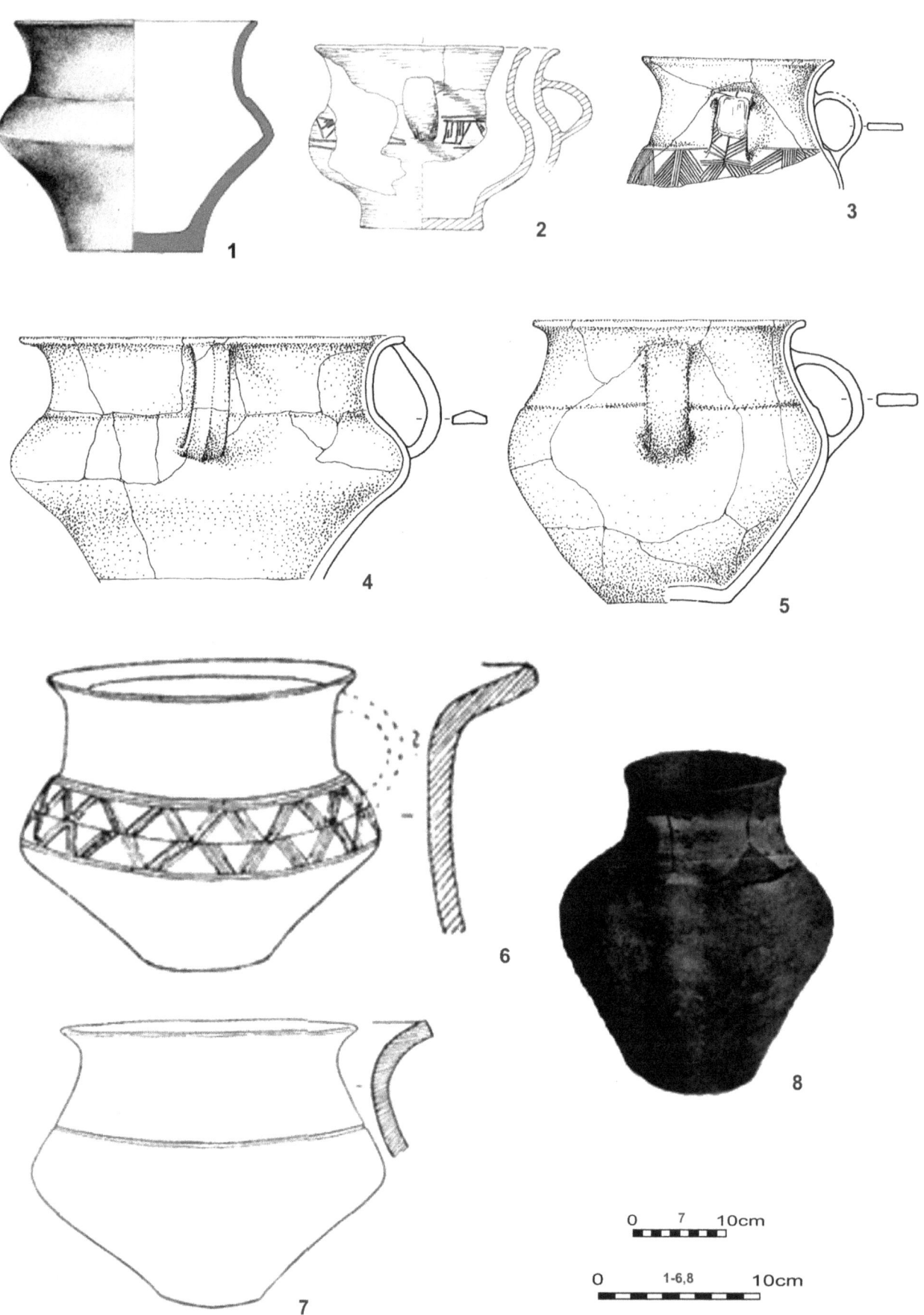

Fig. 11 Jastorf culture dish - a vase with a separate neck. 1 Rumia (after Maciałowicz 2011); 2 – Izdebno Kościelne (after Kołacz 1995); 3, 4. Brześć Kujawski 3 (drow E. Górska); 5-7. Brześć Kujawski 4 (5. draw E. Górska; 6, 7. after Jażdżewski 1940); 8 Karlino (after H. J. Eggers File).

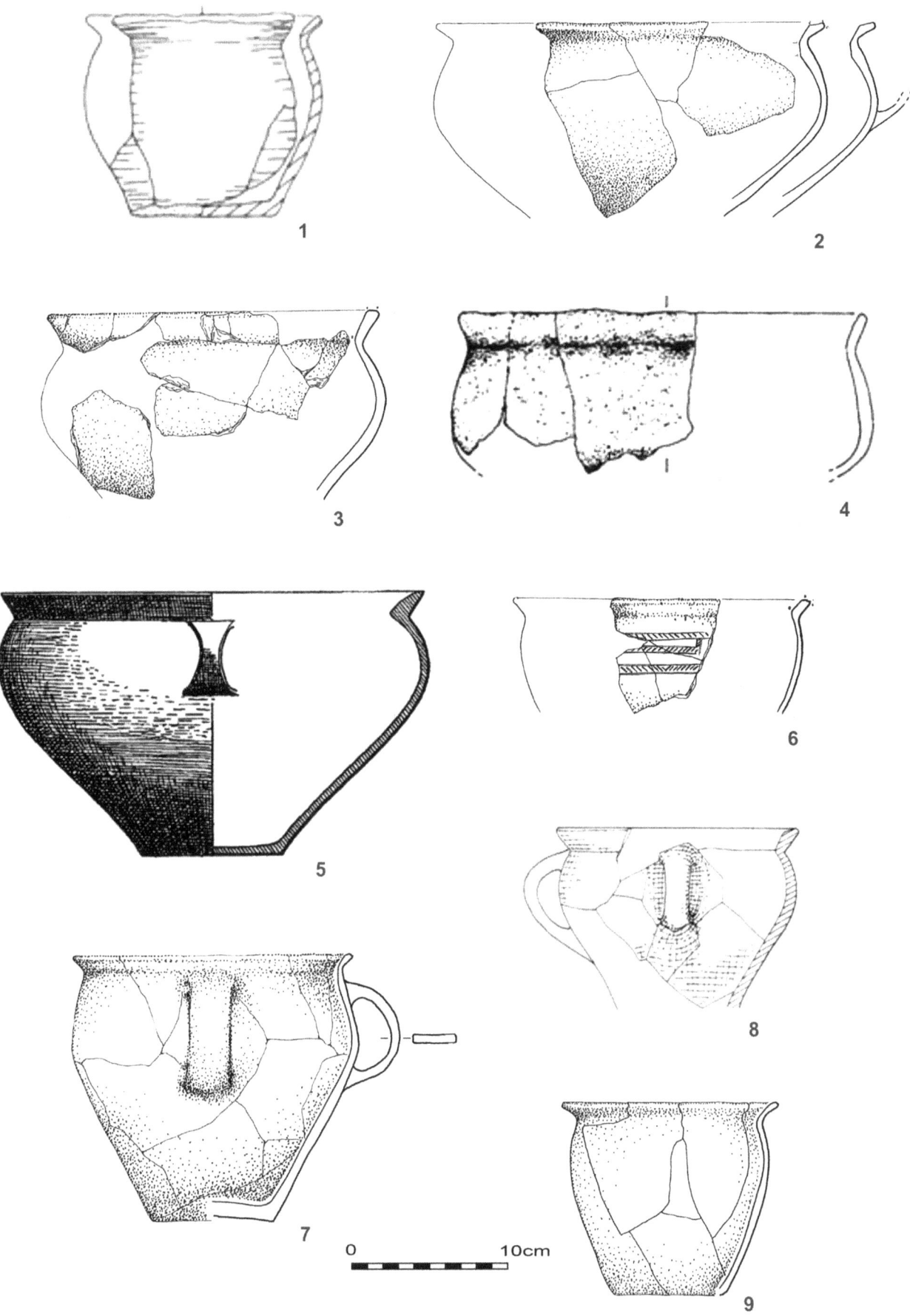

Fig. 12. Jastorf culture dish - a vase without a neck.
1. Izdebno Kościelne (after Kołacz 1995); 2, 3, 6, 7, 9. Brześć Kujawski 4 (draw E. Górska); 4 Wytyczno (after Mazurek 2001); 5 Czarnków (after Michałowski 2006); 8. Piecki (after Bednarczyk, Sujecka 2004).

finished, burnished walls. Among these usually low forms, single slender specimens stand out, resembling reverse pear-shaped vessels known from the younger Pre-Roman period. The rims of the vase-like vessels are usually not marked and sometimes strongly turned outwards, forming funnel-shaped lips. Many of these vessels have an undercut lower belly and handles most often placed where the belly changes into the neck or joining the upper belly with the rim (Fig. 11).[38] Frequent types of finds are a vase-like vessel without a marked neck and, only slightly different, cups with broad openings (Fig. 12).[39] This type of vessel sometimes shows a tendency to undercut the lower belly. Some of the vases/cups had a single handle placed directly below the lip rim. These forms resemble in shape squat cups and goblets, common among Jastorf culture finds, with a roughly globular or barrel-shaped belly (Fig. 13:1-6).[40]

Furthermore, we know of small cone-shaped vessels falling into the category of goblets or cups (Fig. 13:7-1).[41] Bowls are very common. Among them, special attention is deserved by rather deep specimens with their rims turned outwards and cone-shaped or semi-spherical vases with unmarked or poorly marked rims. Some bowls kept their handles located mostly on a belly bent or, in the case of some forms with unmarked rims, on a lower belly (so-called bowls with "hanging" handles - Fig. 14, 15).[42]

---

[38] Examples of vase-like vessels with marked neck. Settlements: Brześć Kujawski, Włocławek district site 3 and 4 – feature 1, 139, 173, 243, 249, 351, 553, 773/774, 856a, 860, 867, 894 (Jażdżewski 1939, Tab. 8.2,4, 9.1, 10.4,18, 11.4; Grygiel 2004, Fig. 2.a,c-e, 3a, 6a,c,e; 2012; unpublished) (Fig. 3.3-7); Dopiewo, Poznań district site 26/29 (Machajewski 2010, ryc. 8.1, 12.10); Izdebno Kościelne, Grodzisk Maz. district site 1 – feature 110 (Kołacz 1995, Tab. XV.d) (Fig. 3.2); Karnin, Gorzów Wlkp. District site 197 – over feature 93 (Grygiel 2012; unpublished); Komorniki, Poznań district site 2 – feature 2 (Kostrzewski 1939); Łagiewniki, Inowrocław district site 5 - feature 87 (Grygiel 2012; unpublished); Łęki Górne, Kutno district site 1 (Grygiel 2012; unpublished); Nowy Drzewicz, Żyrardów district site 5 – feature 839 (Grygiel 2012; unpublished); Otorowo, Szamotuły district site 66 (Żychliński 2004, Fig. 4.6); Pławce, Środa Wlkp. District site 22 (Makiewicz 2004, Fig. 2.1,3); Sychowo, Wejherowo district (Felczak 1985, Fig. 7); Szynych, Grudziądz district site 12 – feature 138, 814(?), 912, quadrat 06/02 I/II cultural layer, quadrat 08/02 I cultural layer (Grygiel 2012; unpublished). Graves: Rumia, Wejherowo district site 1 – grave 46 (Maciałowicz 2011, Fig. 4.a) (Fig. 3.1); Wygoda, Białogard district site 6 – grave 102 (Machajewski 2001, Tab. XXV.102.3). Find with no context: Czarnków, Czarnków-Trzcianka district (Michałowski 2006, Fig. 16)
Examples of slender vase-like vessels. Graves: Karlino, Białogard district – grave of 1934 (Machajewski 1999, Fig. 1.4; H. -J. Eggers's file) (Fig. 3.8); Zarębowo, Aleksandrów Kuj. district site 1 – grave 35 (Tetzlaff 1967, Fig. 23.1-1a) (Fig. 13.9)

[39] Examples of vase-like vessels without a neck/broad opening cups. Settlements: Brześć Kujawski, Włocławek district site 3 i 4 – feature 1, 32, 60, 139, 348a, 845/858, 891, 894, 905 (Jażdżewski 1939, Tab. 8.10,11, 9.8, 12.2, 13.14; Grygiel 2004, Fig. 2b,4d-f, 7d,h, 8j; Grygiel 2012; unpublished) (Fig. 4.2,3,6,7,9); Dobryń Mały, Biała Podlaska district site VII – feature 9 (Bienia&Żółkowski 1994); Dopiewo, Poznań district site 26/29 (Machajewski 2010, Fig. 8.6, 13.5); Gniewowo, Kościan district site 5 – feature 321 (Ciesielski 1980, Tab. XXII.4); Izdebno Kościelne, Grodzisk Maz. district site 1 – feature 110, 301, unattached find (Kołacz 1995, XVI.b, XXVI.d, XXIX.a) (Fig. 4.1); Kałdus, Chełmno district site 1 – feature 23 (Kaszewski 1979, Tab. XIX.13); Karnin, Gorzów Wlkp. district site 197 – feature 99 (Grygiel 2012; unpublished); Łagiewniki, Inowrocław district site 5 – feature 4, 163, 239 (Grygiel 2012; unpublished); Łęki Górne, Kutno district site 1 (Grygiel 2012; unpublished); Nowy Drzewicz, Żyrardów district site 5 – feature 443, 1228, 1377, 1388 (Grygiel 2012; unpublished); Piecki, Inowrocław district site 8 – feature 6, 12, 22 (Bednarczyk & Sujecka 2004, Fig. 214.1,7, 216.1, 218.1) (Fig. 4.8); Poznań Nowe Miasto site 278 – feature A2, A3, A5, A37-38 (Machajewski&Pietrzak 2008a, Tab. 3.3, 14.1, 18.3,, 24.1-3); Poznań Nowe Miasto site 284 – feature 96, 331 (Kasprowicz 2008, Tab. 3.5, 27.13); Strzyżów (Hrubieszów district) – feature 2 (Prochowicz 2006a); Szynych, Grudziądz district site 12/13 – feature 381, quadrat 03/03 IV cultural layer, quadrat 07/01 I/II cultural layer, quadrat 08/02 II cultural layer, quadrat 02/83 VIII cultural layer (Grygiel 2012; unpublished); Wytyczno, Włodawa district – feature 38, 79, unattached find (Mazurek 2001, Fig. 4.30, 5.5,8) (Fig. 4.4); Żółwin, Międzyrzecz Wlkp. district site 3 – cultural layer (Lewczuk 1997, Tab. XXIV.9,11,13). Graves: Chełm-Biełąwin site 7 – grave 1 (Dzieńkowski, Gołub 1999:177, Fig. 2.12) (Fig. 13.3); Drawsko, Czarnków-Trzcianka district site D1 – grave 10 (Dernoga&Gajda 2004, Tab. II.1); Grodziszcze site 12 – grave (feature 263) (Żychliński&Przybytek 2008, Fig.. 2.1) (Fig. 13.2); Niewęgłosz, Radzyń Podlaski district – grave (Kokowski 1991a, Fig. 16) (Fig. 13.1); Nowe Miasto-on-Warta, Środa Wlkp. district site 1 – grave 73 (Machajewski&Walkiewicz 1993, Fig. 3.2); Piaski, Łęczyca district – grave of 1923 (Jakimowicz 1925; PMA Warszawa); Pietrzyków, Września district site 8 – grave 1 (Michałowski 2003, Fig. 4.2); Smólsk, Włocławek district (MAiE Łódź). Find with no context: Czarnków, Czarnków-Trzcianka district (Michałowski 2006, Fig. 15) (Fig. 4.5).

[40] Examples of squat cups/goblets with roughly globular or barrel-shaped belly. Settlements: Brześć Kujawski, Włocławek district site 3 and 4 – feature 78, 173, 553, 731, 867 (Jażdżewski 1939, Tab. 10.6, 11.3, 12.14; Grygiel 2004, Fig. 5c; 2012; unpublished) (Fig. 5.1); Izdebno Kościelne, Grodzisk Maz. district site 1 – feature E/77 (Kołacz 1995, Tab. XXXII.c) (Fig. 5.3); Karnin, Gorzów Wlkp. district site 197 – feature 197 (Grygiel 2012; unpublished); Łagiewniki, Inowrocław district site 5 – feature 87 (Grygiel 2012; unpublished); Nowy Drzewicz, Żyrardów district site 5 – feature 652, 1523, 1633 (Grygiel 2012; unpublished); Obórka, Gniezno district site 2 – feature 92 (Sobucki&Woźniak 2004, Fig. 8.4) (Fig. 5.6); Otorowo, Szamotuły district site 66 (Żychliński 2004, Fig. 7.4) (Fig. 5.4); Piecki, Inowrocław district site 8 – feature 6 (Bednarczyk & Sujecka 2004, Fig. 214.3); Powodów, Poddębice district site 5 – feature A41 (Grygiel 2012; unpublished); Poznań Nowe Miasto site 278 – feature A9 (Machajewski&Pietrzak 2008, Tab. 19.1,8); Poznań Nowe Miasto site 284 – feature 286, 331, 334, 343 (Kasprowicz 2008, Tab. 23.4, 27.11, 28.12, 29.4); Stary Zamek, Wrocław district site 6 – feature of 1972, feature 1, 2 (Domański&Lodowski 1984); Szynych, Grudziądz district site 12 – feature 302, quadrat 03/84 VIII cultural layer (Grygiel 2012; unpublished); Werbkowice, Hrubieszów district site I – feature 44a (Dąbrowska&Liana 1963); Wojnowo, Poznań district site 23 – feature B61 (Kasprowicz 2004, Fig. 11.1); Wytyczno, Włodawa district site 5 – feature 79 (Mazurek 2001, Fig. 5.15) (Fig. 5.2); Żółwin, Międzyrzecz Wlkp. district site 3 – feature 3/62, cultural layer (Lewczuk 1997, Tab. XXII.1,2, XXIV.9,11,13,16). Graves: Dwikozy, Sandomierz district (Pietraszewski 1925, Fig. 5); Iłki, Puławy district (Uzarowiczowa 1970) (Fig. 5.5).

[41] Examples of small conical cups/goblets. Settlements: Brześć Kujawski, Włocławek district site 4 – feature 32 (Jażdżewski 1939, Tab. 12.3); Izdebno Kościelne, Grodzisk Maz. District site 1 – feature 110 (Kołacz 1995, Tab. XVI.a) (Fig. 5.8); Karnin, Gorzów Wlkp. district site 197 – feature 99 (Grygiel 2012; unpublished); Kowal, Włocławek district site 14 – feature 174 (Kurpiewski 2010) (Fig. 5.10); Łagiewniki, Inowrocław district site 5 – feature 105 (Grygiel 2012; unpublished); Nowy Drzewicz, Żyrardów district site 5 – feature 364 (Grygiel 2012; unpublished); Obórka, Gniezno district site 2 – feature 92 (Sobucki&Woźniak 2004, Fig.. 8.3) (Fig. 5.9); Piecki, Inowrocław district site 8 – feature 22 (Bednarczyk & Sujecka 2004, Fig. 218.14) (Fig. 5.11). Graves: Stare Koczargi, Warsaw west district site 6 – feature 3 (Andrzejowska & Andrzejowski 1997, Fig. 10.d) (Fig. 5.7); Żrenica, Środa Wlkp. district site 1 – grave 9 (Dymaczewski 1958, Fig. 13.5).

[42] Examples of bowls with rims turned outwards. Settlements: Brześć Kujawski, Włocławek district site 3 and 4 – feature 32, 139, 243, 553, 564, 731, 773/774, 850, 860, 867, 868, 894, 903, 905, 908 (Jażdżewski 1939, Tab. 9.9-12, 11.5,8, 12.6; Grygiel 2004, Fig. 3.b-d, 4.b,c, 5.a, 7.a; 2012; unpublished) (Fig. 6.3,4,6,8,9); Dobryń Mały, Biała Podlaska district site VII – feature 9 (Bienia&Żółkowski 1994, Fig. 4.1) (Fig. 6.5); Dopiewo, Poznań district site 26/29 (Machajewski 2010, Fig. 8.1, 13.6); Gniewowo, Kościan district site 5 – feature 42, 330, 408, 525, 654, 666 (Ciesielski 1980, Tab. VI.1, VIII.2, XV.1, XXI.1,2, XXIII.5, XXVI.13); Karnin, Gorzów Wlkp. district site 197 – feature 99, 197 (Grygiel 2012; unpublished); Kowal, Włocławek district site 14 – feature 174 (Kurpiewski 2010) (Fig. 6.6); Łagiewniki, Inowrocław district site 5 – feature 105, 239, 247 (Grygiel 2012; unpublished); Nowy Drzewicz, Żyrardów district site 5 – feature 341, 1134, 1633 (Grygiel 2012; unpublished); Pławce, Środa Wlkp. district site 22 (Makiewicz 2004, Fig. 3.2) (Fig. 6.7); Sławsko Wielkie, Mogilno district site 16 – feature 37 (Bednarczyk & Sujecka 2004, Fig. 223.1); Stary Zamek, Wrocław district site 6 – fe-

FIG. 13. JASTORF CULTURE DISH - GOBLET AND CUPS OF SPHERICAL OR BARREL BELLY AND SMALL, CONE-SHAPED CUPS OR GOBLET.
1. BRZEŚĆ KUJAWSKI 4 (DRAW E. GÓRSKA); 2. WYTYCZNO (AFTER MAZUREK 2001); 3. 8. IZDEBNO KOŚCIELNE (AFTER KOŁACZ 1995); 4. OTOROWO ŻYCHLIŃSKI 2004; 5. IŁKI (UZAROWICZOWA 1970); 6, 9. OBÓRKA (SOBUCKI, WOŹNIAK 2004); 7 – STARE KOCZARGI (ANDRZEJOWSKA, ANDRZEJOWSKI 1997); 10. KOWAL (AFTER KURPIEWSKI 2010);
11. PIECKI (AFTER BEDNARCZYK, SUJECKA2 004).

ature 2a (Domański&Lodowski 1984); Strzyżów, Hrubieszów district site 1a/II – feature 2, unattached finds (Kokowski 2006; Prochowicz 2006b); Szynych, Grudziądz district site 12 – feature 165, 224, quadrat 01/82 VIII cultural layer, quadrat 06/90 III cultural layer, quadrat 08/02 I cultural layer, quadrat 13/01 peat earth (Grygiel 2012; unpublished); Wojnowo, Poznań district site 23 – feature B61 (Kasprowicz 2004, Fig. 13.1); Wytyczno, Włodawa district site 5 – feature 79 (Mazurek 2001, Fig. 5.3) (Fig. 6.1); Żółwin, Międzyrzecz Wlkp. district site 3 – cultural layer (Lewczuk 1997, Tab. XXIV.15).

Examples of bowls with unmarked rims, standing upright or bent inwards. Settlements: Brześć Kujawski, Włocławek district site 3 and 4 – feature 1, 173, 773/774, 850, 856 (Jażdżewski 1939, Tab. 8.9, 10.7; Grygiel 2004, Fig. 2.f, 6.d,f) (Fig. 7.2,4,8); Dobryń Mały, Biała Podlaska district site VII – feature 9 (Bienia&Żółkowski 1994, Fig. 4.1) (Fig. 7.7); Dopiewo, Poznań district site 26/29 (Machajewski 2010, Fig. 8.2,4, 12.6,8); Gniewowo, Kościan district site 5 – feature 654 (Ciesielski 1980, Tab. VIII.3); Izdebno Kościelne, Grodzisk Maz. district site 1 – feature 66, 252 (Kołacz 1995, Tab. XI.a, XXIII.b) (Fig. 7.1,6,9); Karnin, Gorzów Wlkp. district site 197 – feature 197 (Grygiel 2012; unpublished); Nowy Drzewicz, Żyrardów district – feature 839, 1447, 1633 (Grygiel 2012; unpublished); Obórka, Gniezno district site 2 – feature 92 (Sobucki&Woźniak 2004, Fig. 8.2) (Fig. 7.5); Piecki, Inowrocław district site 8 – feature 22 (Bednarczyk & Sujecka 2004, Fig. 217.10); Powodów, Poddębice district site 5 – feature A59 (Grygiel 2012; unpublished); Poznań Nowe Miasto site 278 – feature A2, C13, C14 (Machajewski&Pietrzak

Among the above mentioned ceramic forms the bipartite and tripartite vases distinguish themselves in their fine craftmanship, being most often related in technology to that of smooth, thin-walled vessels of the Pomorania-Cloche culture. It is in the same way that some bowls, vases without necks, mugs and cups were also made. It should be noted, however, that among these, in particular neck-less vases and broad-opening mugs, there often occur

2008a, Tab. 3.5, 39.5-7, 40.4); Poznań Nowe Miasto site 284 – feature 130, 141, 169, 267, 331, 343 (Kasprowicz 2008, Tab. 8.6, 11.10, 15.7, 22.12, 27.12, 29.6); Sławsko Wielkie, Mogilno district site 16 – feature 37 (Bednarczyk & Sujecka 2004, Fig. 223.3); Stary Zamek, Wrocław district site 6 – feature 5 (Domański&Lodowski 1984); Strzyżów, Hrubieszów district site 1a/II – feature 2 (Prochowicz 2006a).

Examples of bowls with "drooping" handles. Settlements: Dopiewo, Poznań district site 26/29 (Machajewski 2010, Fig. 8.1, 12.6,8); Izdebno Kościelne, Grodzisk Maz. district site 1 – feature C/77 (Kołacz 1995, Tab. XXXI.a); Nowy Drzewicz, Żyrardów district site 5– feature 1447, 1633 (Grygiel 2012; unpublished); Powodów, Poddębice district site 5 – feature A41 (Grygiel 2012; unpublished); Poznań Nowe Miasto st. 284 – feature 331 (Kasprowicz 2008, Tab. 27.12); Wojnowo, Poznań district site 23 – feature B46 (Kasprowicz 2004, Fig. 6.9,10) (Fig. 7.3); Wytyczno, Włodawa district site 5 – feature 38 (Mazurek 2001, Fig. 4.29).

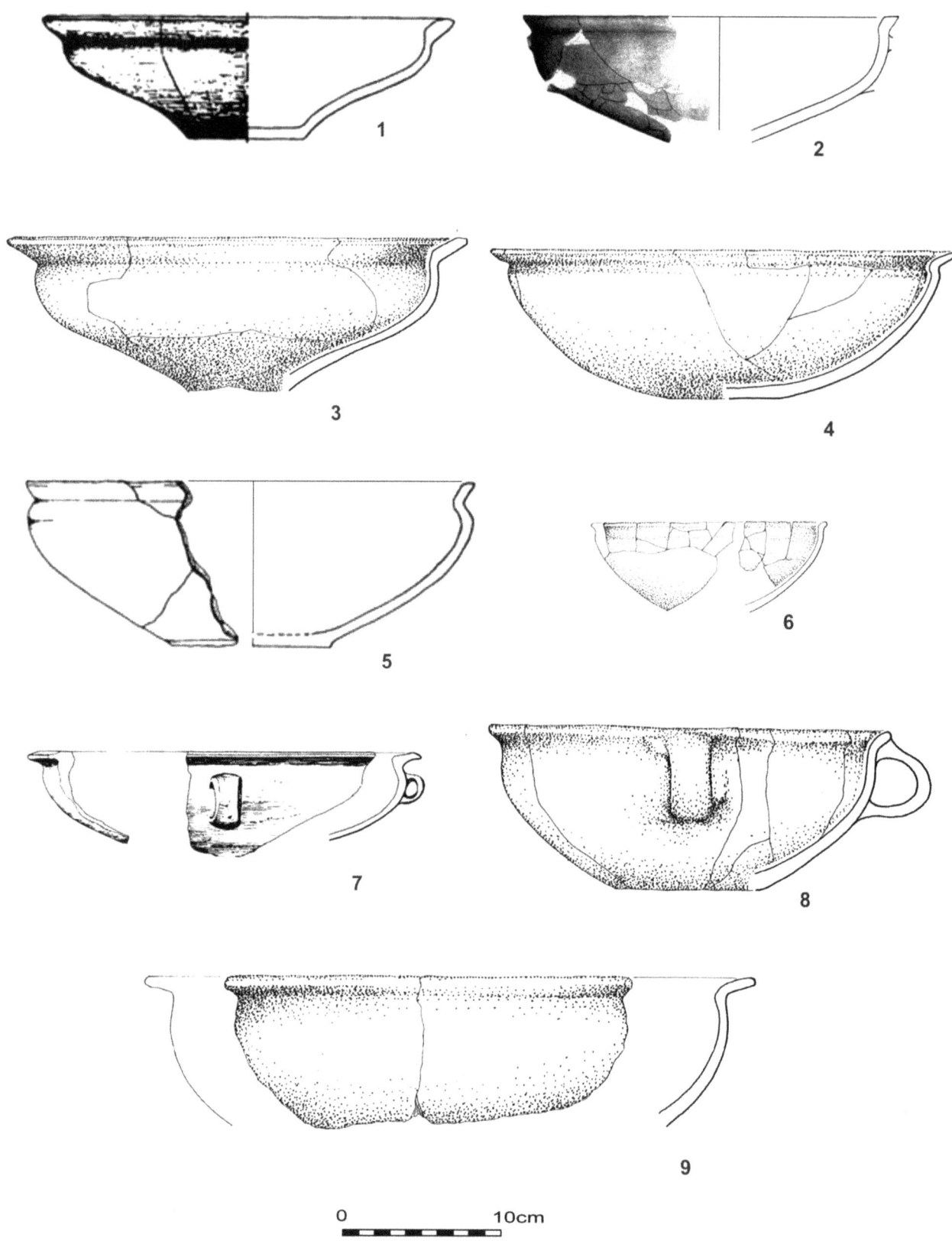

FIG. 14. JASTORF CULTURE DISH – BOWLS WITH OUTSIDE DEFLECTED EDGE.
1 WYTYCZNO (AFTER MAZUREK 2001); 2. KOWAL (AFTER KURPIEWSKI 2010); 3, 4, 6, 9. – BRZEŚĆ KUJAWSKI 4 (DRAWING E. GÓRSKA); 5 – DOBRYŃ MAŁY (AFTER BIENIA, ZIÓŁKOWSKI 1994); 7. PŁAWCE (AFTER MAKIEWICZ 2004); 8.BRZEŚĆ KUJAWSKI 3 (DRAWING E. GÓRSKA).

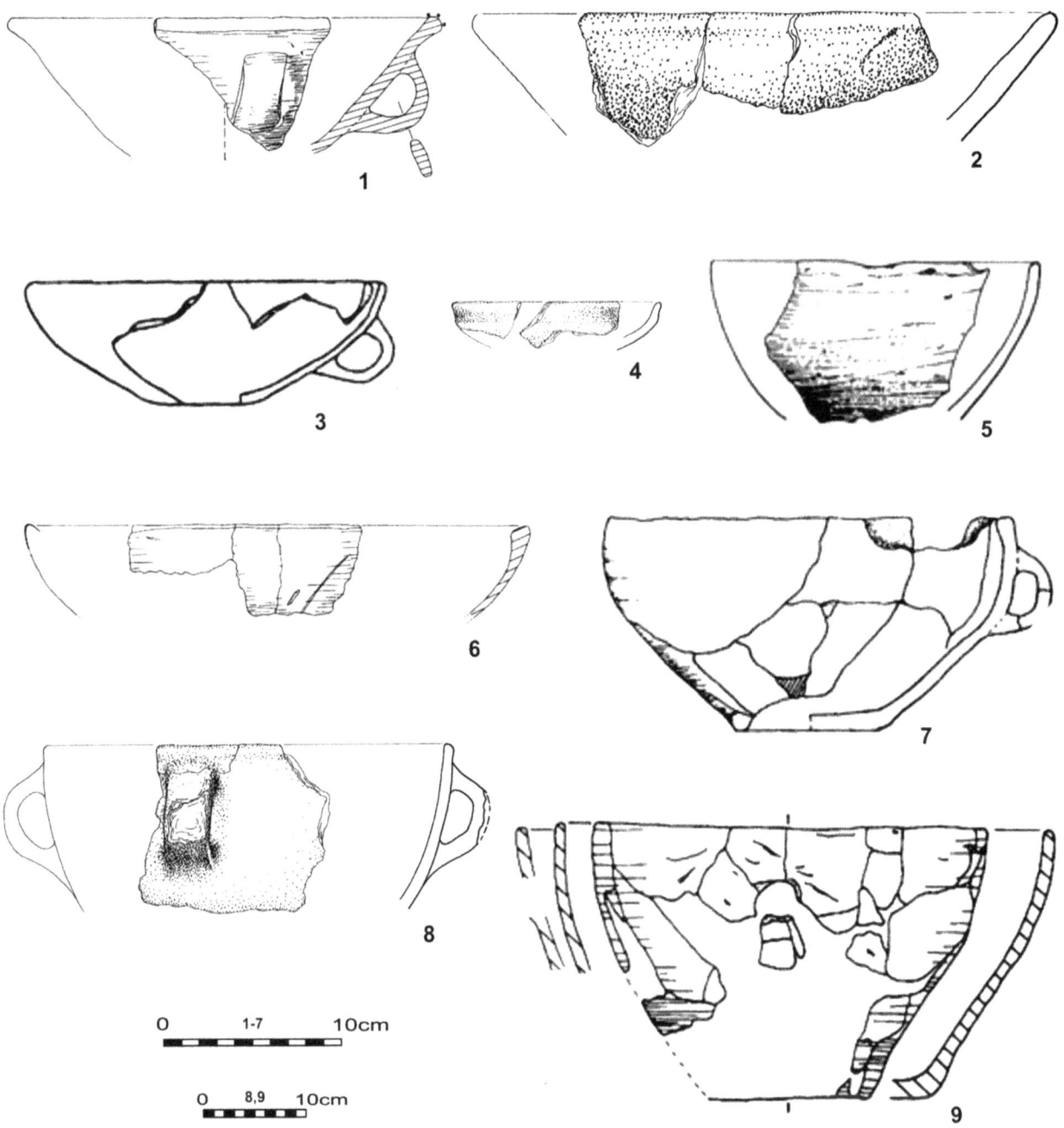

Fig. 15. Jastorf culture dish - bowl without the lip.
1, 6, 9. Izdebno Kościelne (after Kołacz 1995); 2, 4. Brześć Kujawski st. 4 (drawing E. Górska); 3 Wojnowo (after Kasprowicz 2004); 5. Obórka (after Sobucki, Woźniak 2004); 7 Dobryń Mały (after Bienia, Ziółkowski 1994); 8. Brześć Kujawski 3 (drawing E. Górska).

also vessels that can be seen to relate in technology to the oldest "kitchen" ceramic ware of the Przeworsk culture such as vessels featuring smooth, blackened, mat interior surface.

On Jastorf culture settlements, coarse ware dominates, known as kitchen ware, sporadically found also in Jastorf burials. It is almost exclusively represented by two types of vessels: medium-size S-profiled pots and large storage vessels. Among pots, next to numerous broad-opening forms, there are vessels the lips of which have a smaller diameter than a bulbous belly. In some of these vessels, the neck is marked with a clear offset or these are tripartite vessels. Only rarely are egg-shaped pots encountered. Some of the above-named pots have one or two handles (Fig. 16).[43] The storage vessels found on Jastorf culture

[43] Examples of broad-opening pots. Settlements: Brześć Kujawski, Włocławek district site 3 and 4 – feature 139, 144, 173, 773/774, 845/858, 894, 908 (Jażdżewski 1939, Tab. 9.3, 13.1,7,8; Grygiel 2004, Fig. 7.f) (Fig. 8.2,4,5); Ciechanki Łańcuchowskie, Łęczna district – trench 4 (Kokowski 1991a); Dobryń Mały, Biała Podlaska district site VII – feature 9 (Bienia&Żółkowski 1994) (Fig. 8.8); Dopiewo, Poznań district site 26/29 (Machajewski 2010, Fig. 8.3, 9.1, 3, 6, 7); Izdebno Kościelne, Grodzisk Maz. district site 1 – feature 252 (Kołacz 1995, Tab. XXIII.a); Karnin, Gorzów Wlkp. district site 197 – feature 24, 99, 190, 197 (Gry-

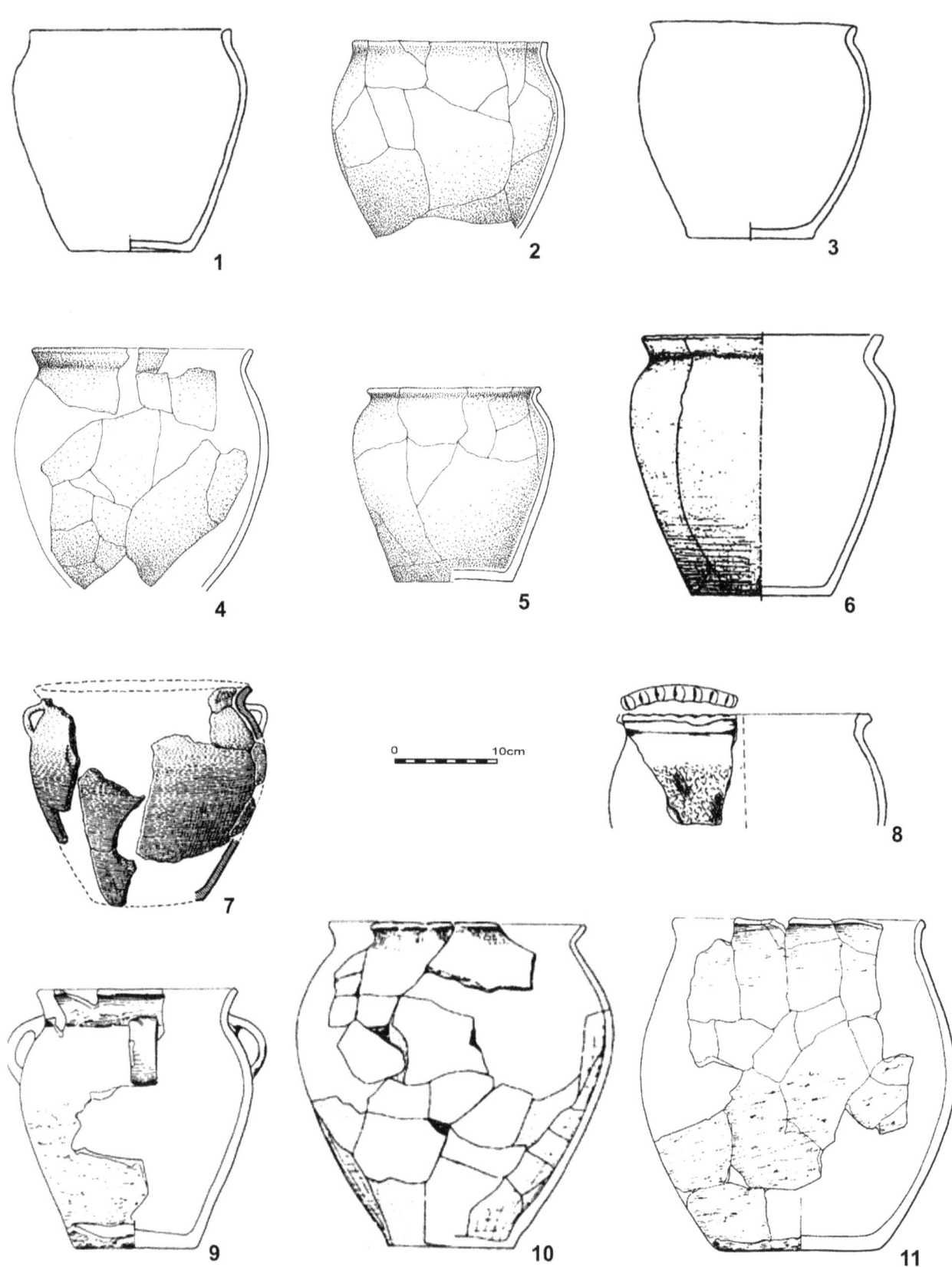

Fig. 16. Jastorf culture dish –pots
1,3 – Wojnowo (after Kasprowicz 2004); 2, 4, 5 – Brześć Kujawski 4 (drawing E. Górska); 6 Wytyczno (after Mazurek 2001); 7 Stary Zamek (after Domański, Lodowski 1984); 8 Dobryń Mały (after Bienia, Ziółkowski 1994); 9 Obórka (after Sobucki, Woźniak 2004); 10 Otorowo (after Żychliński 2004); 11 Pławce (after Makiewicz 2004).

settlements are dominated by slender broad- and narrow-opening S-profiled pot-like vessels with an elevated maximum protrusion of the belly. Other forms are rare,

including specimens with a relatively high funnel-shaped neck and a roughly globular belly, vessels with an undercut belly and squat broad-opening vessels (Fig. 17).[44] Unlike pots, storage vessels are wares most often rough cast on the belly. Only in exceptional cases does the rough-cast reach the lip rim. Equally rare is the custom of burnishing the bottom part of a rough-cast vessel. The rough-casting on storage vessels is not uniform. For we can show vessels smeared with carelessly mixed fat clay and others covered with watered-down clay, forming a characteristic irregular network of veins and small beads after firing (Grygiel 2004, ryc. 4h). In addition there are wares, the rough-cast surfaces of which were burnished before firing (Machajewski, Pietrzak 2008a:163-164). Some storage vessels have small handles on the upper belly (Jażdżewski 1939, Tab. 10.2,3, 11.1, 12.9; Kołacz 1995, Tab. III.a).

Only a small part of the pottery discovered on Jastorf sites does bear any ornament. Ornaments are found, for instance, on bipartite vases the upper bellies of which are covered with subtle incised geometric patterns. The patterns of hatched triangles, herringbone, or simple arrangements of straight lines, most often forming chevrons, hark back to the traditions of the Early Iron Age or Late Bronze Age (Jażdżewski 1939, Tab. 8.2, 10.4; Kołacz 1995, tab. XV.d). Slightly different ornaments are found on vases without a marked neck. These are subtle, incised geometric patterns frequently filled with strokes (jabs) that clearly have affinities with the ornaments of Przeworsk culture ware from the younger Pre-Roman period (Jażdżewski 1939, Tab. 13.15-18; Bienia & Żółkowski 1994, Fig. 4.5, 5.15,17; T.Mazurek & W.Mazurek 1997a, Fig. 4.1,2,4; Dzieńkowski & Gołub 1999, 177, Fig. 2.12; Mazurek 2001, Fig. 4.3, 7, 13, 21-23, 26, 27; Grygiel 2004, Fig. 4.a, 8.j,k; Kasprowicz 2008:229; Machajewski & Pietrzak 2008: 162-163). The coarse 'kitchen' pottery, especially storage vessels, display relief ornaments in the form of circumferential relief strips placed most often on the upper belly and only rarely underneath the lip rim. The strips bear finger-impression ornaments (Richthofen 1931, Tab. III.4; Jażdżewski 1939, Tab. 8.6, 11.6; Kołacz 1995, Tab. III.a; Grygiel 2004, Fig. 11.E; Macha-jewski & Pietrzak 2008a:

---

giel 2012; unpublished); Komorniki, Poznań district site 2 – feature 1 (Kostrzewski 1939); Łagiewniki, Inowrocław district site 5 – feature 105 (Grygiel 2012; unpublished); Nowy Drzewicz, Żyrardów district site 5 – feature 600, 606, 1376, 1388; 1493, 1633 (Grygiel 2012; unpublished); Obórka, Gniezno district site 2 – feature 92 (Sobucki&Woźniak 2004, Fig. 9.5); Otorowo, Szamotuły district site 66 (Żychliński 2004, Fig. 4.1) (Fig. 8.10); Pławce, Środa Wlkp. district site 22 (Makiewicz 2004, Fig. 3.1) (Fig. 8.11); Powodów, Poddębice district site 5 – feature A249, C161, D224, J16 (Grygiel 2012; unpublished); Poznań Nowe Miasto site 278 – feature A2, A85, A109, A117 (Machajewski, Pietrzak 2008a, Tab. 3.2, 5.1, 30.10, 34.3, 35.1); Poznań Nowe Miasto site 284 – feature 130, 267, 322 (Kasprowicz 2008, Tab. 9.8, 22.8, 25.10); Strzyżów, Hrubieszów district site 1a/II – feature 2 (Prochowicz 2006a); Szynych, Grudziądz district site 12/13 – feature 74, 113, 165, 224, 442, 515, 900, quadrat 00/87 XVII cultural layer, quadrat 02/85 VIII cultural layer, quadrat 03/84 VIII cultural layer, quadrat 04/90 III cultural layer (Grygiel 2012; unpublished); Werbkowice, Hrubieszów district site I – feature 61 (Dąbrowska&Liana 1963); Wojnowo, Poznań district site 23 – feature B46, B61 (Kasprowicz 2004, Fig. 6.12,13, 12) (Fig. 8.1,3); Wytyczno, Włodawa district site 5 – feature 79 (Mazurek 2001, Fig. 5.2,4) (Fig. 8.6).
Examples of narrow-opening pots. Settlements: Brześć Kujawski, Włocławek district site 3 and 4 – feature 32, 78, 139, 773/774, 845/858, 902, 903 (Jażdżewski 1939, Tab. 9.7, 12.5,8; Grygiel 2004, Fig. 8.e,g,h; 2012; unpublished) (Fig. 9.1,5); Dopiewo, Poznań district site 26/29 (Machajewski 2010, Fig. 8.5, 9.2,4, 13,4); Gniewowo, Kościan district site 5 – feature 495 (Ciesielski 1980, Tab. XVII.2); Kałdus, Chełmno district site 1 – feature 23 (Kaszewski 1979, Tab. XIX.12); Karnin, Gorzów Wlkp. district site 197 – feature 24, 26, 99 (Grygiel 2012; unpublished); Łagiewniki, Inowrocław district site 5 – feature 105 (Grygiel 2012; unpublished); Nowy Drzewicz, Żyrardów district site 5 – feature 1447 (Grygiel 2012; unpublished); Otorowo, Szamotuły district site 66 (Żychliński 2004, Fig. 4.2) (Fig. 9.2); Poznań Nowe Miasto site 278 – feature A2, A3, A5 (Machajewski, Pietrzak 2008a, Tab. 6.1,2, 15.1, 17.2); Poznań Nowe Miasto site 284 – feature 97 (Kasprowicz 2008, Tab. 2.6; nr kat. II/168); Strzyżów, Hrubieszów district site 1a/II – feature 2 (Prochowicz 2006a) (Fig. 9.3); Szynych, Grudziądz district site 12/13 – feature 224, quadrat 01/93 XVII cultural layer (Grygiel 2012; unpublished); Werbkowice, Hrubieszów district site I – feature 61 (Dąbrowska&Liana 1963) (Fig. 9.4); Wytyczno, Włodawa district site 5 – feature 95 (Mazurek 2001, Fig. 6.15). Grave: Gradowo, Radziejów district (collection of IA UJ ZP 917); Kuny, Turek district site 4a – grave 11 (Skowron 2008, Tab. III.2) (Fig. 9.6).
Examples of pots with marked neck. Settlements: Brześć Kujawski, Włocławek district site 4 – feature 348a, 518 (Jażdżewski 1940, Tab. 13.13; Grygiel 2004, Fig. 2.h, 3.e) (Fig. 9.12); Dopiewo, Poznań district site 26/29 (Machajewski 2010, Fig. 12.3,11); Gniewowo, Kościan district site 5 – feature 127 (Ciesielski 1980, Tab. V.6); Izdebno Kościelne, Grodzisk Maz. district site 1 – feature B/77 (Kołacz 1995, Tab. XXVI.a) (Fig. 9.8); Komorniki, Poznań district site 2 – feature 2 (Kostrzewski 1939) (Fig. 9.11); Łagiewniki, Inowrocław district site 5 – feature 247 (Grygiel 2012; unpublished); Obórka, Gniezno district site 2 – feature 92 (Sobucki, Woźniak 2004, Fig. 9.1) (Fig. 8.9); Powodów, Poddębice district site 5 – feature D283 (Grygiel 2012; unpublished); Piecki, Inowrocław district site 8 – feature 2 (Bednarczyk & Sujecka 2004, Fig. 211.2); Szynych, Grudziądz district site 12 – quadrat 01/91 XVII cultural layer (Grygiel 2012; unpublished). Grave: Równina Dolna, Kętrzyn district site 2 – grave 22 (Gaerte 1938, Fig. 2) (Fig. 9.7)
Example of egg-shaped pots: Brześć Kujawski, Włocławek district site 3 – feature 773/774 (Fig. 9.13,14).
Examples of pots with two handles. Settlements: Brześć Kujawski, Włocławek district site 3 and 4 – feature 139, 144, 249, unattached find (Jażdżewski 1939, Tab. 9.6, 10.1, 13.4; Grygiel 2004, Fig. 4.g,h); Dopiewo, Poznań district site 26/29 (Machajewski 2010, Fig. 9.7, 12.1,2); Obórka, Gniezno district site 2 – feature 92 (Sobucki, Woźniak 2004, Fig. 9.5); Powodów, Poddębice district site 5 – feature A249, C161, J141 (Grygiel 2012; unpublished); Poznań Nowe Miasto site 284 – feature 167 (Kasprowicz 2008, Tab. 6.3); Stary Zamek, Wrocław district site 6 – feature 5, feature of 1972 (Domański&Lodowski 1984) (Fig. 8.7); Szynych, Grudziądz district site 12 – feature 74 (Grygiel 2012; unpublished); Wojnowo, Poznań district site 23 – feature B46 (Kasprowicz 2004, Fig. 6.11) (Fig. 9.10). Graves: Pietryków, Września district site 8 – grave 1 (Michałowski 2003, Fig. 4.1); Wilcza Wólka, Piaseczno district site 14 – grave 1 (Grabarek 2011, Fig. 4-5) (Fig. 9.9).

---

[44] Examples of slender, S-profile storage pot: Brześć Kujawski, Włocławek district site 3 and 4 – feature 1, 249, 553, 773/774 (Jażdżewski 1939, Tab. 8.6, 10.2, 11.1) (Fig. 10.1,4,6,7); Izdebno Kościelne, Grodzisk Maz. district site 1 – feature 1 (Kołacz 1995, Tab. III.a) (Fig. 10.8); Młodzikowo, Środa Wlkp. district 21 – feature 60 (Świerkowska-Brańska 1992); Nowy Drzewicz, Żyrardów district site 5 – feature 842, 886, 1633 (Grygiel 2012; unpublished); Powodów, Poddębice district site 5 – feature A57 (Grygiel 2012; unpublished); Szynych, Grudziądz district site 12 – feature 224 (Grygiel 2012; unpublished); Wojnowo, Poznań district site 23 – feature B46 (Kasprowicz 2004, Fig. 5.3,4) (Fig. 10.2,3).
Examples of squat, S-profile storage pots: Brześć Kujawski, Włocławek district site 4 – feature 78 (Jażdżewski 1939, Tab. 12.9; Grygiel 2004, Fig. 2.g); Poznań Nowe Miasto site 284 – feature 130 (Kasprowicz 2008, Tab. 8.11).
Examples of storage pots with tall, funnel-like neck: Brześć Kujawski, Włocławek district site 4 – feature 139, 249 (Jażdżewski 1939, Tab. 9.2, 10.3) (Fig. 10.5); Szynych, Grudziądz district site 12 – feature 928 (Grygiel 2012; unpublished).
Example of storage pot with undercut belly: Poznań Nowe Miasto site 278 – (Machajewski & Pietrzak 2008a, Tab. 4.2).

Fig. 17. Jastorf culture dish – storage pots.
1, 6 Brześć Kujawski 3 (drawing E. Górska); 2, 3 Wojnowo (after Kasprowicz 2004); 4-7. Brześć Kujawski 4 (after Jażdżewski 1939); 8 Izdebno Kościelne (after Kołacz 1995).

163, Tab. 7.1, 11.2-4, 23.5, 38.5, 40.3; Machajewski 2010, Fig. 9.4,5, 10).

In addition, pot and storage vessel rims were sometimes decorated with finger impressions, corruga-tions or incisions (Fig. 16:8). In this context one should also note examples of hand crafted ceramic ware that was painted, which was discovered in Jastorf settlements in Brześć Kujawski (sites 3 and 4) – to date unknown from other sites on the Lowland (Grygiel 2004: 29).

Some of the above-named Jastorf ware forms have faceted rims on the inside. This is the case with bowls, cups, vases and goblets; among them are specimens with elongated and faceted rims and others with shortened and slightly thickened faceted rims. Facets are also found on some coarse 'kitchen' pottery. However, these rims are made far less carefully than in the tableware mentioned earlier. Sporadically, in Jastorf assemblages, vessels with roll-moulded rims faceted on the outside are encountered. They remind one of the rim shapes of the oldest pottery of the Przeworsk culture. Jastorf pottery has various forms of handles. Relatively frequent, broad band-shaped handles and large handles with a narrowing in their central part stand in contrast to rare handles shaped like a gable roof in cross-section.[45]

Further, Lowland Jastorf culture pottery indicates clear connections to materials from Denmark (Dąbrowska 1988:102-104, 196; 1994:73-74; 2008; Martens 1994:43, 45; Grygiel 2004:22-27; Woźniak 2007a; Machajewski & Pietrzak 2008a; Machajewski 2010:204). Not only do they correspond to Danish finds but also show affinities with ceramic artefacts from the native territory of the Jastorf culture, extending over the drainage basin of the middle and lower Elbe River (Grygiel 2004:27-29; Woźniak 2007a). Within the Lowland pottery, however, no clear affinities with the pottery of the peripheral groups can be readily seen. The peripheral groups of the Jastorf culture in the territory of modern Poland included the Gubin and Oder groups. Any attempts, therefore, to refine the chronology of Jastorf pottery finds on the Lowland can be successful if based on the periodization systems of the Pre-Roman period used in Denmark (Albrechtsen 1954; Becker 1961; Jensen 1996; 1997; 2005; Martens 1996; 1997) and on the chronological schemes of native Jastorf culture materials (Schwantes 1909; 1911; 1958; Hingst 1959).

Lowland Jastorf pottery shows therefore a clear affinity with finds from Jutland traditionally dated to the period spanning phases Ib and IIIa according to Becker (1961:4), which corresponds to phases IB and IIA in the modified division by Martens (1996, Fig. 13-14; 1997, Fig. 16). Also, its similarity, albeit clearly less noticeable, to the pottery style of the Jastorf culture proper from phases Jastorf b and especially from the Ripdorf phase according to Schwantes is nevertheless visible (Grygiel 2004:27-29; Woźniak 2007a: 400-401). If the synchronization of the above-named phases with the chronology of the La Tène culture is correct, the period would roughly correspond to phases LTB and LTC, especially to the older section of the latter (LTC1) (Martens 1994a, Fig. 10; 1997, Fig. 16; Brandt 2001, Fig. 3).

Taking into account the Jutland connections, the earliest elements in the set of Lowland Jastorf pottery would be vase-like wares having bi- or tripartite structure, rims that are not thickened but are often strongly turned outwards, sometimes are fitted with a band-like handle and bear on their bellies an incised ornament, harking back to Hallstatt or Late Bronze patterns. By the same token, early forms should probably include also vases without a neck, broad-opening cups and goblets which bear such stylistic elements as strongly turned rims, band-like handles and peculiar "archaic" ornaments (Fig. 12:6). These ware types have many counterparts in materials coming from Jutland settlements and cemeteries dated to phases Ib and II according to Becker (1961) or to phase IB and the beginning of phase IIA according to Martens, corresponding to phase LTB or, possibly, to the beginnings of LTC1 (Martens 1997; Fig. 16). This is suggested by finds from the settlements at Borremose in Himmerland, in particular vessel forms in the inventory of house XXIII and a deposit found in the moat (Martens 1988:175, 177, Fig. 11.10-11, 19.1, 5,8; 1992a; 1994a; 1997, Fig. 4), Gørding in south Jutland (Becker 1961, Fig. 184, 185), Øster Lem and Grøntoft in west Jutland (Becker 1961, Tab. 74.e; 1965, Fig. 11), Darum II (Becker 1961, Tab. 62.e, 186, 187), Roager (Becker 1961, Fig. 188, Tab. 59.k,l, 60), as well as by sepulchral finds from large south Jutland cemeteries at Aarre, Uldal and Årupgård, and burials discovered at Bjerndrup, Hennekesdam, Vester Vamdrup and Ullemølle (Neergaard 1931, Fig. 2; Becker 1961, Fig. 70.b, 72, 73.b,d,e, 175, Tab. 107.30-27a,30-30a; Museum Sønderjyl-land collections).

A very similar pottery, dated to phases I and II according to Albrechtsen (1954) or to approximately the same chronological period as the named Jutland finds, is found on Fionia (Albrechtsen 1954, Fig. 26, Tab. 13.b,d, 15.a-c; 1973, Tab. 11.f). So early dating of bi- and tripartite vessels with rims that re not thickened is justified by the chronology of stylistic changes of north Jastorf pottery (Grygiel 2004:27-29). Another early and similarly dated form could be large bowls with a broad rim strongly turned outwards (Fig. 14:7,9). They resemble similar bowls occurring among Danish materials associated with phase I according to Becker (1961) and Martens (1997), and phase II according to Albrechtsen (1954) (Albrechtsen 1954, Fig. 13.25-27, 19.j, Tab. 8.b, 15.e, 16.a; Becker 1961, Fig. 140, 145, 146, Tab. 16d, 23j, 24c).

Links to early Danish pottery, i.e. characteristic of the late older Pre-Roman period, can be observed in some forms of coarse "kitchen" pottery as well. Among them are pot-

---

[45] Examples of vessels with handles shaped like a gable roof in cross-section: Brześć Kujawski, Włocławek district site 3 – feature 773/774 (Fig. 3.4); Kuny, Turek district site 4a – grave 11 (Skowron 2008, Tab. III.3); Zarębowo, Aleksandrów Kuj. district site 1 – grave 35 (collections of IAiE PAN, Poznań Branch).

like storage vessels fitted with several small handles or decorated with a relief strip on the upper belly, squat storage pots (Fig. 17:5-8), as well as pots having a relatively tall neck marked by a clear offset and sometimes bearing a deep incised post-Hallstatt ornament (Gaerte 1938, Fig. 2; Kostrzewski 1939, Fig. 28; Jażdżewski 1939, Tab. 8.6, 9.2, 10.3, 11.1, 13.13; Kołacz 1995, Tab. XXVI.a; Grygiel 2004, Fig. 3.e). These pottery forms find their counterparts among finds made on Danish settlements and cemeteries dated to phases Ib and II according to Becker (1961), i.e. phase IB and early phase IIA according to Martens (1997) and phase II according to Albrechtsen (1954) (Madsen & Neergaard 1894, Fig. 5, 6, 13, 14, 17; Albrechtsen 1954, Fig. 24.a,c; Becker 1961, Fig. 66.b,c, 73.a, 161-162, 192, Tab. 4.a, 7.k, 10.e, 22.g, 23.b, 30.b, 65.a, 74.o, 75.a,b, 92.4, 96.179a, 98.261a, 102.340, 104.379, 114.2a; Jensen 2005, Tab. 129).

The same chronological position, i.e. corresponding to the decline of the older Pre-Roman period, seems to be occupied by painted ware fragments unearthed on Jastorf culture settlements in Brześć Kujawski, being linked to painted ware from Schleswig-Holstein of phase Ib and rarely also of phase Ic according to Hingst (Hingst 1974:60-61; Grygiel 2004:29). Most vessel forms found on Lowland Jastorf culture settlements indicate connections to a series of younger Danish wares dated to phase IIIa according to Becker, i.e. phase IIA according to Martens, and north German pottery typical of the Ripdorf phase according to Schwantes or phase IIa according to Hingst (Klindt-Jensen 1949; 1953:82-83, footnote 102; Schwantes 1950; 1958; Becker 1951; 1961:4; Hingst 1959; Bech 1987, Fig. 2; Martens 1988; 1992a, Tab. 2-6; 1997; Dąbrowska 1988, Fig. 13, 16; Jensen 1997; 2005, Tab. 129; Rindel 1997, Fig. 1, 2; Grygiel 2004:33; Woźniak 2007a; Machajewski, Pietrzak 2008a; Machajewski 2010: 212).

Thus, relying on the chronology of the Jutland finds, one can doubtless date the Jastorf materials discussed here to phase A1. The north German connections, however, indicate a slightly shorter chronology, i.e. a dating comprising mainly the inception of phase A1. The links of Lowland Jastorf wares to the finds traceable to the younger phases of the Jastorf circle development, from both north Germany and Jutland, are not as strong as in the case of the forms listed earlier, resembling Danish finds from the older Pre-Roman period. For in this case, there is a similarity only in some general traits of pottery style. They include above all elongated vessel rims faceted on the inside and handles with a narrowing in their central part. A link to a younger series of Danish materials is seen in the ornamentation of some forms of Jastorf tableware – specifically, in subtle incised geometric patterns on the belly frequently filled with strokes (jabs) and in rare cordons under the rim bearing finger impressions found on storage vessels (Müller 1912, Fig. 37; Klindt-Jensen 1949; 1953:82-83, Fig. 25; Hatt 1958, Fig. 195, 247, 248; Becker 1961:4, Tab. 79.n, 83.a,b, 85a,f, 86.e, 88.g, 89.d,e, 90.a,e; Bech 1984, Fig. 7a; Hvass 1985, Tab. 117.g, 126.a, 129a, 130.a, 138.d, 140.e, 144.a, 145.g, 148.a; Martens 1988, Fig. 14, 15, 16.14; 1992a, Tab. 2; 1994a, Fig. 10; 1997, Fig. 5; Dąbrowska 1988:199, Fig. 13, 16; Grygiel 2004:33).

The pottery discussed here also resembles the finds of the Przeworsk and Poieneşti-Łukaševka cultures. The connections to older style Przeworsk wares (Dąbrowska 1988:28-29) are seen in the first place in the above mentioned technological traces and the ornamentation of some forms of Jastorf tableware. Specifically, a particular similarity is observed in a subtle incised geometric pattern filled with strokes and arranged in a narrow band. Another point of convergence is roll-moulded rims faceted on the outside, which are rare on Jastorf wares. In addition, some Jastorf wares – some bowls, slender vases with a marked neck, cups and S-profiled pot-like vessels (Fig. 11:8; 12:6; 13:2, 7; 14:1, 3, 8) – resemble Przeworsk wares subsumed under types I, II, III, VI and VII according to Dąbrowska (1997). In this respect he Lowland Jastorf materials show affinities with the Poieneşti-Łukaševka culture where some of the pottery of the two cultures has large narrowed handles and roll-moulded slanting rims faceted on the inside. Some similarity is also observed between pot-like vessels, bowls with a rim turned outwards and vase-like vessel without a marked neck or cups with broad openings (Babeş 1993: 59-66, Fig. 20.I, II, III.A,B). On the strength of links to the Przeworsk and Poieneşti-Łukaševka cultures, Lowland Jastorf pottery can be broadly dated to a period corresponding to phases A1 and A2.

There are few settlements on the Lowland where both stylistically older and younger Jastorf culture materials have been discovered. A case in point is a complex of settlements in Brześć Kujawski (Kujawy), whence the largest series of Jastorf pottery on the Lowland comes (Jażdżewski 1939; Grygiel 2004). Other settlements that yielded clearly stylistically diversified Jastorf pottery were found in Dopiewo, district Poznań (central Wielkopolska) and Szynych, district Grudziądz (Land of Chełmno) (Machajewski 2010; Grygiel 2012; unpublished finds from Szynych are kept in the collections of the Institute of Archeology, Nicolas Copernicus University in Toruń).

Our knowledge on the chronology of the Jastorf culture settlements on the Lowland is slightly expanded by other more closely dated artefacts, chiefly metal ones, discovered on the sites. On one of such settlements investigated in Szynych (site 12), which yielded a long series of Jastorf materials showing affinities with Danish finds from both the older and the beginning of the younger Pre-Roman periods, a winged pin was discovered (Maciałowicz 2009, Fig. 10), belonging to a rare group of north Jastorf ornaments. They were used, it is believed, in the late older and in the early younger Pre-Roman periods – LTB2-C1 (Maciałowicz 2009: 202-203). The Szynych pin was accompanied by a find of pottery,[46] indicating connections to Jutland materials from the older Pre-Roman period.

---

[46] In the collection of the Institute of Archeology at Nicolas Copernicus University in Toruń

Among them are forms with rims strongly turned outwards and bearing a subtle incised geometric ornament of the "post-Hallstatt" type. Such ornaments are characteristic of early Danish materials associated with phases Ib and II according to Becker, i.e. phase IB and the beginning of phase IIA according to Martens.

Other finds, however, supply less certain data. For some artefacts found within Jastorf settlements are hard to link to specific ceramic assemblages. One is a Holstein pin of the Skovby/Bjerndrup type believed to be a typical north Jastorf artefact, dating to a period which corresponds to the beginning of phase A1 (Schwantes 1958: 365-366; Becker 1961: 255; Hingst 1983: 29; 1986: 36; Prochowicz 2006; Maciałowicz 2009: 197,201). It was discovered at a settlement in Żółwin, district Międzyrzecz Wlkp. (Lubuskie province) (Kres 1965a, Tab. III.2; 1965b: 10-Figure). The settlement also yielded Jastorf pottery resembling the style of Danish materials of phase IIIa according to Becker (1961), i.e. phase IIA according to Martens (Lewczuk 1997, Tab. XXII-XXVII). Other examples include finds from the already mentioned settlement in Dopiewo. Next to a series of Jastorf materials indicating connections do Danish pottery from the end of the older and beginning of the younger Pre-Roman periods, the Dopiewo settlement yielded a fragment of a Celtic glass bracelet of group 6b according to Haevernick (1960) (Machajewski 2010:202). Such bracelets are believed to be characteristic of phase LTC1 (Venclová 1990: 120-122; Karwowski 1997: 51, footnote 12; 2004, Fig. 25; 2005).

A rare Celtic import, which can possibly be associated with the Jastorf culture, comes from a multi-period settlement in Gniewowo, district Kościan (Ciesielski 1980). It is a small bronze fibula, the construction of which follows early or middle La Tène patterns in its elongated stem and two globes, bearing a relief ornament (Gediga 2002, 90, photo.)[47]. This elaborate specimen finds single analogies among Celtic artefacts in the Czech Republic and north Hungary (Hellebrandt 1971:182, Fig. 13.1; Venclová 1990:119, Fig. 16.4, 266. Its structure and ornamentation correspond to the fibulae used by Celts in phase LTC1 (Polenz 1971:32; 1978:188, Fig. 5.1-4; Stöckli 1975:369, Fig. 1.1,7-8; Maute 1994:460). In the past, the fibula was associated with the Pomerania-Cloche culture (Woźniak 1979b:128, footnote 2). However, no traces of settlement by the populations of this culture have been discovered on the Gniewowo site. On the other hand, the site featured the remains of a Jastorf culture settlement including plentiful pottery, having affinities with Danish finds dated to both the late older and early younger Pre-Roman periods (Ciesielski 1980).

A mention is deserved by a set-tlement in Wytyczno, Włodawa district (east Lublin province), which yielded a rich series of Jastorf pottery, exhibiting traits of a younger style (W.Mazurek 1994; 1995a; 2001; T. Mazurek & W. Mazurek 1996; 1997a; 1997b), and a fragment of the long stem of a Celtic iron fibula decorated with a massive globe (T. Mazurek & W. Mazurek 2006: 92, Fig. 9). The fibula must have followed middle La Tène constru-ction patterns, prevailing in phase LTC1 (Polenz 1971:32; 1978:188, Fig. 5.3-4; Stöckli 1974:369, Fig. 1.8; Gebhard 1991:80-81; Maute 1994:460). The link to the Jastorf culture of another more precisely dated artefact, however, seems uncertain. It was found on a multi-cultural settlement in Sowinki, Poznań district (central Wielkopolska), where an indeterminate series of Jastorf pottery was discovered (Makiewicz & Łaszkiewicz 2001). It is an all-bronze fibula, preserved only in fragment and decorated with three massive flattened globes (Makiewicz & Łaszkiewicz 2001, Fig. 1). The artefact shows analogies to cast bronze globe fibulae which are characteristic of the north Jastorf circle and are included in the so-called Danish series. They are popular chiefly, it is believed, in the period corresponding to phase A1 (Albrechtsen 1954, Tab. 19.g; Laursen 1984:128, Fig. 4; Brandt 2001:85-87).

More data for establishing the chronology of Jastorf culture materials is supplied by pottery from Celtic settlements in southern part of Upper Silesia. A small series of such pottery, in the past wrongly associated with the Przeworsk culture (Dąbrowska 1988:112), comes from a La Tène culture settlement in Łany and a settlement in Nowa Cerekwia (Silesia province) (Richthofen 1927; Jahn 1931: 153; Czerska 1959, 1963a; 1963b; 1974; 1976; 1983; Woźniak 1992; Bednarek 1994). These are fragments of vases without necks or broad-opening cups and pots with rims faceted on the inside and sometimes fitted with narrowed handles (house 'a', houses 1, 2, 5, 8, 14, 21, pit 15; Richthofen 1927, Tab. V.8; Czerska 1959, Fig. 9.1,4,8; 1963, Fig. 12.a,b,c,d,f,g,m,n; 1963b, Fig. 4.7; 1976, Fig. 9.o,p; Woźniak 1992, Fig. 4.a,b; Bednarek 1994, Fig. 6; the collection of the MŚO-A-232/70) as well as fragments of tableware decorated with a subtle incised geometric ornament filled with strokes (house 1, 2, 3, pit 4; Czerska 1959, Fig. 11.9, 11, 13.17, 20; 1963, Fig. 20.c-f,h, n, o), and fragments of storage vessels decorated with a relief strip bearing finger impressions under the rim (house 1, 2; Czerska 1959, Fig. 9.9, 13.18).

These pottery items indicate connections to the style of younger Jutland pottery dated to phase IIIa according to Becker (1961), i.e. phase IIA according to Martens (1997) and to the earliest vessels of Przeworsk culture. In the case of finds from the Łany settlement, their chronology cannot be made any more precise, because the dating of this settlement is based only on La Tène pottery discovered there, which resembles ceramics occurring on other Celtic settlements in Upper Silesia and Moravia used in horizons 3-5 according to Meduna (1980), synchronized with the end of early La Tène period and the whole middle La Tène period. More closely dated materials, however, come from Nowa Cerekwia. The chronology of most features discovered at the site and containing Jastorf pottery can be made more specific thanks to the Celtic artefacts that have been unearthed in their fills. Precisely dated, the

---
[47] The artefact is held in the collections of the Institute of Prehistory, AMU.

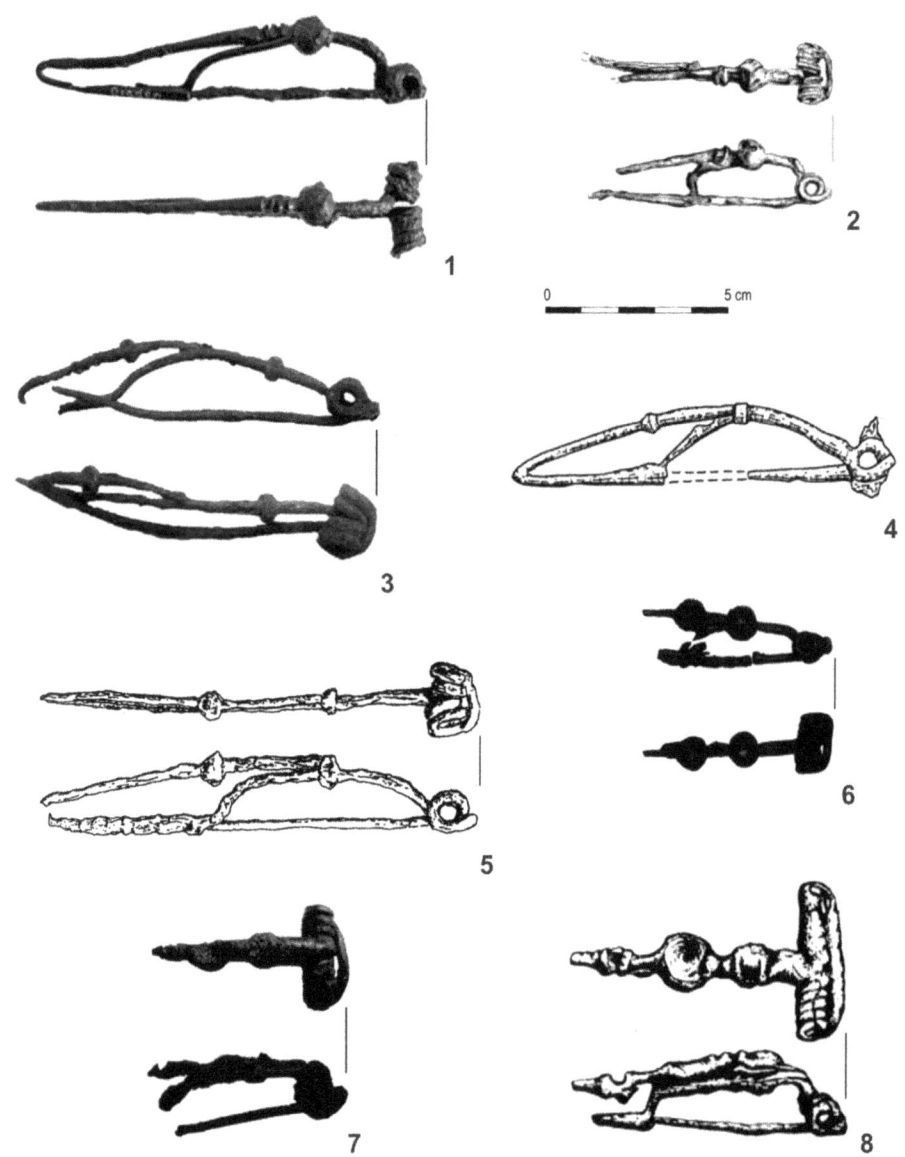

FIG. 18. CELTIC ORIGIN IRON BROOCHES FOUND IN JASTORF CULTURE GRAVES.
1 GRADOWO (INSTITUTE OF ARCHAEOLOGY UJ COLLECTIONS); 2 WILCZA WÓLKA (AFTER GRABAREK 2011); 3 ZARĘBOWO (INSTITUTE OF ARCHAEOLOGY AND ETHNOLOGY POLISH ACADEMY OF SCIENCES, POZNAŃ BRANCH COLLECTIONS); 4 KARLINO (AFTER MACHAJEWSKI 1999); 5 STARE KOCZARGI (AFTER ANDRZEJOWSKA ANDRZEJOWSKI 1997); 6 NOWE MIASTO (POZNAŃ ARCHAEOLOGICAL MUSEUM COLLECTION); 7 PIETRZYKÓW (POZNAŃ ARCHAEOLOGICAL MUSEUM COLLECTION); 8 CHEŁM BIEŁAWIN (ARCHIVE MUSEUM IN CHEŁM).

artefacts include in the first place fragments of iron fibulae, following middle La Tène construction patterns and dated to phase LTC1[48], fibulae of group 1b according to Gebhard (1991:7-8, 87, Fig. 1) (Mötschwil type), characteristic of phase LTC2[49] as well as fragments of glass bracelets/armlets believed to be typical of phases LTC1 and C2 (Woźniak 1992; Karwowski 1997, Tab. 1). [50]

---

[48] House 1 – frag. of a fibula resembling the fibulae of group 15 according to Gebhard (1991) (Czerska 1959, 30, no. 3, Fig. 15.2; Museum of Opole Silesia (MŚO) – A-232/5), frag. of a stem of an iron fibula with a large globe bearing a relief ornament (unpublished artefact in the MŚO collections).
House 2 – frag. of a fibula resembling the fibulae of group 15a according to Gebhard (Czerska 1959: 36, Fig. 15.1; MŚO-A-232/14)
House 14 - frag. of a fibula resembling the fibulae of group 13b according to Gebhard (Czerska 1963b:141, Fig. 5.1; MŚO-A-232/150)
Pit 10 – frag. of a fibula resembling the fibulae of group 14 according to Gebhard (Czerska 1963a:293, 298, Fig. 6d; Woźniak 1970, Tab. XX.1; 1971:507, Fig. 2.2), frag. of an iron fibula decorated with a large globe on a stem (MŚO-A-232/126)

[49] House 3 – 1 specimen (Czerska 1963a:293, Fig. 6.i; Woźniak 1970, Tab. XX.5; 1971:507, Fig. 2.3; Bednarek 1994:504, Fig. 9.f; MŚO--A-232/37)
House 8 – 1 specimen (Czerska 1963a:293, 297, Fig. 6f; Woźniak 1970, Tab. XX.3; 1971:507, Fig. 2.1; MŚO-A-232/108)

[50] House 2 – frag. of a bracelet/armlet of group 15 according to Haevernick (Czerska 1959, 36, Fig. 14.18; Karwowski 1997:60, no. 17, Fig. 5i, Tab. 1a; 2005, Fig. 1b, 3b; MŚO-A-232/12);
House 3 – frag. of a bracelet/armlet of group 7b according to Haevernick (Czerska 1963a:291, Fig. 3a; Bednarek 1994:504, Fig. 9.a; Karwowski 1997:60, no. 17, Fig. 2e, Tab. 1d), frag. of a bracelet/armlet of group 8b according to Haevernick (Czerska 1963a:291, Fig. 3.e; Karwowski

The above comments on the chronology of Lowland Jastorf settlement finds can be supplemented by a single radiocarbon date from the settlement in Karnin (Lubuskie province). The settlement yielded stylistically younger Jastorf pottery, i.e. having affinities with Danish finds from phase IIIa according to Becker (1961) or phase IIA according to Martens (1997).[51] One of the more probable ranges of this measurement (59.7% of probability) covers the period of 330-200 BC, which corresponds to the absolute dating of phases LTB2 and C1 (Brandt 2001:67, Tab. 1b).

More data for establishing the chronology of the Lowland Jastorf culture are supplied by its grave complexes. Sepulchral materials, however, form only – as already mentioned – a small group when compared to relics from settlements (Grygiel 2012, list 28). These are most often single burials sometimes found at the same sites where grave finds of Pomerania-Cloche culture were exposed or even much older graves, belonging to the Lusatian culture and dated to the Late Bronze and Early Iron Ages. Strangely enough, Jastorf culture grave features are rarely found on the burial grounds of the early Przeworsk and Oksywie cultures[52]. Among the few Jastorf culture grave complexes that have been accurately dated, one should mention burials from Chełm-Bieławin grave 1 (east Lublin province), Grodziszcze, district Świebodzin feature 263 (Lubuskie province), Zarębowo, district Aleksandrów Kuj. grave 35 and Smólsk, Włocławek district (Kujawy), Nowe Miasto-on-Warta, Środa Wlkp. district grave 73, Źrenica, Środa Wlkp. district grave 9 and Pietrzyków, Września distr. grave 1 (central Wielkopolska), and Stare Koczargi, Warsaw west district feature 3 and Wilcza Wólka, Piaseczno district grave 1 (western Mazovia). In the graves from Zarębowo and Stare Koczargi (Fig. 18: 3,5), discoveries were made of long ornamented fibulae of type A according to Kostrzewski (1919a, Fig. 1) (Tezlaff 1967, Fig. 24; Andrzejowska & Andrzejowski 1997, Fig.

1997:60, no. 17, Fig. 5g),
House 8 – frag. of a bracelet/armlet of group 8b according to Haevernick (Czerska 1963a:291, Fig. 3l, 296; Karwowski 1997:61, no. 17, Fig. 5h), frag. of a bracelet/armlet of group 11 according to Haevernick (Czerska 1963a:291, 296, Fig. 3o; Karwowski 1997:61, no. 17, Fig. 5b; MŚO- -A-232/114)
House 14 – frag. of a bracelet/armlet of group 7a according to Haevernick (Czerska 1963b:141; Karwowski 1997:61, no. 17, Fig. 2a, Tab. 3c)
House 21 – frag. of a bracelet/armlet of group 7a according to Haevernick (Czerska 1974:34, Tab. X.b; 1976:113, 123, no. 3, Fig. 3; Karwowski 1997:61, no. 17, Fig. 2b, Tab. 3b)
Pit 4 – frag. of a bracelet/armlet of group 7b according to Haevernick (Czerska 1963a:291, Fig. 3d; Karwowski 1997:61, no. 17, Fig. 2d; MŚO- -A -232/45), frag. of a bracelet/armlet of group 6a according to Haevernick (Czerska 1963a:291, Fig. 4i; Karwowski 1997:61, no. 17)
Pit 10 – frag. of a bracelet/armlet of group 8a according to Haevernick (Czerska 1963a:291, Fig. 3j, 298; Karwowski 1997:61, no. 17, Fig. 5f, Tab. 2c; MŚO-A-232/124)
[51] Unpublished materials from rescue investigations kept in the Historical and Archaeological Museum in Głogów. The radiocarbon measurement (MKL-21) was made by Prof. Marek Krąpiec, AGH in Kraków, on a selected wood sample taken from the fill of a feature interpreted to have been a well (feature 275).
[52] Kuny, Turek district site 4a (Skowron 2008), Rumia, Wejherowo district site 1 (Pietrzak 1987; Maciałowicz 2011), Wygoda, Białogard district site 6 (Machajewski 2001), Źrenica, Środa Wlkp. district site 1 (Dymaczewski 1958).

10. b-c) which are linked to the Celtic fibulae of group 15a according to Gebhard, characteristic of phase LTC1 (Gebhard 1991:17, 80-81, Fig. 5). The burials from Chełm-Bieławin and Pietrzyków (Fig. 18:7, 8) are dated using fibulae of the middle La Tène construction and ornamented with a plate on a stem (Michałowski 2003: 67, Fig. 3; Mazurek T. & Mazurek W. 2006:93, photo 11). They point to connections with the Celtic fibulae of group 13b according to Gebhard (1991:15, 80-81, Fig. 5) characteristic of phase LTC1. In a Jastorf culture grave in Wilcza Wólka (Fig. 18:2), a ball fibula was found and classified as Beltz (1911, Fig. 46) variety F (Grabarek 2011, Fig. 6, 7). It is similar to an unornamented fibula of type B according to Kostrzewski discovered in a grave in Źrenica (Dymaczewski 1958: 17-18, Fig. 13.1). Both forms resemble the fibulae of group 13c according to Gebhard (1991: 15, 80-81, Fig. 5) occurring in phase LTC1. Doubtless contemporary with the above finds, Jastorf burials in Nowe Miasto and Smólsk (Fig. 18:6) yielded short ball fibulae of variety F according to Beltz (1911) (Machajewski & Walkiewicz 1993, Fig. 3.1; collections of the MAiE in Łódź). They correspond to the rare forms of Celtic fibulae encountered on La Tène culture cemeteries in Slovakia in phase LTC1 and included in group EF H/ L3-B, C according to Bujna (2003, Fig. 65). It is with these La Tène artefacts that a small fibula of type A or A/B according to Kostrzewski shows affinity. It was found in a Jastorf grave in Grodziszcze (Żychliński & Przybytek 2008, Fig. 2.2, photo 2.4-5).

Possibly, the list of graves containing Jastorf pottery and dated to the same period ought to be expanded by adding a complex from Gradowo, Radziejów Kuj. district (Fig. 18:1). It features a long iron globe fibula, covered with fire patina and classified as variety F according to Beltz (Kostrzewski 1919a:17, Fig. 35),[53] suggestive of the Celtic specimens of group 13c according to Gebhard.

A mention should also be made of Jastorf culture graves located on the Lowland, far from the zone of frequent occurrence of other Jastorf materials. One such is a grave unearthed in Równina Dolna, Kętrzyn district (Old Prussian Plain), on the territory of the Western Baltic Kurgans culture (Gaerte 1938; Maciałowicz 2009). The grave inventory, next to an urn having a Jastorf form, included a winged pin of the Danish type (Gaerte 1938, Fig. 1), similar to the already mentioned specimen of the same type from the settlement in Szynych. The winged pin from Równina Dolna represents a type of north Jastorf ornament that was used towards the end of the older and in the early younger Pre-Roman periods (Maciałowicz 2009:202-203). Another grave find of the Jastorf culture, discovered in a place far away from its home ground, comes from Karlino, Białogard district, on the lower Parsęta River, in the borderland between west and east

---

[53] The Institute of Archaeology, Jagiellonian Univ., holds in its collections, next to the discussed fibula, a fragment of a Jastorf vessel, allegedly found together with it (gift of T. Lange-ZP 917) (Undset 1882:111). Both artefacts bear traces of burning on a pyre, which indicates their connection to the inventory of a cremation grave.

Pomerania (Machajewski 1999; Eggers's card file). This is an urn grave dated by reference to a long decorated A type fibula (Fig. 18:4) according to Kostrzewski (Machajewski 1999, Fig. 1.1). Having Celtic provenance, the fibula resembles the fibulae of group 15b according to Gebhard, popular in phase LTC1 (Gebhard 1991:17, 80-81, Fig. 5). The youngest Jastorf grave comes, as it seems, from Drawsko on the Lower Noteć River (north Wielkopolska) (Dernoga & Gajda 2004). In it, a type B fibula (according to Kostrzewski) was found (1919a, Fig. 2) (Dernoga & Gajda 2004, Tab. II.2), resembling the Celtic fibulae of group 19b according to Gebhard, believed to be characteristic of phase LTC2 (Gebhard 1991:18-20,82, Fig. 6).

The above mentioned precisely dated burials yielded, *inter alia*, broad-opening cups, small conical cups and vase-like vessels of various sizes without a neck.[54] In addition, these complexes included pots with an egg-shaped belly fitted with two handles,[55] a fragment of an S-profile, narrow-opening pot,[56] slender vases with a marked neck, resembling reverse pear-shaped vessels,[57] a bowl with the rim turned outwards[58] and a poorly preserved vessel with a marked neck that must have been one of vase-like forms.[59] All these vessels have mostly faceted rims on the inside, some have narrowed handles and a subtle incised geometric pattern sometimes arranged in a narrow ornamentation band. They correspond in terms of their character to other younger Jastorf materials from the Lowland having affinities with the Danish finds of phase IIIa according to Becker (1961), i.e. phase IIA according to Martens (1997) and with the materials of Przeworsk culture early phases (Dąbrowska 1988:28-29). What clearly stands apart from the above named forms is only a pot-like urn from a grave in Równina Dolna, which has a neck marked with an offset (Gaerte 1938, Fig. 2). It is important to note that the urn has counterparts among stylistically older Lowland Jastorf pottery (Maciałowicz 2009: 206).

The set of forms of Jastorf pottery found in graves on the Lowland corresponds to ceramic artefacts discovered on settlements. The only differences, however, are noticeable in the incidence of some vessel types, specifically in the smaller amount of coarse kitchen ware in graves. The grave complexes containing Jastorf pottery that were precisely dated and discussed here bear out earlier comments about the chronological differentiation of Lowland Jastorf materials. These finds indicate that stylistically younger Jastorf vessels should be dated to the early younger Pre-Roman period.

Jastorf culture sites on the Lowland yielded, besides pottery, few metal artefacts of north Jastorf provenance. These are the two Danish-type winged pins mentioned earlier; one of which was found on the Jastorf culture settlement in Szynych in the Land of Chełmno, while the other was discovered in a grave in Równina Dolna on the Old Prussian Plain, distant from the Jastorf material home ground (Fig. 14.1, 2) (Gaerte 1938, Fig. 1; Maciałowicz 2009, Fig. 10). Another artefact of north Jastorf provenance, mentioned already earlier, is a Holstein pin of the Skovby/Bjerndrup type found on the Jastorf settlement in Żółwin (Lubuskie province) (Kres 1965a; 1965b). Furthermore, it is probably with the Jastorf culture that two pins of the same type should be associated. They were unearthed without a context in Łuszczewo and Sobiejuchy, in the borderland between Wielkopolska and Kujawy (Fig. 14.3) (Erzepki 1890, Tab. XXI. 6, 7). The same attribution should be given to an iron pin with a fluted head and a sabre-curved stem found in Zarębowo (Kujawy).[60] Other north Jastorf artefacts include crown neck rings discovered on the Lowland. Among them, according to Kostrzewski (1919a:73-79) ,a distinction is made between type I/II flat forms with a plate covering the hinge pin (Fig. 19:7-9) and type III/IV specimens featuring a thinned ring decorated with triangular protrusions, known as toothed-crown necklaces type D, E (Fig. 19:10, 11) according to M. Babeş (Dąbrowska 1988: 180-183; Babeş 1993:107-108; Maciałowicz 2011: 89-100).

For the most part, these are unattached finds. Hence, the connection of all these necklaces to the Jastorf culture is by no means certain. The more so as one of the toothed-crown necklaces was discovered in the burial of a Przeworsk culture man on a cemetery in Błonie, Sandomierz district (Mycielska & Woźniak 1988:83, Tab. CXXXVII.3). In addition, several fibulae were found on the Lowland, representing forms known chiefly from Jutland and the Danish-German borderland. One such is a bronze fibula, mentioned already earlier, from the settlement in Sowinki (central Wielkopolska), indicating connections to globe fibulae of the Danish series (Makiewicz & Łaszkiewicz 2001, Fig. 1). Another, similar fibula was discovered unattached on a burial ground in Luszyn, Gostynin district (Kostrzewski's card file, file no. 69), which has been used by the populations of the early phases of the Przeworsk culture (see Fig. 19:5). A connection to north Jastorf goods is indicated also by two small cast bronze fibulae with a frame-shaped stem found in Wszedzień, Mogilno district cemetery I and Kałdus (Fig. 19:4), Chełmno district (Erzepki, Kostrzewski 1914, Tab. LX.7; Bokiniec 2008, Tab. XXI.3, LXI.2). Similar fibulae, sometimes likened to typical Jastorf fibulae with a step-like bow, can be rarely found among the finds from the Lower Elbe area

---

[54] Chełm Biełwin grave 1 (2 specimens) (Dzieńkowski & Gołub 1999:177, Fig. 2.12; collections Chełm Museum); Drawsko grave 10 (Dernoga & Gajda 2004, Tab. II.1); Grodziszcze feature 263 (Żychliński & Przybytek 2008, Fig. 2.1); Nowe Miasto on Warta grave 73 (2 specimens) (Machajewski & Walkiewicz 1993, Fig. 3.2, 3); Pietrzyków grave 1 (2 specimens) (Michałowski 2003, Fig. 4.2; collections of Archaeological Museum in Poznań); Smólsk (collections of MAiE in Łódź); Stare Koczargi feature 3 (Andrzejowska & Andrzejowski 1997, Fig. 10.d); Źrenica grave 9 (Dymaczewski 1958, Fig. 13).
[55] Pietrzyków – grave 1 (Michałowski 2003, Fig. 4.1); Wilcza Wólka – grave (Grabarek 2011, Fig. 4, 5).
[56] Gradowo (IA UJ ZP 917)
[57] Karlino – grave of 1934. (Machajewski 1999, Fig. 1.4; H. J. Eggers's card file); Zarębowo – grave 35 (Tetzlaff 1967, Fig. 23.1-1a)
[58] Zarębowo – grave 35 (Tetzlaff 1967, Fig. 23.2).
[59] Zarębowo – grave 35, collections of IAiE PAN, Poznań Branch.

[60] Unpublished artefact in the collections of Institute of Archaeology and Ethnology Polish Academy of Sciences, Poznań Branch (no. 5489).

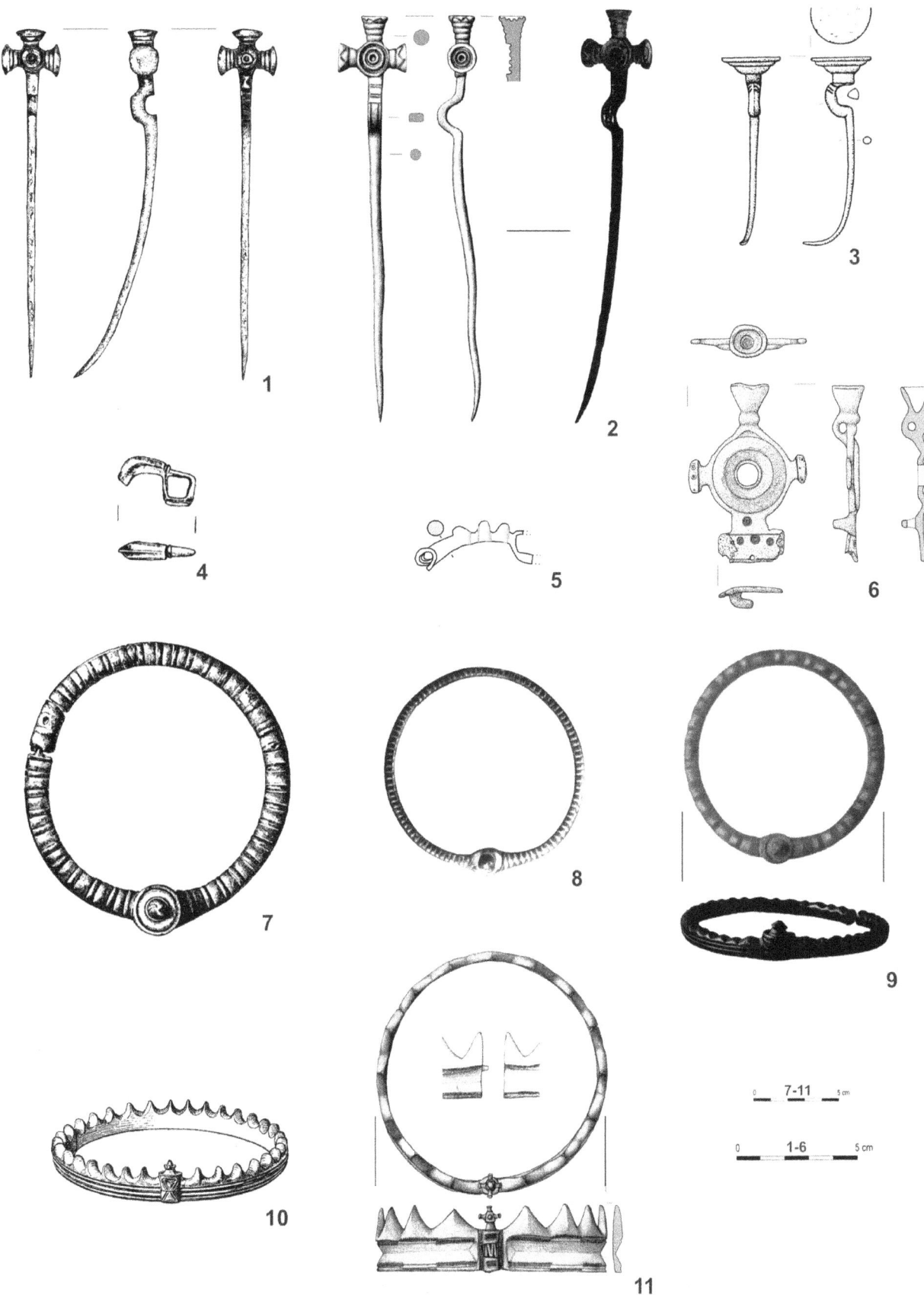

Fig. 19. Bronze finds with the Jastorf culture origin from Poland.
1. Szynych (after Maciałowicz 2009); 2. Równina Dolna (after Maciałowicz 2009); 3. Łuszczewo (after Prochowicz 2006); 4. Kałdus (after Bokiniec 2008); 5. Luszyn (after J. Kostrzewski Archiv); 6. Pręgowo Dolne (after Prochowicz 2011); 7. Piasutno (after Gaerte 1929); 8. Piekło (after Brutzer 1942); 9. Milczek (after J. Kostrzewski Archiv); 10. Wybranowo (after Seger 1899); 11. Kluczewo (after Dąbrowska 2008).

and Jutland (Bech 1975, Fig. 8; Wendowski-Schünemann 2000). The cultural attribution of mentioned artefacts from Luszyn, Wszedzień and Kałdus is hard to establish as they come from destroyed sites that were amateurishly investigated already prior to the First World War.

Other Jastorf provenance artefacts – not representative of, however, typical Jutland forms – are believed to include pins discovered unattached in Kamieńczyk, Wyszków district and Tomasze, Ostrołęka district (east Mazovia) (Dąbrowska 2008:35). Cast in full in bronze and having a small conical head (Prochowicz 2006, Fig. 1.a), the specimen from Tomasze can be likened to early Holstein-type pins common in the north part of the Jastorf culture oecumene (Holstein pins of series A-B according to Hingst 1986)). This is not, however, a typical Jastorf ornament, which is evidenced by the shape of its stem – it is bent sail-like below the head. The Kamieńczyk pin, in turn, (Nowakowski 2006, Fig. 1a) is one of the winged pins of the east Mecklenburg-Vorpommern type, which are almost never encountered beyond these two regions (Schubart 1957:87; Schoknecht 1991, Fig. 1).

Another artefact of Jastorf provenance was found without any context in Pręgowo Dolne, Gdańsk district (Gdańsk Seaboard) (Prochowicz 2011). It is a bronze fibula with a large circular ring and trumpet-shaped head classified under the Zachow type (Fig. 19:6). It is believed to be a variety of fibulae deriving from winged pins popular on the lower Elbe River (*Flügelnadelfibeln*) (Schubart 1953: 65-66; 1957: 90; Prochowicz 2011: 237). Zachow-type fibulae were unearthed on few Jastorf sites in northeast Germany: north Brandenburg, east Mecklenburg and Vorpommern (Schubart 1957, map 2; Keiling 1969, map 9; Prochowicz 2011, Fig. 2). Visibly removed to the east of this zone, the finds of several fibulae of this type from Lubieszewo and Żółte, Drawsko district, West Pomerania (Merkbuch für Ausgrabungen 1914, Tab. 9.41; Wołągiewicz 1997, Tab. IV.21b, c) are related to the Oder group. The Pręgowo Dolne fibula with a massive head, broad ring and stamp ornament differs, however, from Zachow-type specimens, known from the Jastorf culture oecumene. The fibula finds, however, constitute an analogy in respect to a fibula of this type discovered in Gröstorp (southeast Scania) (Montelius 1896, Fig. 6). The similarity between the fibulae from Pręgowo Dolne and Gröstorp is so remarkable that it can be assumed that these ornaments were made in the same workshop (Prochowicz 2011:239).

The above-named north Jastorf artefacts, from both Jutland and northeast Germany, should be associated with the end of the older and the beginning of the younger Pre-Roman periods. The oldest of these seem to be crown neck rings with plates, showing connections to some necklace forms of Celtic origin dated to phase LTB, Danish type winged pins and Zachow-type fibulae used, it is believed, since the end of the older Pre-Roman period (Keiling 1970:170; Wołągiewicz 1981a, Tab. XXVII.3; Brandt 2001:99-100; Maciało-wicz 2009:202-203; 2011:100-103; Prochowicz 2011:239). Possibly to this period or the beginning of phase A1 should be dated the Kamieńczyk pin, indicating connections to Danish specimens and classic winged pins from the lower Elbe (Schoknecht 1991:77; Maciałowicz 2009:200). To the beginning of phase A1 one can date Skovby/Bjerndrup-type Holstein pins and the pin with the fluted, elongated head from Zarębowo, which is suggested by the chronology of identical or similar pins occurring in Jastorf culture materials in Holstein and dated to phase IIa according to Hingst or to a period roughly corresponding to phase LTC1 (Hingst 1959:17a.65-74; 1986:35; Maciałowicz 2009:201). It is also most probably from this period that the atypical Tomasze pin originates. Its manufacture time cannot be too remote from the period of occurrence of early Holstein pins, being its prototypes, dated to phase Id and, to a lower degree, to phase IIa according to Hingst (1959, Fig. 17a. 57, 58; Maciałowicz 2009:201) on the lower Elbe.

A slightly broader chronology is characteristic of the north Jastorf globe and frame-like stem fibulae found on the Lowland that are among the forms dated mainly to phase A1 (Bech 1975; Wendowski-Schünemann 2000; Brandt 2001:85-87). The least precise, it seems, is the chronology of the toothed-crown necklaces, which, unlike their prototypes with plates, do not indicate any closer connection to Celtic ornaments. Toothed crowns are generally believed to be later than necklaces with plates – the former were manufactured and used chiefly in phase LTC (Shchukin et al. 1992; Babeş 1993:107-108; Brandt 2001:100). This dating is based, however, on very weak arguments almost exclusively limited to the analysis of the stylistic traits of the artefacts in question. In the lands of present-day Poland, one may expect that toothed crowns were in use for longer. An argument in favour of this view is provided by the grave find of the Przeworsk culture from Błonie, mentioned earlier, dated to phase A2. The dating is supported above all by the chronological brackets of the use of the burial ground there (Woźniak 1994).

In summary, the dating of Jastorf culture finds on the Lowland is based for the most part on the analysis of connections between the most popular Lowland Jastorf pottery and Jutland materials as well as in part north Elbe ones. Primarily on the strength of such analyses and the dating of a few Celtic artefacts and some Jastorf metal ornaments co-occurring with the pottery, an attempt may be made to segregate the materials into older and younger ones. The older ones, i.e. dated to the end of the older Pre-Roman period, include bi- and tripartite vases, broad-opening cups and goblets featuring rims that have not been thickened but have been strongly turned outwards and sometimes featuring band-like handles, covered in subtly incised geometric ornamentation. These forms indicate affinities with Jutland finds of phases Ib and II according to Becker (1961). The same affinities are shared by bowls with a broad, markedly turned outwards or even horizontal rim. The north Jastorf pottery from the end of the older Pre-Roman period is resembled by pot-like storage vessels, featuring several handles or relief strips placed on the upper belly, and by pots with a tall neck marked by clear offset and a deeply incised post-Hallstatt ornament.

In turn, other pottery forms should be treated as younger materials among Lowland Jastorf finds, indicating connections to north Jastorf goods dated to a later period, i.e. the beginning of the younger Pre-Roman period; distinguished by rims faceted on the inside and handles narrowed in the middle. These are above all various tableware forms: vases with no neck, cups and bowls with rims turned outwards as well as slender vase-like vessels with a marked neck, resembling reverse pear-shaped vessels. On some, chiefly vases, there appears, encountered also on younger Jutland pottery, a subtle incised geometric pattern sometimes filled with strokes and arranged in horizontal ornamentation bands. The younger Jastorf forms should encompass some coarse kitchen wares of which few survive. These are pots with faceted rims with two narrowed handles and pot-like storage vessels decorated with a relief strip bearing finger impressions and placed beneath the rim.

The distinction between older and younger Lowland Jastorf culture materials made on the strength of connections to the north Jastorf zone is borne out by few co-occurring artefacts that can be dated using the system of La Tène culture chronology. In this context, one could mention both younger Lowland Jastorf pottery finds, including the fibulae of type A and B according to Kostrzewski (1919a) and variety F fibulae according to Beltz (1911) – indicating connections to the Celtic fibulae of phase LTC1, as well as materials of this type occurring on Celtic settlements in Upper Silesia dated to the middle La Tène period, specifically its older section (LTC1). Another argument in favour of the chronological differentiation of the Lowland Jastorf pottery is the links of its younger forms to the materials of the Przeworsk and Poieneşti-Łukaševka cultures. However, the dating is not accurate as it covers a period corresponding to phases A1 and A2.

The Jastorf pottery pointing to connections with north Jastorf finds from the end of the older Pre-Roman period is known from a few settlements in central and north Wielkopolska, Kujawy, the Land of Chełmno and western Mazovia. In addition, single finds of this type were found in the north of the Lowland – the Gdańsk Seaboard, Parsęta River drainage basin and Old Prussian Plain (Grygiel 2012, list 28a).[61] Contemporary with these finds, two Danish-type winged pins were discovered together with the older Jastorf pottery in the Land of Chełmno (Szynych settlement) and in the territory of the Western Baltic Kurgans culture (grave in Równina Dolna). It is also with the end of the older Pre-Roman period that north Jastorf crown neck rings with plates, also occurring mainly along the Baltic Coast, should be associated. The younger, more numerous, Jastorf pottery is spread over a larger territory. For it was found on the sites, chiefly settlements and few burials, which are located in part in the same regions where older finds were discovered, as well as in others where no older materials have been recorded – in the Land of Lubusz, south Wielkopolska, southeast Lower Silesia, central Poland, right-bank Mazovia, Podlassia and the east Lublin province. Moreover, such materials were discovered on mentioned above Celtic settlements in south Upper Silesia (Grygiel 2012, list 28b).[62] Contemporary with the younger Jastorf pottery, few metal relics originating from the Danish-German borderland were discovered in various parts of the Lowland but predominantly in Wielkopolska, Kujawy and Mazovia. They include Holstein pins, a pin with a fluted head, toothed-crown necklaces and single bronze fibulae of northern origin.

The question of Jastorf culture relationships with other Lowland cultures

In the Pre-Roman period, on the Lowland, four large cultural units thrived: the 'post-Hallstatt' Pomerania-Cloche culture, the more archaic Western Baltic Kurgans culture, Przeworsk culture remaining under a strong La Tène impact, and related Oksywie culture (Kozłowski & Kaczanowski 1998:212-230). There is no evidence of any ties between the Pomerania-Cloche culture and Lowland Jastorf culture. The reason may be, to some extent, the difficulties in the dating of relics assigned to the younger development phase of the Pomerania-Cloche culture. The

---

[61] Examples of sites with older Jastorf culture pottery: Brześć Kujawski site 3 and 4 (Kujawy) (Jażdżewski 1939; Grygiel 2004), Czarnków (north Wielkopolska) (Michałowski 2006, Fig. 16), Dopiewo site 26/29 (central Wielkopolska) (Machajewski 2010), Izdebno Kościelne site 1 (west Mazovia) (Kołacz 1995), Komorniki site 2 (central Wielkopolska) (Kostrzewski 1939), Obórka site 2 (central Wielkopolska) (Sobucki, Woźniak 2004), Otorowo site 66 (north Wielkopolska) (Żychliński 2004), Pławce site 22 (central Wielkopolska) (Makiewicz 2004), Równina Dolna site 2 (Old Prussian Plain) (grave 94) (Gaerte 1938), Rumia site 1 (grave 46) (Gdańsk Seaboard) (Maciałowicz 2011), Szynych site 12 (Land of Chełmno) (Grygiel 2012; unpublished), Wygoda site 6 (Parsęta River drainage basin) – grave 102 (Machajewski 2001).

[62] Examples of sites with younger Jastorf culture pottery. Settlements: Brześć Kujawski site 4 (Kujawy) (Jażdżewski 1939; Grygiel 2004), Czarnków (north Wielkopolska) (Michałowski 2006, Fig. 15), Dobryń Mały site VII (Podlassia) (Bienia&Żółkowski 1994), Dopiewo site 26/29 (central Wielkopolska) (Machajewski 2010), Gniewowo site 5 (south-west Wielkopolska) (Ciesielski 1980), Izdebno Kościelne site 1 (west Mazovia) (Kołacz 1995), Karnin site 197 (Land of Lubusz) (Grygiel 2012; unpublished), Młodzikowo site 21 (central Wielkopolska) (Świerkowska-Barańska 1992), Poznań Nowe Miasto site 278 and 284 (central Wielkopolska) (Machajewski & Pietrzak 2008a; Kasprowicz 2008); Piecki site 8 (Kujawy) (Bednarczyk&Sujecka 2004), Stary Zamek site 6 (Lower Silesia – Wrocław district) (Domański&Lodowski 1984), Strzyżów site Ia/II (Lublin province) (Kokowski 2006; Prochowicz 2006a), Szynych site 11-13 (Land of Chełmno) (Grygiel 2012; unpublished), Werbkowice site I (Lublin province) (Piętka-Dąbrowska&Liana 1962; Dąbrowska&Liana 1963), Wojnowo site 23 (central Wielkopolska) (Kasprowicz 2004), Wytyczno site 5 (east Lublin province) (Mazurek 2001), Żółwin site 3 (Land of Lubusz) (Lewczuk 1997). Graves: Chełm-Bieławin site 7 (east Lublin province) – grave 1 (Dzieńkowski&Gołub 1999), Grodziszcze site 12 (Land of Lubusz) – feature 263 (Żychliński&Przybytek 2008), Karlino (Parsęta River drainage basin) – grave of 1934 (Machajewski 1999), Kuny site 4a (north east Wielkopolska) – grave 11 (Skowron 2008), Niewęgłosz (Podlassia) (Kokowski 1991a), Nowe Miasto upon Warta site 1 (central Wielkopolska) – grave 73 (Machajewski&Walkiewicz 1993), Piaski (central Poland) – grave of 1923 (Jakimowicz 1925), Pietrzyków site 8 (central Wielkopolska) – grave 1 (Michałowski 2003), Stare Koczargi site 6 (west Mazovia) – feature 3 (Andrzejowska&Andrzejowski 1997), Wilcza Wólka site 14 (west Mazovia) – grave 1 (Grabarek 2011), Zarębowo site 1 (Kujawy) – grave 35 (Tetzlaff 1967)

latest, accurately dated finds of this culture come from phase LTB and, there are grounds to believe, mainly from its older section (Grygiel 2004:45-50; Woźniak 2007a:396-397). Hence, there is no evidence of any settlement traces by Pomerania-Cloche populations contempo-rary with the occurrence of Jastorf materials on the Lowland. However, it cannot be theoretically excluded that the older phase of the Jastorf culture on the Lowland was contemporaneous with the decline of the Pomerania-Cloche culture. Adopting this hypothesis, one should note, however, that Pomerania-Cloche materials (in this case pottery only) broadly dated to the younger section of the culture's development, do not show any traits that would point to contacts with the Jastorf culture on the Lowland. Attempting to define possible relationships between the Pomerania-Cloche and Jastorf cultures on the Lowland, one should remember, however, that we face major obstacles following from the nature of the sources being compared. While the Pomerania-Cloche culture is known chiefly from sepulchral finds, the Jastorf finds for the most part come from settlements. Furthermore, it must be observed that a comparison of the two units is to some extent hampered by their affiliation to the same post-Hallstatt cultural circle.

By contrast, clear connections are observed between the Jastorf and Przeworsk cultures. They are seen above all in the similarity of many pottery characteristics (Grygiel 2004; Woźniak 2007a; Dąbrowska 2008:95). The ties between the two cultures are possibly illustrated also by certain common characteristics of funeral rites. The Lowland Jastorf culture features include cremation burials placed in large pits which are filled with pyre remains, almost completely cremated human remains, and comminuted pottery that has been secondarily burned. Such burials correspond to typical Przeworsk culture graves from the early phases of the culture's lifetime (Godłowski 1977: 172-173).[63] In addition, the connection between the two cultures seems to be borne out by the occurrence of similar house remains, the basements of which are sunk into the ground, and dog burials on settlements associated with them (Andrałojć 1986; Makiewicz 1987; 1993; Dąbrowska 1988:146; Michałowski 2010:187).[64] Further, in respect to ties linking the Jastorf and Przeworsk cultures on the Lowland there are clear indications of a 'cross-pollination' of materials of both cultures on settlement and sepulchral sites (Grygiel 2004:32-34; Dąbrowska 2008:95, 98; Machajewski&Pietrzak 2008b:307-308).

The period when the Przeworsk culture crystallized, according to hitherto held views, is synchronized with phase LTC1. This period of the Przeworsk culture lifetime is associated with the early relics of Celtic provenance from phase LTC1. They are believed to include above all the long decorated fibulae of type A according to Kostrzewski (1919a, Fig. 1) and some weapons indicating connections to La Tène specimens known from the latest celtic grave finds in Bohemia, Moravia, and Slovakia (Godłowski &Woźniak 1981: 52-53; Godłowski 1981: 59; 1985: 13; Dąbrowska 1988: 15-19, 55-56). Such goods, however, do not occur on Przeworsk burial grounds, but, for the most part, these are single finds or finds made in poorly furnished graves of indeterminate cultural attribution or in Jastorf settlements and graves mentioned earlier (Grygiel 2012).[65]

---

[63] Examples of such Jastorf culture graves come, for instance, from Kuny – grave 11 (Skowron 2008:18), Nowe Miasto-on-Warta – grave 73 (Machajewski&Walkiewicz 1993), Pietrzyków – grave 1 (Michałowski 2003).

[64] A dog burial, which can possibly be associated with the Jastorf culture, was found on a settlement in Karnin, near Gorzów Wielkopolski, in the remains of a house (feature 99) – collections of the Historical and Archaeological Museum in Głogów.

[65] Among artefacts having Celtic affinities discovered on the Polish Lowland, forms characteristic of phase LTC1 include: long, frequently decorated iron fibulae, of types A and B according to Kostrzewski (1919a), having an elongated stem and showing affinities with the Celtic fibulae of groups 13-15 according to Gebhard (1991) (e.g. Stare Koczargi, Warsaw west district (Andrzejowska & Andrzejowski 1997, Fig. 10. b-c)); short type A or B iron fibulae according to Kostrzewski and small iron ball fibulae of variety F according to Beltz similar to those encountered on Celtic cemeteries in Slovakia and included in group EF H/L3-B, C according to Bujna (2003, Fig. 65) (e.g. Rosko, Czarnków-Trzcianka district (Kostrzewski 1914:115, Fig. 349) and Nowe Miasto-on-Warta, Środa Wlkp. district (Fig. 12.6)); iron globe fibulae of variety F according to Beltz (1911), having counterparts among the Celtic fibulae of groups 13-15 according to Gebhard (1991) (e.g. Bierutów, Oleśnica district (north Lower Silesia) (Langenhan 1890, Tab. I. 8), Bieżyń, Kościan district (southwest Wielkopolska) (collections of AMU Institute of Prehistory in Poznań) and Gradowo, Radziejów Kuj. district (Fig. 12.1)); fibulae following middle La Tène construction patterns with a stem, having counterparts among the Celtic fibulae of groups 13b according to Gebhard (1991) (e.g. Chełm Bieławin (Fig. 12.8)); iron fibulae following middle La Tène construction patterns with a low pin, resembling the fibulae of type D/E according to Kostrzewski (1919a, Fig. 4, 5), finding analogies among eastern Celtic fibulae found on La Tène culture cemeteries in Slovakia in the period covering the end of phase LTB2 and phase LTC1 (Bujna 2003, Fig. 65) (e.g. Wólka Zamkowa, Siemiatycze district (Rosen-Przeworska 1948, Fig. 27.1, Tab. VII.4)); an ornamented bronze fibula from Gniewowo (see above); a type of bronze ring ornament decorated along its circumference with oval bosses, a fragment of which was unearthed in Legnickie Pole (Legnica) (Jahn 1931:37-38, Fig. 40). It is reminiscent of the so-called *Buckelringe* that imitate Celtic products and are known in the Jastorf environment (Brandt 2001:107). As artefacts pointing to connections to the Celtic goods of phase LTC1 in the Przeworsk culture certain weapons come into consideration as well. These are scabbards of double--edged swords decorated with a curvilinear ornament and band-like bosses and related bosses of the Bartodzieje type (Dąbrowska 1988, 55-56). In the light of recent findings, however, the chronology of most of these artefacts needs to be corrected. As a typologically early relic, it is only a scabbard for a Celtic sword found in a grave in Warsaw-Żerań that can be taken into consideration. It is decorated at its opening with the motif of a pair of fantastic creatures arranged antithetically and an elaborate *chagrinage* ornament placed below (Jakimowiczowa 1930; Tomaszewska 1997; Bochnak 2005:41-43). The scabbard finds analogies in the few finds of the La Tène culture of phase LTB2 (Krämer 1985::25, 82, Fig. 12, Tab. 16; Bujna 1994, Tab. 6-7). Accompanying it, a double-edged sword has two rectangular openings in the broadened transition of the blade into the handle bar and corresponds to the form of Celtic swords occurring in the period covering phases LTB2 and LTC1 (de Navarro 1959, Tab. 1.2, 9.1, 12.3, 13.1?, 14.1, 17.6; Horvath 1987, Tab. XVII.2, XXXVII.3, XXXIX.4,5?; Kelemen 1987, Tab. XVIII.2; Pare 2003: 55, Fig. 4.1). Probably later are band-like bosses occurring in the Przeworsk oecumene, resemble shield ferrules used by Celts in phases LTC2 and D1 (Bochnak 2005:110; Łuczkiewicz 2006:207). It is doubtless from the same period that single Bartodzieje-type bosses come, which are related to the band-like bosses mentioned earlier. This view is supported by the chronology of a ferrule of this type from the cemetery in Bartodzieje, Góra district, discovered in a complex dated by reference to a fibula of type B/C according to Kostrzewski (Seger 1902:41, Fig. 41; collections of the Archaeological Museum in Wrocław MAW/III/26). The fibula indicates connections to the Celtic fibulae of group 19c/d according to Gebhard (1991:18-20, 82, Fig. 6), considered to be typical of phase LTC2, or the decline of phase A1. Possibly, a boss of the type discussed here, from an extensively excavated cemetery in Wymysłowo, Gostyń district, can be dated still later. In this respect the cemetery has not yielded any

For this reason, as the earliest Przeworsk culture features, graves should be taken which are furnished with pottery characteristic of this culture and, in addition, containing fibulae of Celtic provenance. The fibulae resemble the specimens of groups 16-19 according to Gebhard (1991:17-20,81, Fig. 6) and are considered characteristic of phase LTC2. It can be claimed, therefore, that the period when the Przeworsk culture crystallized did not cover the beginnings of phase A1 but started only towards the end of this phase. So dated graves, both single ones and forming part of larger Przeworsk burial grounds, are known from north Lower Silesia, south and east Wielkopolska, central Poland, Kujawy, and west and north Mazovia (Grygiel 2012).

It follows from the above that the Jastorf culture settlement covered some regions of the Lowland prior to the crystallization of the Przeworsk culture, the formation of which was to a degree influenced by the Jastorf culture. In north Lower Silesia, south and east Wielkopolska, Kujawy, central Poland and in west and north Mazovia, the inception of Przeworsk culture crystallization is marked, as has already been mentioned, by graves with Przeworsk pottery dated by referring to the relics of Celtic provenance characteristic of phase LTC2, hence, somewhat younger than the very beginning of the younger Pre-Roman period.

In other regions of the Lowland where Jastorf materials are encountered, the so called rhythm of cultural transformations is different. This is true, for instance, of east Mazovia, Podlassia and the Lublin province where the Przeworsk culture appeared relatively late – only in the end of phase A1 or more probably in phase A2 (Godłowski 1985:29-30; Dąbrowska 1988:73-74; 2001; 2008:101-104). It would appear that the Jastorf settlement could have survived there until a slightly later time than in the other regions of the Lowland. This view is supported by the character of one of the larger series of Jastorf materials unearthed on the settlement in Werbkowice-Kotorów, Hrubieszów district (Piętka-Dąbrowska & Liana 1962; Dąbrowska & Liana 1963). These are strikingly similar to the pottery of the Poienești-Lukaševka and Przeworsk cultures dated to both phase A1 and phase A2 (Dąbrowska 1988:28-29; Babeș 1993:59-69). It would be reasonable to expect a longer duration of Jastorf settlement also in north Wielkopolska and the Land of Lubusz, where almost no typical phase-A1 Przeworsk materials have been recorded. Instead, we know of a relatively large number of Jastorf finds recorded in the two regions, in particular in settlement clusters on the middle and lower Noteć River, dated to the end phase A1 or phase A2 (Godłowski 1985, s. 19-20; Dąbrowska 1988, map 23; Gałęzowska 1996; Lewczuk 1997; Dernoga & Gajda 2004; Michałowski 2006; Machajewski 2010:199). Moreover, in phase A1, dispersed Jastorf settlement could have subsisted in east Lower Silesia, on the left bank of the Oder River, where the Przeworsk culture must have

materials older than phase A2 (Jasnosz 1951).

emerged only in the end of phase A1 and in phase A2 (Godłowski 1985:23-24; Dąbrowska 1988:74).

It is harder to assess the significance of few dispersed Jastorf finds for the cultural transformations taking place in the north of the Lowland – in the Land of Chełmno, Gdańsk Seaboard, Parsęta drainage basin or on the Old Prussian Plain. It cannot be excluded that the populations that produced these finds, hailing from the territory of today's Denmark or neighbouring areas of north Germany, took part in the crystallization of the Oksywie culture which, like the Przeworsk culture, considerably differs from the Pomerania-Cloche substratum (Maciałowicz 2011:111-112). A detailed reconstruction of the role the northern societies could have played in the cultural transformation is not possible due to the still meagre amount of sources that can be linked to the end of the older and the beginning of the younger Pre-Roman periods, and that have been recorded in the areas where the Oksywie culture arose (Wołągiewicz 1979; Stąporek 1995; Dąbrowska 2003; Dąbrowska&Woźniak 2005; Bokiniec 2008). Still less can be said of the changes that could have occurred in the neighbouring Western Baltic Kurgans culture in the territory of which single Jastorf finds are encountered, testifying no doubt to contacts with the populations of northern origin.[66] This is a result of inaccurate dating of the materials of this cultural unit. Consequently, the dating cannot be more closely correlated with the inter-regional chronology in question.

Conclusion

It follows from the above comments that, contrary to earlier views, the Jastorf culture settlement was not a short-lived episode on the Polish Lowland. The sojourn of this culture's populations can be synchronized in the first place with phase LTC. However, the few oldest relics of this culture can be dated to the period corresponding with phase LTB2. The Lowland Jastorf culture does not show any clear connections to two other Jastorf groups from the territory of modern-day Poland – the Gubin and Oder groups.[67] By way of contrast, its materials show

---

[66] These are a Jastorf burial from Równina Dolna, Kętrzyn district (Gaerte 1938; Maciałowicz 2009) and a crown neck ring with a plate (type I according to Kostrzewski) found in Piasutno, Szczytno district (Gaerte 1929, Tab. III; Maciałowicz 2011, Fig. 7).

[67] Possibly, with the Jastorf culture on the Lowland, only few relics can be associated that come from the areas on the Oder River. They were found on damaged and poorly explored cemeteries on the middle Noteć River, where typical Przeworsk materials are rare. They include winged pins with a perpendicular plate on the head from the necropolis in Biała, Czarnków-Trzcianka district (Kostrzewski 1914, Fig. 334; Kostrzewski's card file, file 33) as well as a necklace discovered on the same site and characterized by butt-shaped endings classified as type I by Kostrzewski (Kostrzewski 1914, Fig. 336; 1919). Doubtless western imports found in the Noteć concentration include one-piece buckles of type Ia according to Kostrzewski (Biała, 2 specimens; Kuźnica Żelichowska, Czarnków-Trzcianka district, 3-4 specimens) (Kostrzewski 1914, Fig. 358; Gałęzowska 1996), long iron three-piece buckles of type I according to Kostrzewski (Biała, 2 specimens; Rosko, Czarnków-Trzcianka district (Kostrzewski 1914, Fig. 361; 1919:273, list 27; Michałowski 2006, Fig. 4.1), long and slender fibulae with a step-like bow (Biała, 2 specimens) (Kostrzewski 1914, Fig. 356; Kostrzewski's card file, file 33) and iron chains attached to clothing (Rosko; Machajewski, Maciejewski & Nie-

surprisingly strong and far-reaching ties with the north Jastorf zone, especially Jutland. Such ties are visible chiefly in pottery, the most numerous category of Jastorf relics on the Lowland, and few, rare metal artefact forms, derived from Jutland and the Danish-German borderland. They include, in the first place, crown neck rings, Danish winged pins and Skovby/Bjerndrup-type Holstein pins. Close ties with the Danish zone are testified to by the character of the oldest Jastorf materials on the Lowland dated to the end of the older Pre-Roman period. They come from a few settlements and single graves spread over central and north Wielkopolska, Kujawy, west Mazovia, the Land of Chełmno, Gdańsk Seaboard, drainage basin of Parsęta and the Old Prussian Plain.

A slightly different character is shared by far more numerous younger Jastorf finds dated to the early phase of the younger Pre-Roman period. Among them in addition, in relatively weaker northwest connections, one can notice affinities with the Przeworsk culture and similarities to the Poienești-Lukaševka culture. Such finds are encountered in a vast area, covering – besides the regions where older finds are discovered – territories that were not settled earlier by Jastorf populations, including the Land of Lubusz, south Wielkopolska, southeast Lower Silesia and central and east Poland. The proof of Jastorf culture society extensive contacts, in the beginning of the younger Pre-Roman period is testified to by the presence of younger Jastorf pottery in the remote Celtic settlements in south Upper Silesia that were occupied in phase LTC. This area is clearly isolated from the Jastorf settlement zone, which may indicate that the above mentioned ceramic ware did not find its way solely as a result of intra-cultural contacts, but also as a result of the presence itself of peoples of a northern provenance in the upper drainage basin of the Oder.

The presence of Jastorf culture settlement on the Lowland is related, as mentioned in the introduction, to the trek of the Germanic Bastarnae who in the 3rd century BC supposedly moved southeast across the drainages of the Oder and Vistula rivers, heading for the Black Sea coast. As a result of this trek, in the borderland between Romania and Moldova, the Poienești-Lukaševka culture emerged, which is associated with these peoples. The materials of this culture, in particular those related to the older phases of its development, exhibit clear connections to what is broadly understood as Jastorf circle (Babeş 1993). What clearly stands out is the similarity of the Poienești-Lukaševka materials to the younger Lowland Jastorf finds. It does not seem probable, however, that Lowland Jastorf populations played any role in the origins of this cultural unit. The founders of the Poienești-Lukaševka culture rather it would appear originated from the home ground of the Jastorf culture. This view is supported by characteristic burial rites observed on cemeteries of this culture where clearly dominating urn graves are very often covered with bowls and also by the nature of many belt buckles and fibulae used for female dress, resembling chiefly Jastorf finds from Brandenburg, Holstein, Mecklenburg and Vorpommern (Babeş 1993:34-52, 154-162).

Jastorf culture populations settling the Lowland, however, contributed towards the rise of the Przeworsk culture in late phase A1. This is especially seen in the similarities between the pottery of the two cultures. There is no sufficient evidence, however, to believe that the rise of the Przeworsk culture on the Lowland was a direct continuation of the older Jastorf culture settlement, which, supposedly, at the threshold of the younger Pre-Roman period underwent fundamental transformations mostly due to a La Tène impact (Grygiel 2004, Tab. II). What we moreover observe, is a considerable difference between the amounts of finds of both cultures. Far more numerous and covering a larger area than Jastorf finds, are Przeworsk culture materials dated to phases A1-A2 (Dąbrowska 1988, Map 2), which doubtless testifies to a greater demographic potential of the culture. Hence, it can be expected that a share to its rise was contributed, besides the arrivals from the northwest, by local populations identified with the Pomerania-Cloche culture. We are not able, however, to assess the extent of this contribution, primarily because of the difficulties mentioned earlier in determining the settlement potential of the youngest phases of the last mentioned culture.

---

dzwiecki 2004, Fig. 1A). Both three-piece buckles and fibulae with a step-like bow discovered on the Noteć River differ from the relics of the same type found on the sites of the Oksywie culture on the lower Vistula River and on the Gulf of Gdańsk (Stąporek 1995:29-32, 39-41; Bokiniec 2005; 2008:26-28, 73-74), which rules out their eastern provenance.

Chapter 3

The Jastorf Culture in Northwest Poland

Henryk Machajewski

In northwest Poland, the Jastorf culture, reaching here its east limits, was hitherto present as the Gubin and Oder groups, as well as many unattached finds scattered throughout Wielkopolska, Kujawy and Mazovia (Fig 20). Attempts to determine its relations with the culture of the Hallstatt and La Tène cycles and to define the cultural picture of its several groups initially dominated the study of the Jastorf culture in Poland (Domański 1975; Wołągiewicz 1970:43-66; 1981b:192-196; Woźniak 2007a:390-397; Dąbrowska & Woźniak 2005:87-101). Later, its study was expanded to include an analysis of various aspects of settlement transfor-mations and recently an attempt has been made to trace whence it came to the present-day Polish territories. A relatively short history of research into the Jastorf culture, leaving aside the question of the Gubin group (discussed separately, Domański in this volume), was divided in today's northwest Poland into the following stages:

(a) Prior to the middle of the 20th century – the distinguishing of a Central Pomerania group based on the results of investigations at a burial ground in Długie, West Pomerania province (Eggers 1936:128-139; 1955:13-16). One reason for the distinction was stylistic affinities of pottery and metal dress accessories from the burial ground to the finds encountered west of the lower Oder River, on Jutland and Bornholm. A correction to these findings was made by Gustaw Schwantes (1958:334-388) by including the group in the Jastorf circle in its Ripdorf phase. This stage is associated with the investigations by Józef Kostrzewski (1919a; 1923; 1955) who pointed to the participation of northwest European or 'west Germanic' cultural elements in the history of Pomerania and Wielkopolska societies in the Pre-Roman period. First, Kostrzewski (1919a) systematized typologically some metal dress accessories dating to the Pre-Roman period to be later considered classically Jastorfian (e.g. pins, neck rings). Next, Kostrzewski (1923: 137-145) distinguished a 'Walled-In Grave culture', later renamed 'West Pomeranian culture' (Kostrzewski 1955:206-207), in northwest Wielkopolska. The later name referred to an earlier designation "Central Pomerania group" as used by Eggers (1936: 19-22). Such characteristics of this culture as the form of graves, style of pottery and metal dress accessories unequivocally suggested links to the areas on the lower and middle Elbe River, Mecklenburg and Branden-burg, hence areas identified with the rise of the Jastorf culture in the Pre-Roman period. Józef Kostrzewski stressed the exceptional character of the Noteć marginal stream valley that served as a contact zone between the Elbe circle and the Polish Lowland in the Pre-Roman period. The work of this scholar is characterized by an inconsistency in the cultural classification of Pre-Roman finds. This can be seen in some metal dress accessories, especially pins, neck rings, or belt clasps, that are associated alternately with the Jastorf or Przeworsk cultures. This practice must have followed from his conviction that the La Tène impact had followed a single route, namely via south European cultural centres, in its spread among Pre-Roman societies (Kostrzewski 1923:155-157; 1955:196, Fig. 562).

(b) By the end of the 20th century, fundamental changes occurred in the ways of analyzing this culture (Wołągiewicz 1968:168-170; 1970:43-66; 1981b:191-196; 1989:307-321). First, the scope of its observation was expanded to cover areas located outside of Pomerania and Wielkopolska. More and more often, findings concerning this culture were placed against a broader European background in the Pre-Roman period (Wołągiewicz 1968:178-191; Woźniak 1977:269-287; Dąbrowska 1994:71-79; Domański 1999:179-184). This was helped by the advances in the study of cultural relations between northwest and southeast Europe (Kasparowa 1981:57-79; Dąbrowska 1988; Babeş 1993; Martens 1997).

In Pomerania, referring to the previous idea of the Central Pomerania group (Eggers 1936:13-16), an Oder group was distinguished, having a Jastorf tradition similar to that encountered in Mecklenburg and Brandenburg (Wołągiewicz 1981b:191-196). A thesis was offered that its earliest elements emerged on the local Late Bronze cultural substrate of the West Pomerania group of the Lusatian culture. The rise of the Oder group was preceded by the Marianowo horizon (HD2 – HD2/LTA) that displayed Hallstatt characteristics and those of a Late Bronze group of the West-Pomeranian Lusatian culture, preserved only in a vestigial form. Successive stages, associated with the development of the already classic Oder group (horizon I a – III) were synchronized, in turn, with phases Jastorf a–c, Ripdorf and early Seedorf (Wołągiewicz 1981b:193, Tab. XXVIII). The group thrived at the decline of phase Jastorf c and in the Ripdorf phase, which was synchronized with the spreading of La Tène patterns across the North European

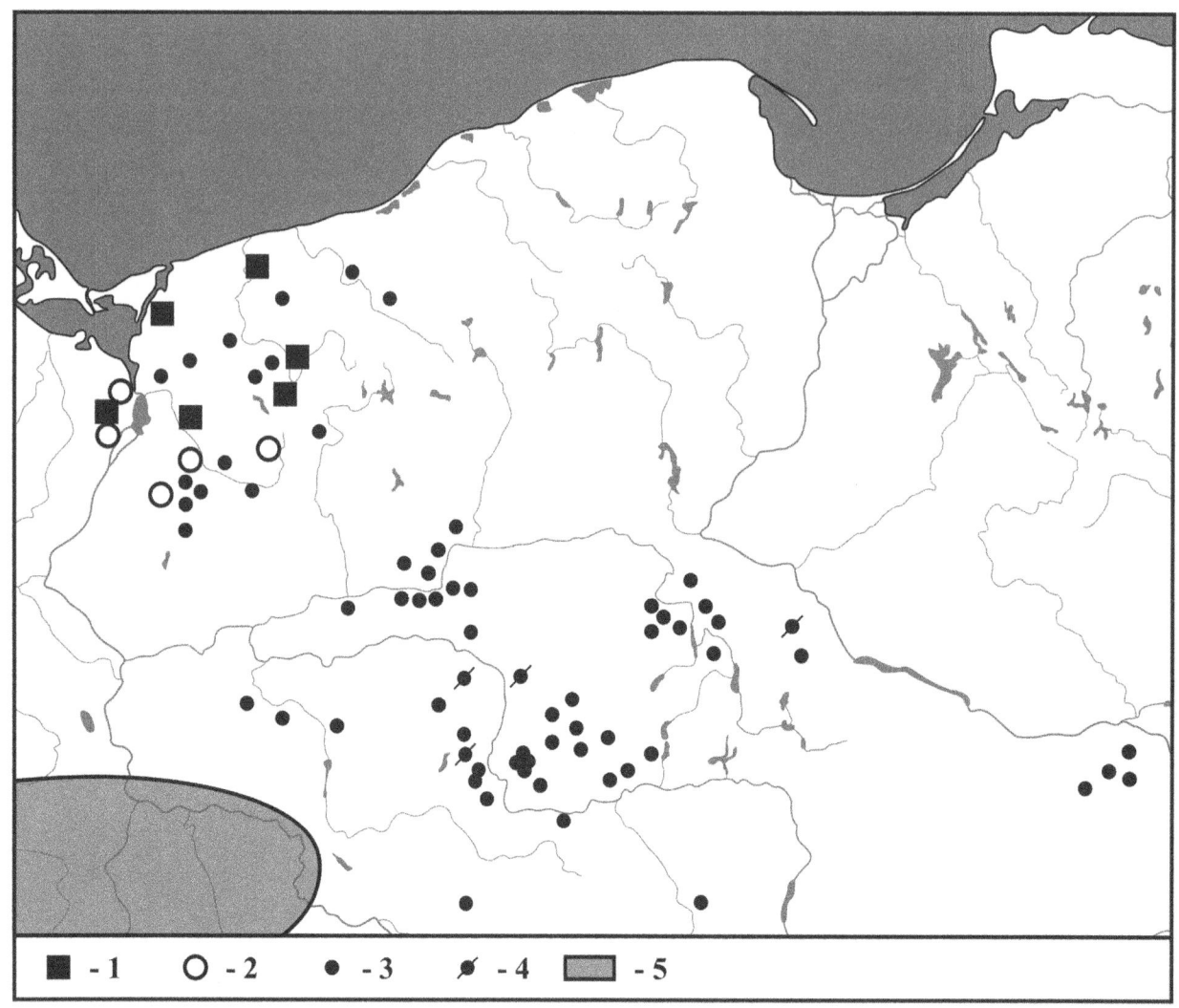

FIG. 20. JASTORF CULTURE SETTLEMENT IN NORTHWEST POLAND.
MARIANOWO; TROSZYN; LUBISZEWO; ŁOBŻANY; WĄWELNICA; ŁUBIEŃ DOLNY; SZCZECIN – POGODNO; SZCZECIN – NIEMIERZYN; BABIN; KUNOWO; DŁUGIE; BRZEŚĆ KUJAWSKI; DOPIEWO; WOJNOWO; OTOROWO; 4 – BARNISŁAW; BIAŁA; BISKUPICE; BORZEJEWO; BORUSZYN; BRONIEWICE; BUKOWICE; CHOMĘTOWO; CZARNE PIĄTKOWO; CZARNKÓW; CZARNKÓW - VICINITY; ĆMACHOWO; DOBIESZOWICE; DOBROPOLE GRYFISKIE; DRAWINGSKO; DUNIEWO; DZIERZNICA; GINAWA; GOLENIÓW; GOLINA; GRZĘPY; IZDEBNO; JABŁONOWO; KARLINO; KARNICE; KŁĘBY; KOMORNIKI; KONINKO; KOZIELICE; KRZEPOCIN; KUŹNICA ŻELICHOWSKA; KÓRNIK; MILCZEK; MODLISZEWO; NOWA WIEŚ; NOWE MIASTO; NOWY DRZEWICZ; OBÓRKA; OGNICA; OSŁONKI; PŁAWCE; POZNAŃ-NOWE MIASTO, SITE 150, 226, 278, 284; ROSKO, SITE 4; ROSKO, SITE 7; RUSOWO; SOBIEJUCHY; SOKOŁOWICE; SOWINKI; STARE BABICE; STAW; SULĘCIN; ŚWIERKOWIEC; WAPNIARNIA; WIĘCKOWICE; WŁOSZAKOWICE; WOJNOWO; WÓJCIN; WSZEDZIEŃ; WYTOMYŚL; ZAGÓRZYN; ŻÓŁWIN).
LEGEND: 1 – SITES ASSOCIATED WITH THE MARIANOWO HORIZON (HAD2 – JASTORF B); 2 – SITES DATED TO THE PERIOD FROM HAD3/JASTORF B/LT.A-B1 TO RIPDORF/SEEDORF/LT. C2; 3 – SITES DATED TO THE PERIOD FROM HAD3/JASTORF B/LT. B2 TO RIPDORF/SEEDORF/LT. C2/D1; 4 – PRESUMED EARLIER JASTORF SETTLEMENT HORIZON IN NORTH WIELKOPOLSKA AND KUJAWY; 5 – GUBIN GROUP RANGE

Plain. In the early Seedorf phase (horizon III), the Oder group dispersed while almost all Pomerania came under the influence of the Oksywie culture (Wołągiewicz 1981b: 195). It was assumed that one of more important links in the formation of this culture was the Jastorf culture. It could have filled the hiatus between the Pomerania and Oksywie cultures as, supposedly, there was no continuity between the two cultures in LTB2 and LTC1 (Jastorf/c – Ripdorf) (Wołągiewicz 1979: 56-57).

In Poland, the significance of the Jastorf culture, except for Pomerania, despite advances in research, was not appreciated and downplayed by being treated only as a centre from which imports flowed to the milieu of the Pre-Roman settlement of the Pomerania culture and to Oksywie and Przeworsk cultures, i.e. in the period from LTB2 to LTD1 (Wołągiewicz 1979: 39; Michałowski 2008: 89).

At this stage, the milestones of research into the Jastorf culture in Poland were works by Grzegorz Domański (1975) on the Gubin group, Teresa Dąbrowska (1988; 1993) on the ties between the Przeworsk culture and the Jastorf circle, as well as Zenon Woźniak (1977) on the east frontier of the Jastorf circle. Attention was attracted by finds from southeast Poland (Czopek 1991a), which were preliminarily classified as close to the traditions of this culture. A common denominator of research at this stage, following from the nature of sources but also from the prevailing opinions on the directions along which new cultural patterns spread in Poland in the Pre-Roman period, was relegating the Jastorf culture to a secondary role in the rise of La Tène-ized non-Celtic cultures on the Polish Lowland. The culture's secondary role also resulted from it being treated as a short-lived, episodic occurrence.

(c) Prior to the beginning of the 21st century – a new opening in the study of the Jastorf culture was made by an incredible growth in the amount of archaeological sources in Wielkopolska, Kujawy, west Mazovia and in southeast Poland (Machajewski 2004: 7-11; Michałowski 2008: 89-100). This growth was brought about by many field investigations preceding great construction projects. A number of vast settlements were discovered and single graves were unearthed as well. However, no large burial grounds were found (Grygiel 2004: 50-59), which as it seems was not an entirely chance result, but could have reflected a peculiar characteristic of settlement transformation trends in this culture. What strikes the eye on the settlements is a dense grid of houses and exceptionally rich pottery assemblages. The latter display styles hitherto completely unknown in Wielkopolska, Kujawy and west Mazovia. Earlier, as already mentioned, numerous metal dress accessories of the Jastorf origin encountered in these regions were treated only as imports within broadly understood Pre-Roman settlement, which not always was clearly defined in terms of culture (Wołągiewicz 1979:56, Fig. 14; Machajewski 1986, map 2). A preliminary chronological classification of the pottery that was discovered in the discussed area helped to distinguish at least its two horizons, showing affinities to a broadly treated Jastorf circle. To the older horizon corresponds pottery in the type of Jastorf b (LTB1-LTB2) phase ,while the younger one is associated with pottery displaying characteristics of the Ripdorf and early Seedorf phases (LTC1-LT D1). In the older horizon, one can notice elements evocative of lower Elbe and Jutland pottery whereas the younger horizon pottery shows affinities to Jutland but also to early Przeworsk material (Dąbrowska 1994:71-78; Grygiel 2004:59-65; Machajewski & Pietrzak 2004:89-102). The already-mentioned Jastorf imports, especially from Wielkopolska and Kujawy, were easily synchronized with the older and early younger pottery horizons.

Attempts made at this stage to interpret the elements of the Jastorf culture exposed in northwest Poland resulted in the formulation of at least two different opinions. The first (Grygiel 2004; Machajewski & Pietrzak 2004; Jurkiewicz & Machajewski 2008; Michałowski 2008:100-102) stresses their connections to the birthplace of the Jastorf culture (Jutland, areas on the Elbe River) whereas the second (Woźniak 2007a:404-405), while not denying these connections, admits the possibility that a substantial share in their dissemination east of the Oder River belonged to local Pre-Roman culture groups.

The advances in the study of the Jastorf culture in northwest Poland verified many earlier findings about the cultural and settlement scene in the Pre-Roman Period (Michałowski 2008:87-105). It appeared that it was necessary to build an almost entirely new scenario of this culture's formation. In fact, new findings were adopted concerning cultural and settlement transformations, taking place at least in two chronological sequences. The first followed cultural changes taking place in the Late Bronze and Early Hallstatt milieu while the second traced settlement re-organizations witnessed in the Hallstatt and La Tène periods. New chronological relationships were established between the Jastorf culture and the local Pomerania culture, undergoing dispersion at the decline of the older Pre-Roman period (LTB2), and the Oksywie and Przeworsk cultures (LTC1-C2). Thus, the chronological hiatus between these cultures, observed in LTB2 and LTC1, was "closed" (Woźniak 1979b: 147, Fig. 3). Consequently, the thesis proposing that the Jastorf culture was only an inspirer facilitating the dissemination of La Tène patterns was discarded and, instead, it began to be regarded as an important factor in the rise of the culture of the younger Pre-Roman period (Woźniak & Dąbrowska 2005: 92).

Thus, the very definition of the La Tène impact came under review. A realization came that it had spread across Poland not only via south Europe but also from the west of the continent through the agency of none other than the Jastorf culture. The approach to the emergence of the Przeworsk and Oksywie cultures (Lt C1-C2) was adjusted and moved their rise to a slightly later time, coinciding with phase A1b or even late phase A1 and early phase A2 (Lt. C2/D1) (Grygiel 2004: 50-56). As a result, as Teresa Dąbrowska and Zenon Woźniak (2005: 92) stress, taking into account the many stages of cultural and settlement changes of this culture, a need arose in Poland to distinguish (next to the already distinguished Gubin and Oder groups) yet another group of the Jastorf culture that functioned in Wielkopolska, Kujawy and west Mazovia. All the facts mentioned here make it necessary to build a new chronology of the Pre-Roman period in Poland. Any effort to this end should attempt to distinguish a middle Pre-Roman period, being a stage that would define the relationships between the Hallstatt and La Tène styles, with the latter being observable in the tradition of the Jastorf culture (Machajewski 2011: 209-210).

Any attempt to explain the phenomenon of the Jastorf culture in northwest Poland would therefore require a critical review of its source base, which greatly varies from region to region. In West Pomerania, this culture is identified primarily on the basis of burial grounds (numbering from 50 to 150 graves) (Rogalski 2010:551-

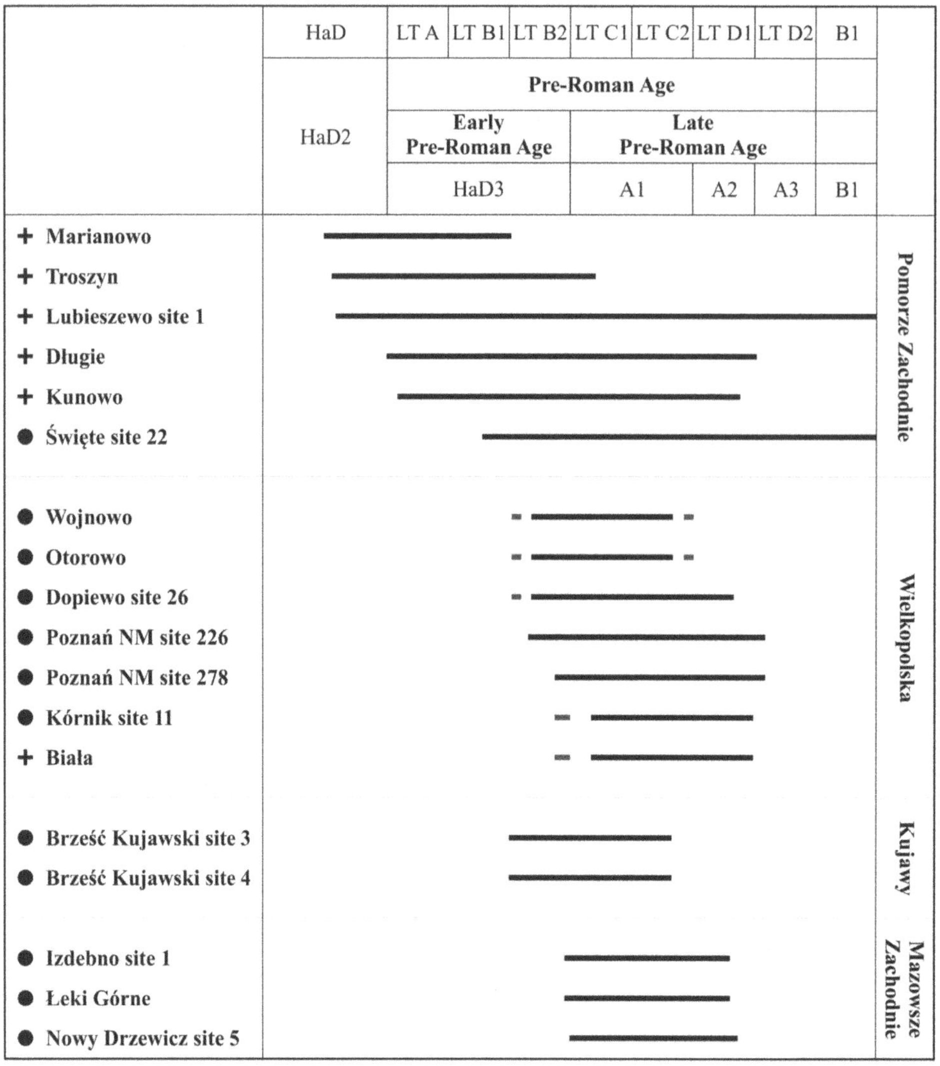

The Jastorf Culture in Poland

	HaD	LT A	LT B1	LT B2	LT C1	LT C2	LT D1	LT D2	B1	
		Pre-Roman Age								
	HaD2	Early Pre-Roman Age			Late Pre-Roman Age					
		HaD3			A1		A2	A3	B1	
+ Marianowo										Pomorze Zachodnie
+ Troszyn										
+ Lubieszewo site 1										
+ Długie										
+ Kunowo										
● Święte site 22										
● Wojnowo										Wielkopolska
● Otorowo										
● Dopiewo site 26										
● Poznań NM site 226										
● Poznań NM site 278										
● Kórnik site 11										
+ Biała										
● Brześć Kujawski site 3										Kujawy
● Brześć Kujawski site 4										
● Izdebno site 1										Mazowsze Zachodnie
● Łęki Górne										
● Nowy Drzewicz site 5										

Fig. 21. Chronology of selected Jastorf culture sites in northwest Poland

556). In the rest of northwest Poland, it is above all identified by its settlements that sometimes are over 1 ha large and by a small number of single graves (Machajewski 2004:9, Fig. 1; Michałowski 2006:183, Fig. 1). The reasons for these differences are given as the state of field exploration (however, to a smaller degree), and different rates of cultural and settlement transformations taking place in this culture in individual regions of northwest Poland. Further differences follow from the scope of dissemination of Jastorf patterns among local cultural traditions (Wołągiewicz 1979:35-36; Machajewski & Pietrzak 2004:96-102; Michałowski 2008:88-89). Finally, not entirely insignificant was the different nature of Jastorf elements, associated with either the Hallstatt or La Tène tradition, found scattered across northwest Poland.

In northwestern Poland, the dating of Jastorf elements, due to the different places they were found (Fig. 21) at, followed two different principles. In the Oder group, the principle relied on arguments resting on the association of grave assemblages, correlated with similar procedures performed with respect to Brandenburg and Mecklenburg (Wołągiewicz 1981b: 192-193; Wołągiewicz 1989: 311-319). In Wielkopolska, Kujawy and west Mazovia, however, because of the availability of many pottery assemblages found at settlements, an attempt was made to trace the variability of the stylistic traits of the pottery. This was done separately for materials from Kujawy (Grygiel 2004:20), Wielkopolska (Machajewski & Pietrzak 2004: 96-97; Machajewski 2010: 202-214) and west Mazovia (Dąbrowska 1994: 71-79; Jurkiewicz & Machajewski 2008: 84-88; Machajewski & Rozen 2011). The results obtained were comparable in the sense that at least two groups of pottery were distinguished that differed in their style, namely, an older and a younger one. Next, these findings were compared with results obtained in similar procedures performed for the Elbe circle (Schwantes 1911; Hingst 1959).

The research into the chronology of Jastorf culture traits in northwestern Poland have resulted so far in the distinguishing of least three groups within the culture. The first, dated to HaD2-HaD3/Jastorf A/Lt A, is associated with squat jugs sometimes bearing a festoon ornament (Fig. 22:2, 8), poorly profiled pots with large, flat, slightly-dimpled bosses (Fig. 22:5, 7), barrel-shaped pots with a

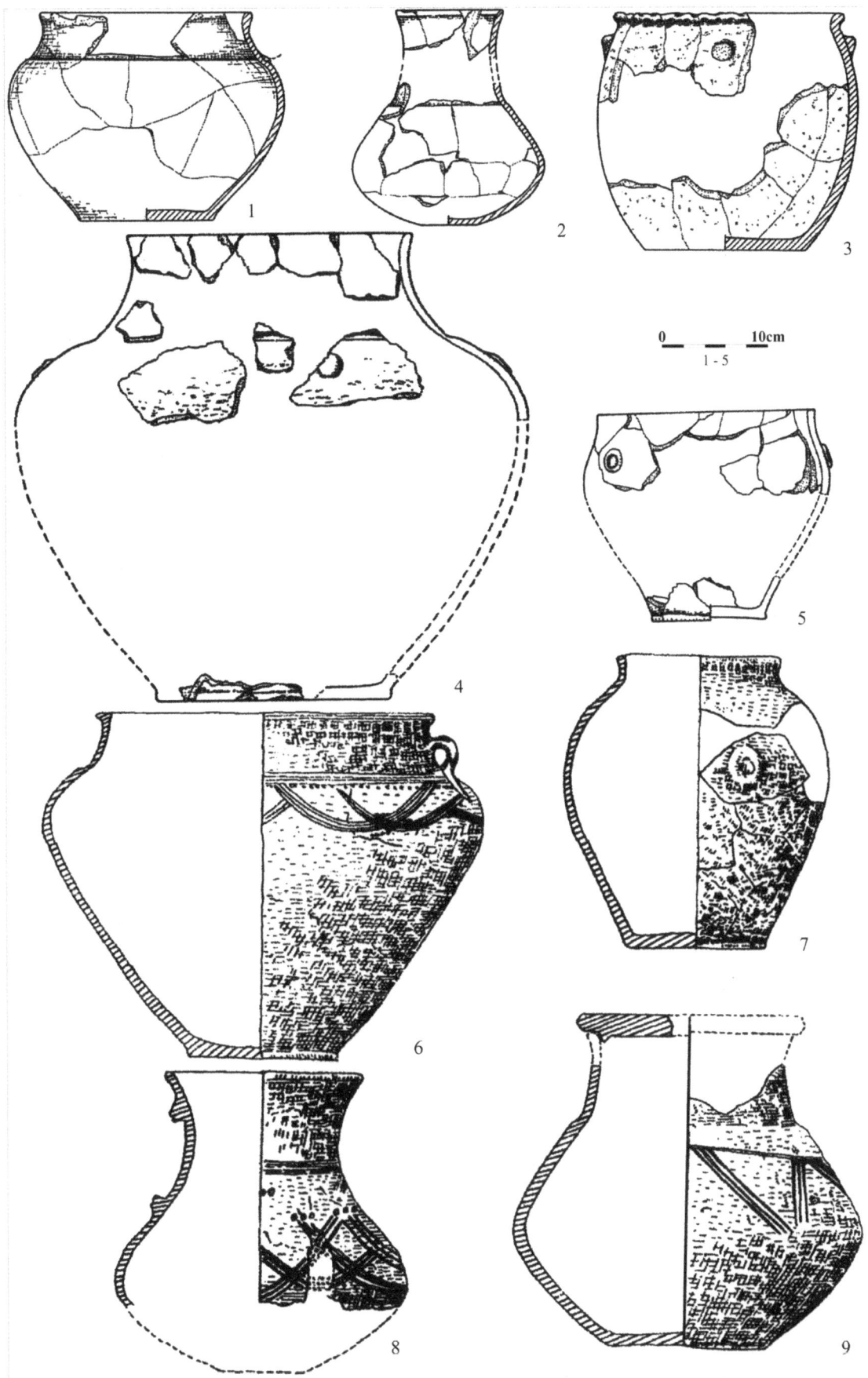

Fig. 22. Group I of Jastorf culture ceramics in northwest Poland.
1 Troszyn, grave 21; 2 Troszyn, grave 51; 3 Troszyn, grave 4; 4 Troszyn, grave 137; 5 Troszyn, grave 150; 6 Marianowo, grave 7; 7 Marianowo, grave 19; 8 Marianowo, grave 27; 9 Marianowo, grave 43

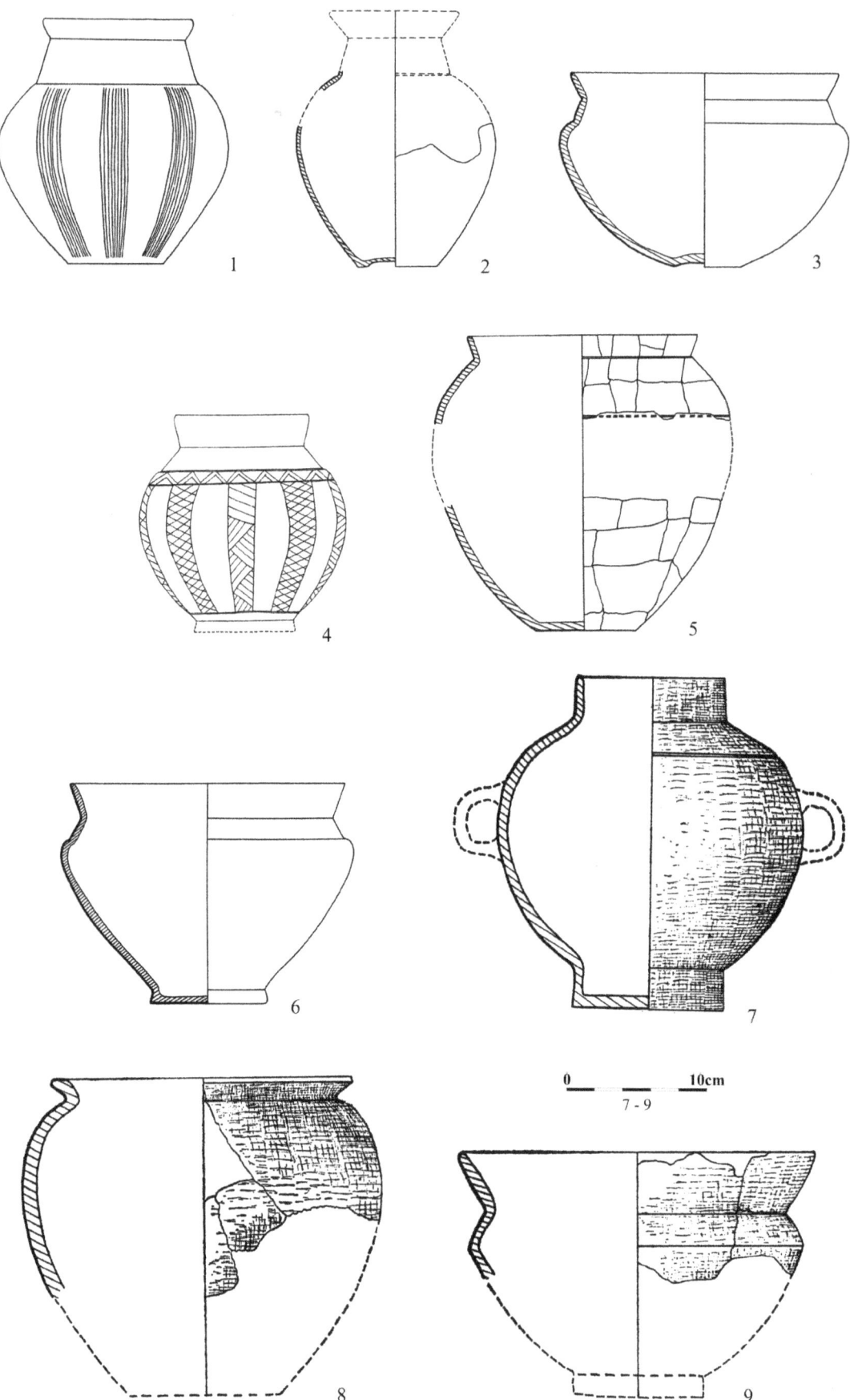

Fig. 23. Group II of Jastorf culture ceramics in northwest Poland. 1 – Długie, grave 96; 2 – Długie, grave 101a; 3 – Długie, grave 122; 4 – Kunowo, grave 20; 5 – Kunowo, grave 24 b; 6 – Kunowo, grave 31; 7 – Szczecin, ul. Traugutta, grave NN; 8 – Szczecin – Niemierzyn; 9 – Szczecin – Niemierzyn.

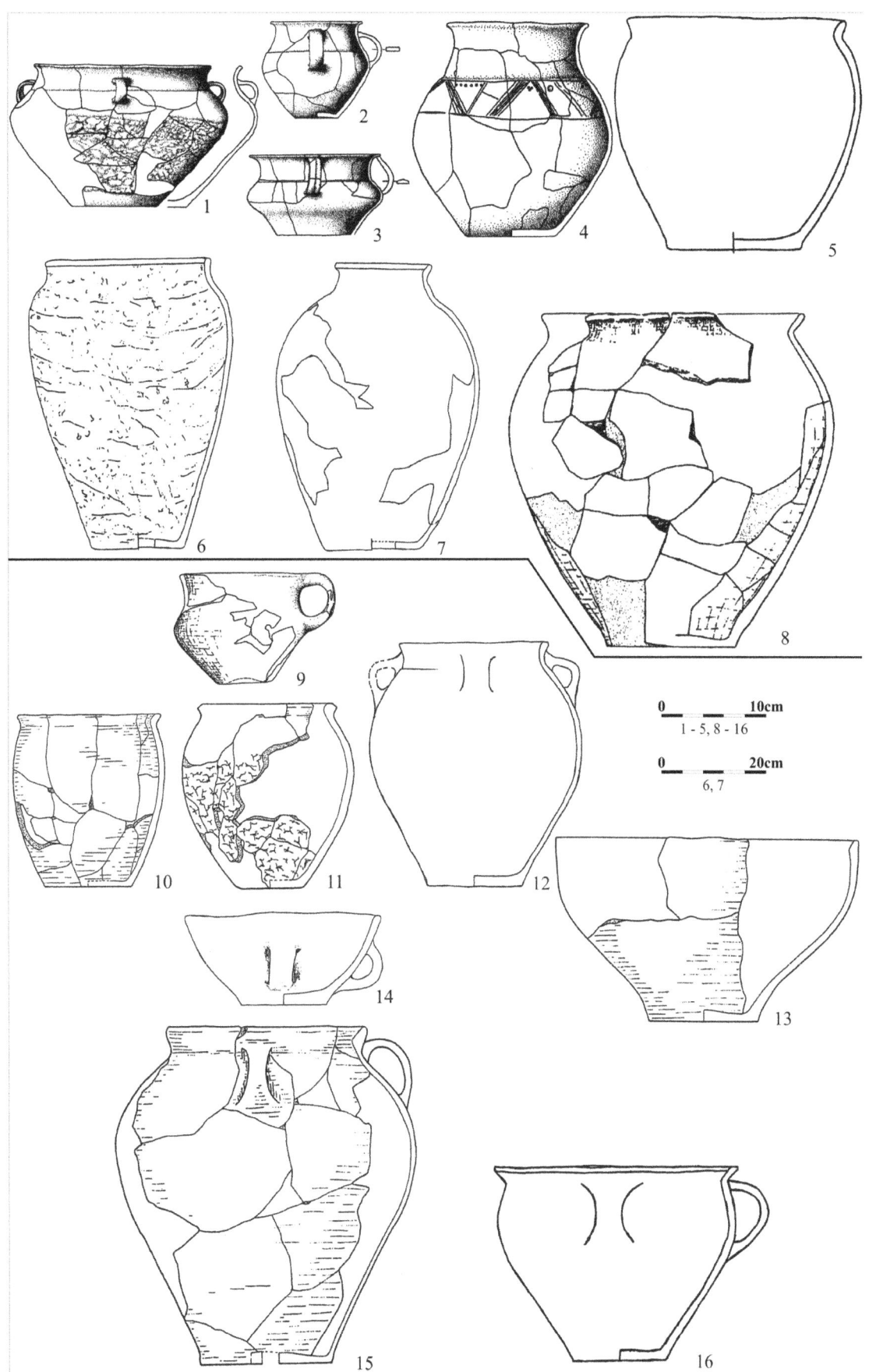

Fig. 24. Group III of Jastorf culture ceramics in northwest Poland. (1 - 4 Brześć Kujawski, site 3 & 4, vessel selection; 5 - 7 Wojnowo, site 23, feature B 46; 8 - 9 Otorowo, site 66; 10 Poznań – Nowe Miasto, site 226, feature A 109; 11 – Poznań – Nowe Miasto, site 226, feature A 126; 12 Poznań – Nowe Miasto, site 284, feature A 284; 13 Poznań – Nowe Miasto, site 226, feature A 115; 14 Poznań – Nowe Miasto, site 284, feature A 331; 15 Poznań – Nowe Miasto, site 278, feature A 5; 16 Poznań – Nowe Miasto, site 284, feature A 267.

corrugated lip rim and flat bosses (Fig. 22:3), globular vessels with a marked neck, sometimes bearing a festoon ornament or appliqué bosses (Fig. 22:1, 4, 6), bi-conical vessels with a cylindrical neck bearing a chevron ornament and covered with a lid (Fig. 22:9). Some of these forms find their counterparts among group A vessels, having Hallstatt characteristics, according to Rogalski (2010: 699). The metal dress accessories include ear bands of the *Bandohrring* type and hooked pins with an hourglass or spade-like head (Wołągiewicz 1989: 311; Machajewski 2006: 83-86; Pawlak 2009). What also can be noticed in this group is a share of local characteristics traced to the Late Lusatian and Pomerania cultures (Fig. 22:9).

The dead were buried in cinerary-urn graves, less frequently without cinerary urns, without pyre remains, usually lined with stone. Only exceptionally were the dead buried in pit graves with pyre remains. In the graves, next to human remains, there are sometimes found many burned animal bones, usually horse bones, exceptionally those of sheep/goat, as for instance in Troszyn.

The general character of archaeological material from this research stage, correlated with the Marianowo horizon by Wołągiewicz (1989: 314), suggests a possibility of synchronizing the first group with the Jastorf culture markers of its early style in Brandenburg (phase I a-b according to Seyer 1982).

The second group, dated from HD3 (LTA-B1) to phase A2 of the younger Pre-Roman period (LTD1), is distinguished by bi- or tripartite pots with tall lips, sometimes bearing a vertical band ornament made with a comb (Fig. 23: 1, 2, 3), bipartite vases with tall rims (Fig. 23: 6, 9), globular pots with a cylindrical neck and handles placed on the greatest protrusion of the belly (Fig. 23:7), and globular vessels with tall lips (Fig. 23:4, 5, 8). All these vessels find their counterparts among the specimens of groups B, C, and D in Rogalski's approach (2010: 700-705). The style of the vessels belonging to the second group reminds one of specimens typical of Mecklenburg and Brandenburg from the end of phase I c to phase II b according to Seyer (1982) and Keiling (1969). The vessels are accompanied

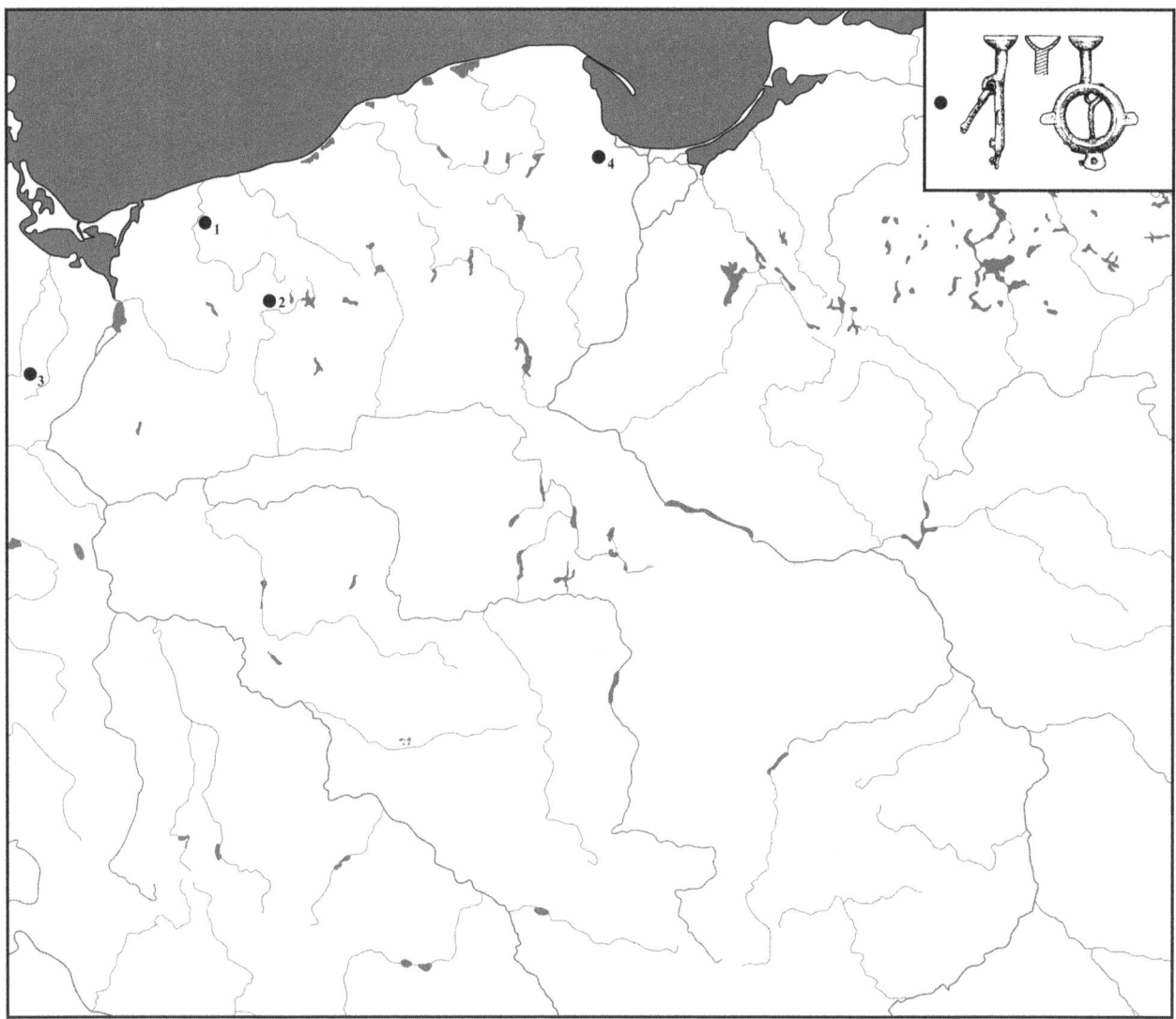

Fig. 25. Distribution of Zachow type fibulae in northwest Poland. 1. Lubiszewo; 2. Żółte; 3. Blankenburg; 4. Pręgowo Dolne.

by fibulae of the Zachow type (Fig. 25), their origins are traced to the Mecklenburg Lake District (*Mecklenburgische Seenplatte*), winged pins with a perpendicular plate of type III according to Kostrzewski (1919a), corresponding to 'Oder' specimens (Schubart 1957) (Fig. 27) encountered in Mecklenburg and north Brandenburg, and long belt clasps. Possibly, the second group should comprise crown neck rings of type I (Fig. 29) according to Kostrzewski (1919:73-76). Generally speaking, this group may be synchronized with phases Ic and IIa, according to Seyer's approach (1982), west of the Oder River.

The most common type of grave continued to be a cinerary urn type lined with stones; rarely did there occur graves without a cinerary urn but only with a small heap of bones lying on a flat stone.

The third group, dated from the late older and early younger Pre-Roman period (LTB2 /LTC1) to the late phase A2 and early phase A3 (LTD1/LTD2), comprises two different stylistic subgroups (Fig. 24). The first consists of low vase-like vessels with two handles (Fig. 24:1), S-profiled pot-like vessels sometimes bearing zigzag ornaments (Fig. 24:4), vase-like vessels with single band-like handles (Fig. 24:2, 3), tall pots with broad (Fig. 24:6) and narrow (Fig. 24:7) openings, and globular pots with tall lips (Fig. 24:8). Most of the vessels had lips that were not thickened while their rims were either rounded or cut off at the top. The vessels were rarely decorated with multi-line zigzags or horizontal lines. The second sub-group, in turn, embraced pots with a globular belly and a short lip (Fig. 24:10, 11), tall pots with two handles (Fig. 24:12), tall jugs with slightly narrowed handles (Fig. 24:15), vase-like vessels with a single handle (Fig. 24:9), low bowls with 'hanging' band-like handles placed on the belly (Fig. 24:14), tall bowls (Fig. 24:13), low vases with narrowed handles (Fig. 24:16). Almost all sub-group 2 vessels had thickened lips and faceted rims on the inner side. The

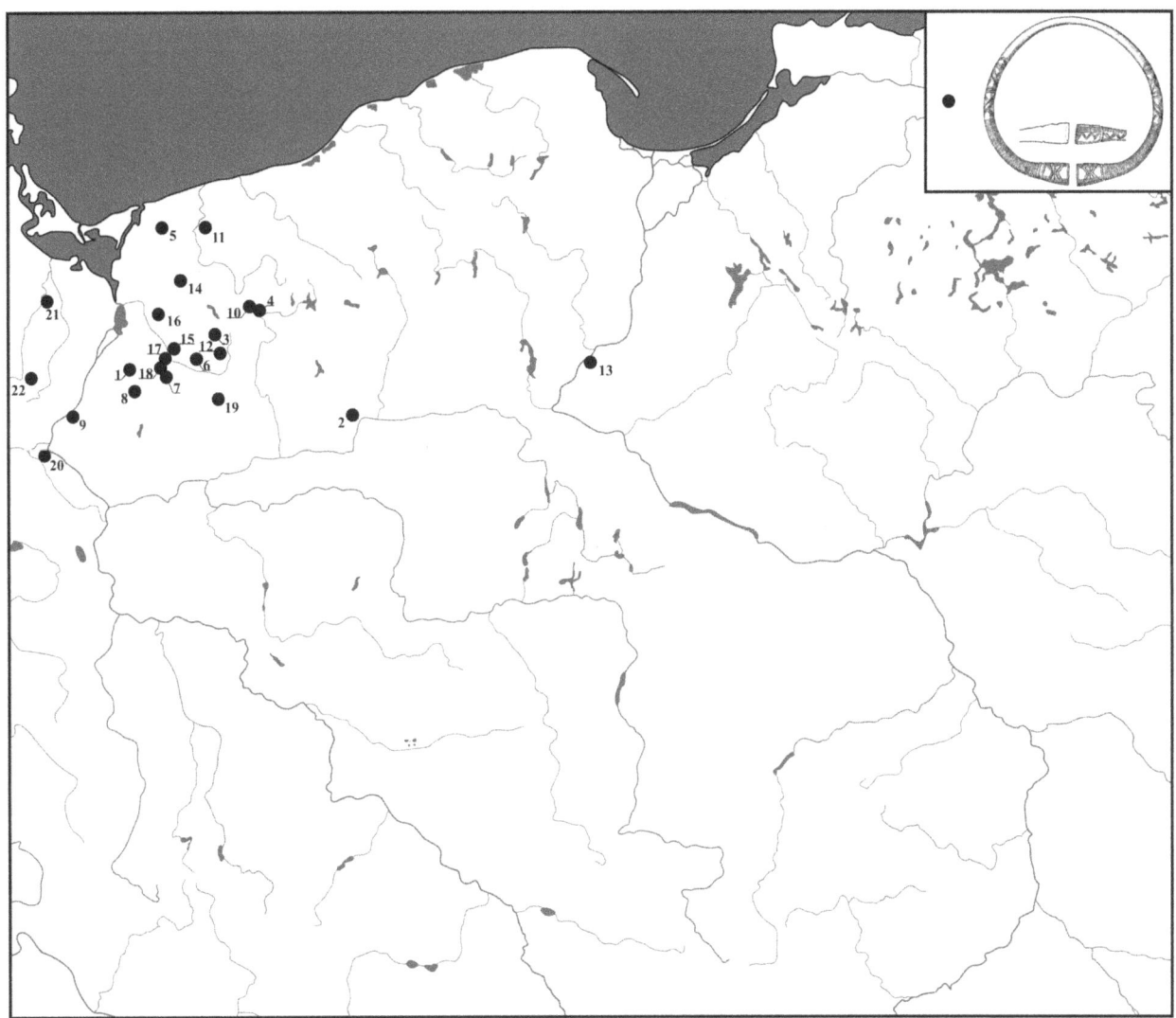

FIG. 26. DISTRIBUTION OF NECK RINGS WITH CYLINDRICALLY THICKENED ENDS IN NORTHWEST POLAND. 1. BABIN; 2. BIAŁA; 3. DŁUGIE; 4. DRAWINGSKO; 5. DUNIEWO; 6. GOLINA; 7. KŁĘBY; 8. KOZIELICE; 9. KRAJNIK DOLNY; 10. KRĘGLI; 11. LUBIESZEWO; 12. OGNICA; 13. PODWIESK; 14. SĄPOLNICA; 15. STARGARD; 16. TARNÓWKO; 17. WITKOWO; 18. WÓJCIN; 19. ŻEŃSKO; 20. HOHENWUTZEN; 22. PASEWALK; 21. SCHMIEDEBERG.

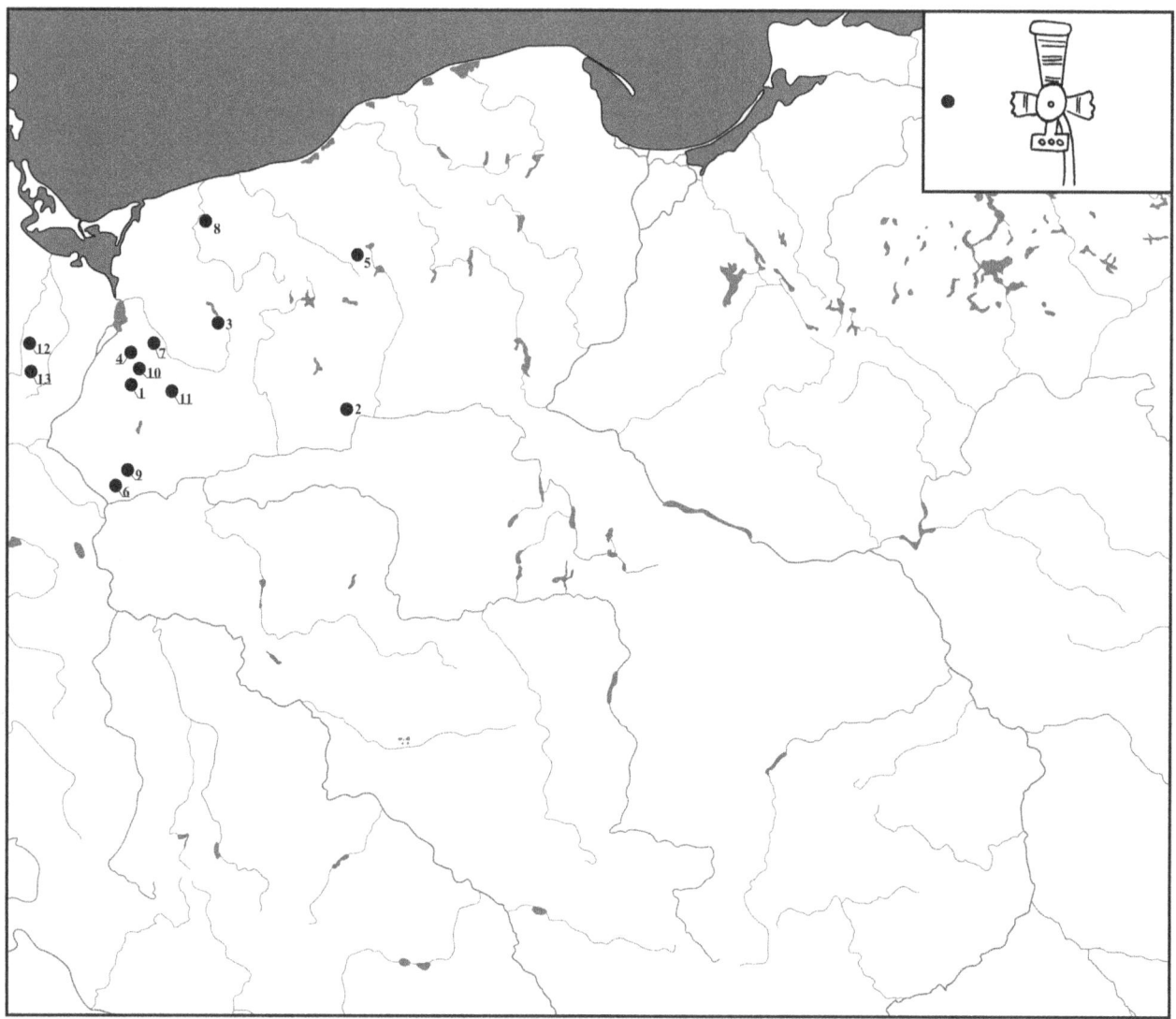

FIG. 27. DISTRIBUTION OF WINGED PINS WITH A PERPENDICULAR PLATE IN NORTHWEST POLAND. 1. BABIN; 2. BIAŁA; 3. DŁUGIE; 4. DOBROPOLE; 5. GAŁOWO; 6. KAMIEŃ MAŁY; 7. KUNOWO; 8. LUBIESZEWO; 9. MOŚCICE; 10. STARE CZARNOWO; 11. WÓJCIN; 12. BIETIKOW; 13. RÖPERSDORF.

vessels were rarely decorated with relief strips, 'fingernail' ornament or geometric elements arranged horizontally (Machajewski & Pietrzak 2004:120, Tab. XII). In both stylistic subgroups, one can see inspirations coming from various cultural trends. In the case of the first sub-group, these are affinities with ceramics encountered in Jutland (pots with a cylindrical neck, relief strip ornaments, tall pots with broad and narrows openings) and on the lower Elbe (S-profiled pot-like vessels, vase-like vessels with two handles). Chronologically speaking, these affinities should be dated to the decline of the Jastorf and the beginning of Ripdorf phases (LTB2–LTC1).

In the second stylistic subgroup, in turn, one can notice, next to affinities with ceramics from Jutland, some stylistic traits already typical of early Przeworsk ceramics (low vases with narrowed handles, ornament of a narrow band filled with a meander). These affinities should be dated to the beginning stages of the younger Pre-Roman period (LTC2–LTD1).

The third group should be associated with neck rings with cylindrically thickened ends (Fig. 26), likely a form typical of Vorpommern and West Pomerania, crown neck rings of types II, III and IV according to Kostrzewski (1919a:73-76) (Fig. 29), traced to Jutland, and iron fibulae of variety A according to Kostrzewski. They are sometimes joined by a chain (site 7, Rosko) and resemble chain-like and plate-like ornaments found in the Havel-Middle Elbe group (Keiling 1968:163, Abb. 2). The group also comprises fibulae of varieties A and B according to Kostrzewski, decorated with a pair of beads on the bow (Fig. 28) and traceable to the Middle Elbe traditions (Keiling 1968: 198, Abb. 2; Begier 2003, Karte 3-4). Finally, bi- and tripartite clasps are included in the third group as well. In Seyer's approach (1982), the third group should be synchronized with the decline of phase IIa and with phase IIb.

The funerary rite made use of urn cremation graves, containing pyre remains or not, and less frequently pit graves. Exceptional in northwest Poland, the cemetery in

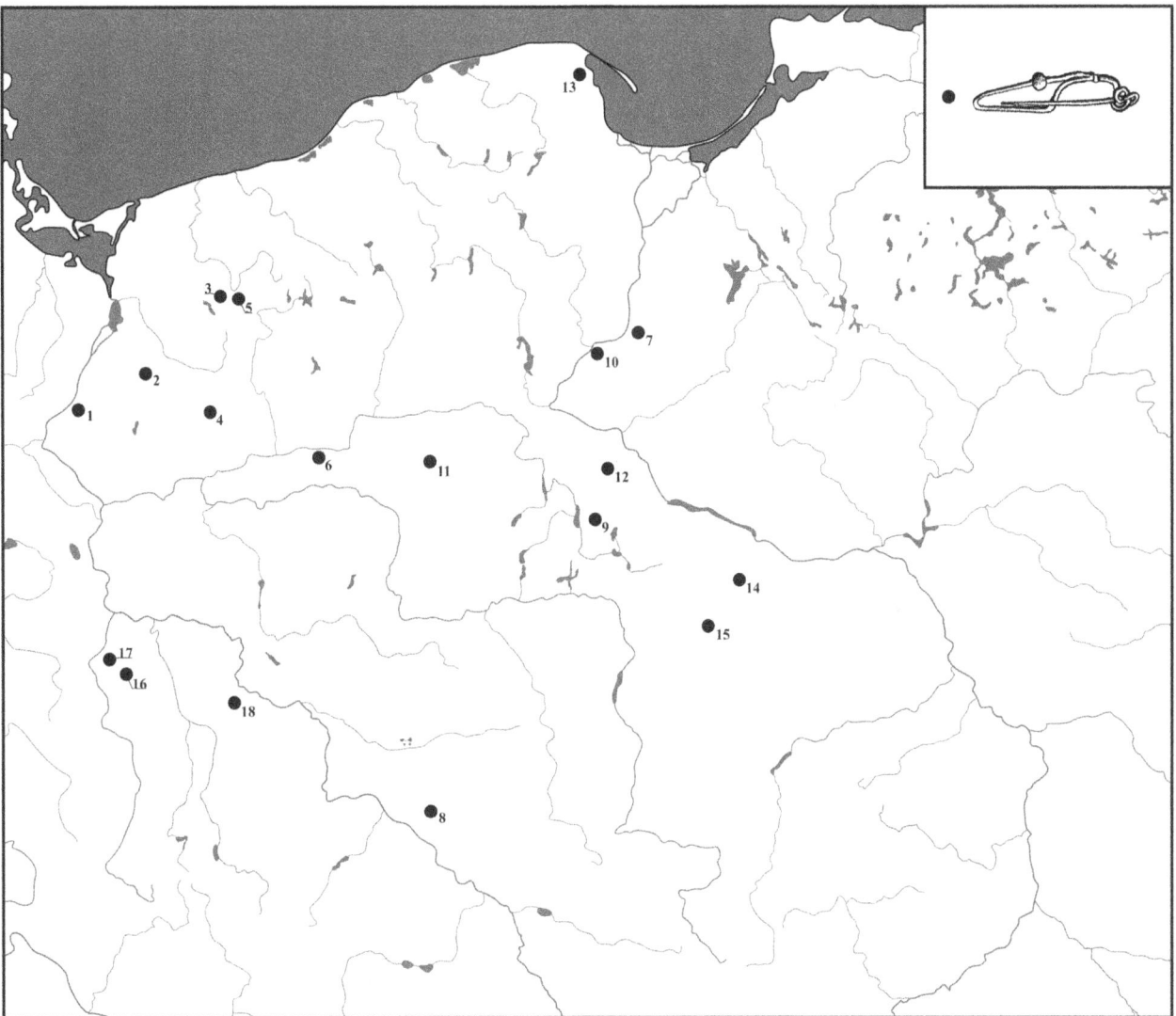

Fig. 28. Distribution of fibulae with a pair of beads reminiscent of types A and B according to Kostrzewski (1919) in northwest Poland. Będargowo; Biernatów; Brzeźniak; Dąbrowa Biskupia; Brody; Gradowo; Krajnik Dolny; Kunowo; Luboszyce; Luszyn; Maruna; Nowe Dobra; Nowe Miastko; Podlesie Kościelne; Połchowo; Rosko; Rumia; Witaszewice.

Biała, Trzcianka-Czarnków district, site 1, consists of urn graves containing no pyre remains and covered by earthen barrows, and pit graves without pyre remains and covered by stone mantles (Machajewski 2002: 14-15; Michałowski 2006: 185-189).

An attempt to synchronize the three consecutive stylistic groups of this culture with the Jastorf settlement exposed in northwest Poland, produced the following comments (Fig. 20-21). The first group, dated to HD2–HD3-/Jastorf a/LTA phase, synchronized with the Marianowo horizon, is noticeable only in northwest West Pomerania. Almost all sites associated with this group are found in the area of the decline-Bronze West Pomeranian Lusatian culture (Wołągiewicz 1989:309, Fig. 1; Machajewski 2006:83-86; Machajewski 2011:214, Table 1). Some of them were abandoned in the late older and early younger Pre-Roman period (LTB2–LTC1) (Marianowo, Troszyn, Wąwelnica), others functioned even until the early period of Roman impact (site 1, Lubieszewo). The earliest elements of the Jastorf culture in northwest Poland show affinities with artefacts from the Mecklenburg Lake District and north Brandenburg. This is a result of a similar dissemination process of Hallstatt stylistic patterns among Late Bronze groups on the south coast of the Baltic Sea (Wołągiewicz 1989:316-318). It is hard to tell, however, whether early Jastorf patterns were received then through the agency of local Late Bronze groups or whether there were some settlement shifts. The version involving only pattern reception seems to be more likely as besides West Pomerania it also took place in Brandenburg (Wołągiewicz 1989:314-317).

The second group of Jastorf culture materials was formed on the substratum of classic Hallstatt and La Tène patterns. It is still connected to West Pomerania where, as late as HD3, there could have functioned the vestiges of the West Pomerania group of the Lusatian culture and the Górzyce group while from the east, the Pomerania culture began to spread (Griesa 1982; Wołągiewicz 1989:309, Fig. 1). It was then that next cemeteries were founded (e.g. Długie, Kunowo) which were used until the decline of the Ripdorf phase and the beginning of the Seedorf phase (LTD1). There are also records of settlements of which some thrived until phase B2 of the early Roman period (e.g. Święte, Stargard district, site 22) (Machajewski 2011:217, Table IV). In this respect clear settlement clusters took shape in the drainage basins of the Ina, upper Drawa, Rega and middle Parsęta rivers (Eggers 1955:16, Taf. 4; Wołągiewicz 1959:135, Fig. 2; Machajewski 1999:234-235). Quite possibly, in this group should be included the earliest Jastorf elements from north Wielkopolska, originating from the Noteć marginal stream valley (Michałowski 2006: 195-196; Woźniak 2007a: 404). At that time, the Jastorf culture continued to be influenced by the Hallstatt style, as in the first stage, traced to Mecklenburg and Brandenburg and next by the early La Tène style, having its roots west of the middle Oder (Seyer 1982). At this stage, settlement shifts took place, which are particularly well noticeable in the Ina and Drawa drainage basins.

The elements of the third group, dated from the late older and the early younger Pre-Roman periods (LTB2-C1) to late phase A2 and early phase A3 of the younger Pre-Roman period (LTD1), emerged above all in Wielkopolska, Kujawy and west Mazovia. Relying on the chronology of settlement, it is presumed that Jastorf elements in this area surfaced first in Kujawy (Brześć Kujawski) and in north Wielkopolska (Otorowo, Wojnowo and Dopiewo). It is with these sites that the first stylistic assemblage of vessel ceramics is associated. Sometime later, however, elements of this culture spread to the rest of Wielkopolska and west Mazovia. These later sites therefore, it can be argued, must correspond to the ceramics of the second stylistic assemblage.

The rise of the Jastorf culture in northwest Poland took place in many stages from Hallstatt to the developed stages of the younger Pre-Roman period. Its dissemination, as mentioned earlier, coincided with the time when two separate cultural cycles related to the Hallstatt and La Tène traditions continued here. The first cycle was made up of the Lusatian culture, specifically of its pattern of traits typical of its decline, and the Pomeranian culture together with the so-called Cloche Grave culture, whereas the second cycle comprised Oksywie and Przeworsk cultures. With respect to the cultures of the first cycle, it is observed that the final stage of the Lusatian culture (Gedl 1972: 311, Fig. 1), if one were to rely with respect to northwest Poland on findings regarding the Górzyce (Górzyce – I and II) and West Pomeranian groups (Griesa 1982: 23, Abb. 4; Woźniak 2010:55, map 2), may be set at HC–HD1 or HD2.

A precise determination of the range of the Pomerania culture together with the so-called Cloche Grave culture, due to the unsatisfactory state of analysis of its archaeological sources, is still not possible. Despite the outlined narration about the three stages of its dissemination, continuing from phase HaC until HD3/LTB2 (phases I–III) (Petersen 1929a: 116-118; Malinowski 1989: 571, map 27), it is assumed that what we have is only a vague idea of its maximum range and not its successive development stages. In this approach, its more dynamic development in HD (phases II and III), judged by the strength of impact from the west Hallstatt circle, was well documented only in southwest Wielkopolska (Woźniak 2010: 47, map 1). This, however, does not mean that in the other regions the culture dissipated at this time. It could have remained already then under the influence of an entirely different inspiration: the Jastorf culture. This supposition is in part borne out by the poor reception of the La Tène patterns by the Pomeranian culture, especially in LTB, and the dynamic expansion of the Jastorf patterns of phase Jastrof b (?)–c at that time. The latter are encountered also east of the lower Oder, in areas not occupied by the Pomeranian culture (Wołągiewicz 1979:55-56; Woźniak 1979:146-148; 2007:396). Hence, it can be presumed that in West Pomerania (Wołągiewicz 1979:54-55) the Pomeranian culture developed from HaC to Lt.B, while outside of this region, it thrived from HaD to the decline of phase LTB2.

In turn, the arrival of the elements of Oksywie and Przeworsk cultures, associated with the second cycle, at West Pomerania took place in phase A2 (LTD1) of the younger Pre-Roman period. At that time, West Pomerania as far as the Rega and Drawa drainage basins was occupied by the Oksywie culture (Wołągiewicz 1979:48; Machajewski 1999: 241–242; Strobin 2011: 84-85). Almost at the same time or slightly earlier, Przeworsk culture elements made their way to this part of Pomerania. They included weapons and vessel ceramics. The native area of the Przeworsk culture, beginning already with the decline of phase A1 of the younger Pre-Roman period, was the Polish Lowland (Dąbrowska 1988: 64, map). The sources that stimulated the dynamic development of the Oksywie culture are linked to the Przeworsk and Jastorf cultures. In the case of the latter culture, the sources included new dress accessories (fibulae, bi- and tripartite belt clasps and neck rings) and a number of new types of behaviour connected with the funerary rite (Wołągiewicz 1979: 48-49).

The cultural re-organizations, taking place in the younger Pre-Roman period, triggered settlement changes that brought about, except for small areas on the Szczecin Lowland, where settlements and cemeteries were used without any interruption throughout the Pre-Roman period (e.g. site 1, Lubiszewo, site 22, Święte), a new settlement network, which took shape in phase A2 of the younger Pre-Roman period (Machajewski 2011: 209-219).

The outlined picture of northwest Poland at the time when the Jastorf culture developed, shows a similar pattern of transformations. First, intercultural relations were established, chiefly through the reception of alien stylistic patterns, next, contacts were expanded through the settlement re-organization of already settled areas; areas that had not been settled earlier were affected by reorganizations only to a small extent. Thus, the transformations took place along almost all the directions

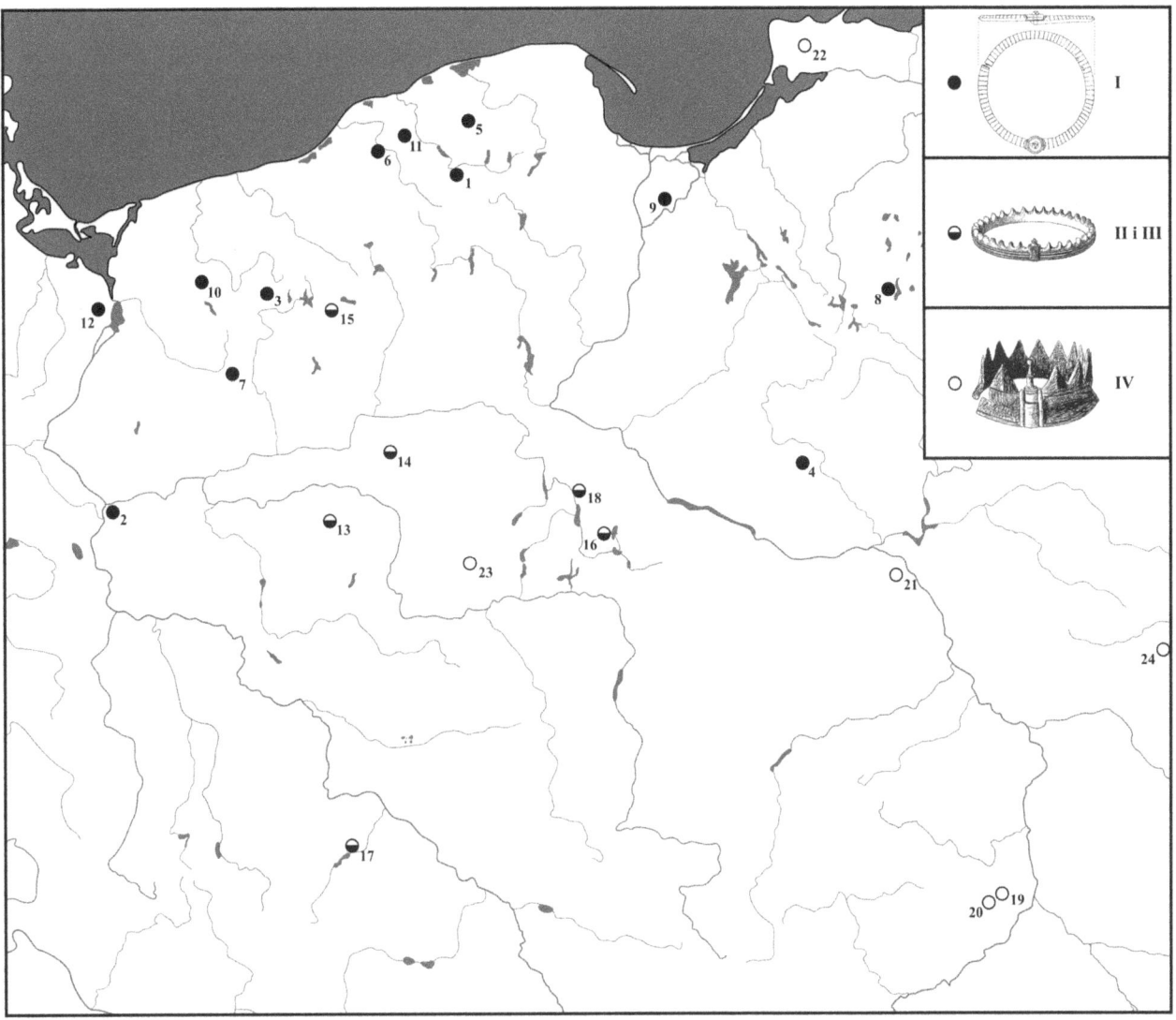

FIG. 29. DISTRIBUTION OF CROWN NECK RINGS, FOLLOWING KOSTRZEWSKI'S TYPOLOGY (1919), IN NORTHWEST POLAND. *TYPE I* – 1. CHOCIELEWKO; 2. CZARNÓW; 3. KARNICE; 4. KLUCZEWO - ?; 5. KOPANIEWO; 6. KRUSZYNA; 7. OGNICA; 8. PIASUTNO; 9. PIEKŁO; 10. REDŁO; 11. RUNOWO; 12. SZCZECIN – POGODNO; *TYPE II & III* – 13. ĆMACHOWO; 14. MILCZEK; 15. RĘDOWO; 16. SYNOGAĆ; 17. ŚWIDNICA; 18. WYBRANOWO; *TYPE IV* – 19. BŁONIE, GRAVE 151; 20. DWIKOZY; 21. IZDEBNO, SITE 1; 22. LÖCHSTÄDT (GERMAN NAME); 23. STAW; 24. ZALESIE.

where the culture was disseminated, limited only by the Baltic coastline, as well as the Noteć and Warta marginal stream valley.

If one accepts the findings about the chronology of cultures associated with the first and second cycle, an inescapable conclusion is that in northwest Poland, the Jastorf culture developed in three stages, 'driving' a wedge between the cultures of the two cycles. The first stage, corresponding to the earliest elements of this culture (the first group, Marianowo horizon; HD2-HD3/Jastorf A/LTA), is characterized by affinities to Jastorf materials found in Mecklenburg and north Brandenburg. East of the lower Oder River, they surfaced by being adapted in the local milieu of the Late Bronze West Pomeranian and Górzyce groups (Fig. 20). Possibly, in a similar way, but slightly later (HaD2), such elements could have appeared in the Pomeranian culture. The scale of adaptation of elements coming from beyond the Oder River by local groups varied. This is illustrated by the differences in grave goods and types in Troszyn and Marianowo. It is rather doubtful that any settlement shifts took place at that time, although this cannot be excluded in the case of lands lying immediately west of the lower Oder River (Wołągiewicz 1968:185, Abb. 2).

The arrival of the Jastorf culture in West Pomerania around that time was not a local development but a fragment of a broader process of its dissemination across the lands between the lower Elbe and Oder rivers in HaD (Keiling 1968: 169, Abb. 5).

The second stage of the emergence of the Jastorf culture (the second group; HD3/LTA-B1-A2 of the Pre-Roman period) is still noticeable only in West Pomerania, but it cannot be excluded that it had already spread to north

Wielkopolska and into the middle Noteć marginal stream valley (Fig. 21). It continued to spread in the time when the settlement of decline Lusatian culture groups still existed accompanied by that of the Pomeranian culture advancing from the east of Pomerania as far as the drainage basins of the Rega, Drawa and the middle Noteć rivers (Fig. 21). It must have been then or slightly later that local groups began to receive Jastorf elements (e.g. Zachow type fibulae, type III winged pins, long belt clasps, type I crown neck rings), which also made their way to the Słowińskie Coast and the Noteć marginal stream valley. The co-occurrence of Jastorf and Pomerania culture elements on the same sites, although still little evidence is available to support this finding, indirectly indicates a possibility that the settlement of these cultures co-existed especially between the Parsęta and Gwda, and the Rega and Drawa rivers in HD3 (LTB). This situation could have triggered a deeper penetration of east Pomerania by Jastorf culture communities.

The Jastorf cemeteries that were laid out at this stage, which usually functioned until phase A2 (LTD1), could have been related to the influx of populations from beyond the Oder River (Keiling 1968:169, Abb. 5). The influx, as in the first stage, was a fragment of more general developments in the Jastorf circle involving major population shifts from the German Lowland south and southeast.

A consequence of the two earlier stages of Jastorf culture development in northwest Poland was its third stage that witnessed its dynamic growth (LTB2/C1-LTD1) (Fig. 21). Elements of this culture appeared in Wielkopolska, Kujawy and west Mazovia. This stage, on the strength of stylistic differences visible in vessel ceramics, reflecting cultural traditions hitherto unknown here, can be divided into two segments in terms of chronology and style (stage IIIa and IIIb). The earlier one (stage IIIa) shows affinities to Jutland and the areas on the lower and middle Elbe, while the later one (stage IIIb) brings to mind the Jutland tradition already accompanied by early Przeworsk elements from the Polish Lowland. Meanwhile pottery from West Pomerania stayed away, as it were, from these stylistic novelties by continuing to adhere to the style prevailing in Mecklenburg and north Brandenburg. Only in the younger Pre-Roman period (LTD1) did new elements come to light there in the form of the early Przeworsk style (Machajewski 2011:212-213).

In turn, metal dress accessories, although all of them bear out the preference for Jastorf patterns in northwest Poland, the scale of their dissemination varies locally. An example in point is neck rings with cylindrically thickened ends derived from trans-Oder traditions (Fig. 26) but encountered only in West Pomerania. In turn, as far as crown neck rings, originating in Jutland (Babeş 1993:108, Abb. 28), are concerned, it is noticeable that earlier type I specimens according to Kostrzewski are found only in Pomerania whereas others, in particular those of type IV (Fig. 29), are more frequent in the Jastorf culture on the Polish Lowland. Fibulae of variety A and B with a pair of beads on the pin (Fig. 28) are, instead, quite uniformly spread over almost the whole territory occupied by the Jastorf culture in northwest Poland.

At this stage, the Jastorf culture spread chiefly over the Polish Lowland as far as the peripheries of the Przeworsk culture settlement.

This dynamic expansion of the Jastorf culture in northwest Poland came in the aftermath of exceptional developments – the spread of first Hallstatt and then La Tène traditions over the North European Plain. Consequently, the Jastorf culture must have spread in two directions. The first, observing the Hallstatt and early Jastorf traditions, penetrated north Pomorze and Wielkopolska (Noteć marginal stream valley), while the other, following the La Tène tradition and enriched by Jutland and lower Elbe elements, headed for Wielkopolska, Kujawy and west Mazovia or, in broader terms, towards southeast Europe. These differences must have been instrumental in the development of the varieties of this culture encountered in West Pomerania and on the Polish Lowland.

If the Jastorf culture transformations were relatively not very dynamic in the Hallstatt period, they greatly accelerated in the La Tène period as a result of cultural changes taking place in the territories that until recently had been under the influence of Celtic traditions.

Considering the Jastorf culture in northwest Poland and the term 'Jastorf settlement', which is applied to ever greater number of sites with the progress of research, a special effort should be made to find an answer to the question whence "Jastorf" populations could have come in such a relatively short period of time. For west of the Oder River no settlement destabilization of such magnitude is observed to explain the movement of people to other locations. The answer to this question is the major research problem concerning the study of the Jastorf culture in Poland.

Chapter 4

Jastorf Culture in Wielkopolska

Andrzej Michałowski

Wielkopolska of the older Pre-Roman period is usually associated with a single dominant component, i.e. Pomerania culture that emerged there, both in its classic and cloche grave variant, already in the Hallstatt C period (Kaczmarek 1995:117). However, if not in the twilight of the Hallstatt C, then surely in the early younger Pre-Roman period, Wielkopolska lost its homogeneity to become a scene of various cross-cultural interactions. Parties to these interactions were communities which, as proved by their material culture traits, belong to separate archaeological units such as the Pomerania/Cloche Grave, Przeworsk, and Jastorf cultures. Basically, these cultures should be perceived as fully equal formations making up a final picture of the then existing settlement of Wielkopolska. At that time, Wielkopolska was accommodating, in addition to old inhabitants identified as belonging to the Pomerania/Cloche horizon, also groups of newcomers who, sometimes following very far-reaching routes of migration, were bringing a fully-developed model of representative cultural behaviour reflected in material remnants left upon their withdrawal. Arriving to Wielkopolska, presumably from homelands in Lower Silesia, were people whose cultural pattern, otherwise known as the Przeworsk culture, exhibited strong La Tène influences. Other newcomers came from western regions that were settled by the broadly understood Jastorf circle which, at that time, was also intensively transforming towards the La Tène model. Settlements of these two groups spreading to Wielkopolska show some similar instability over time combined with considerable scattered migrations during the early younger Pre-Roman period (Michałowski 2008:101).

It was already Kostrzewski in the early 20th century who pointed to Jastorf elements occurring at the sites of Wielkopolska, and mentioned some 'West Germanic' elements present not only on metalwork but also on pottery (Kostrzewski 1919b:341). These elements were similarly viewed also by Petersen (1929b). After the 2nd World War, scholars tended to relegate both the influence of the Germanic civilizational circle on, and its significance for, transformations occurring in the younger Pre-Roman period in Wielkopolska. The role of the Germanic component was reduced solely to imports (Wołągiewicz 1979: 36) recovered both from late Pomerania (Kaczmarek 1999:149-150) and early Przeworsk contexts (Bednarczyk & Sujecka 2004:419; Dąbrowska 1988:192-204). Recently collected material (Machajewski 2004) permits the conclusion that the opinion of Wołągiewicz may be ruled out (1979:63 et seq.) for settlements, particularly those in the Noteć River region and initially identified as belonging to the Przeworsk culture of strong Jastorf influences (Dąbrowska 1988:67), were in fact manifestations of the actual presence of the Jastorf circle population as originally postulated by Kostrzewski (1955: 206).

Jastorf influences affecting the development of cultural complexes located to the east of the Jastorf circle are noticeable already at the close of the Hallstatt period. At that time, the area occupied by the Jastorf tribes must have constituted what may be called a transmission zone for certain late Hallstatt and early La Tène elements to proliferate from Thuringia into the late Lusatian and early Pomerania cultural zone. An indicator of these relations may be distribution of ornamented foot fibulae (Woźniak 1995:202). Also Doppelpaukenfibeln found at the graveyard at Kietrz, grave no. 2044, provide important information on contacts between the aforesaid cultural zone and regions of the Jastorf culture, for such fibulae commonly occur in Brandenburgian contexts dated to Phase Ia (Seyer 1982:15), this corresponding to Jastorf a in Schwantes' chronology (Seyer 1982:21, Abb.[Fig.] 2). A large difficulty in determining the onset of the Jastorf component penetration into the Pomerania culture settlement zone (including penetration into Wielkopolska) during the late Pre-Roman Period posed by similarity between Jastorf and Pomerania elements (Czopek 1991a; 1992a; 1992b). In Wielkopolska, the early horizon of Jastorf manifestations specific to Jastorf b and, first and foremost, Jastorf c is connected with single finds, such as band earrings, paddle-shaped pins, disc-headed pins, and tongue buckles, which have been identified in Pomerania culture contexts (Kaczmarek 1999:150; Wołągiewicz 1979:67-68). Owing to their considerable dispersion, the finds cannot serve as evidence for any independent groups of settlers existing at that time. A qualitative change did not occur until the end of the older Pre-Roman period / beginning of the younger Pre-Roman period, i.e. late Jastorf c / early Ripdorf according to Schwantes' chronology (1950).

The settlement pattern of the Jastorf culture in Wielkopolska becomes particularly clear for Phase A1 of the younger Pre-Roman period (Michałowski 2005:171-176). However, the available evidence allows for dating an actual increase in prominence of civilizational influences from what is now north-western Germany and Denmark already to the end of the older Pre-Roman period / beginning of younger Pre-Roman period (Dąbrowska 1988:192-204; Kostrzewski 1914:109-110; 1923:143; Machajewski

Fig. 30. Individual stone-curbed graves 1., 2. Koninko (after Blume 1911); 3. Wierzenica (after Kostrzewski 1919-1920).

1986:274-276). Such an increase might be due to some groups of the Jastorf culture population penetrating as far as Wielkopolska (Woźniak 1979: 283), for most artefacts identified as belonging to the Jastorf culture show stylistic features typical of the late Jastorf c and Ripdorf stages. Dominant are elements datable to the younger Pre-Roman period, i.e. Phase A1. Phase A1 corresponds to late Lt C1 and most of Lt C2 (Dąbrowska 1988:62), which can be correlated with the aforesaid Ripdorf stage in the Jastorf culture chronology.

The above-mentioned horizon may be also assumed for the commencement of the process of establishing settlements in Wielkopolska by newcomers of the Jastorf circle origin. The settlements at issue include: Borzejewo 22; Komorniki 39; Pławce 22; and Poznań Nowe Miasto 226, 278, and 284. The settlements yielded mainly objects of pottery that find parallels in the Jastorf culture assemblages datable to late Jastorf/early Ripdorf, as well as in Ib/IIa pottery from Kraghede according to Martens' chronology (Chłodnicki & Pietrzak 2004:172; Kasprowicz 2008:232-233; Makiewicz 2004:242; Machajewski & Pietrzak 2008a:165, 167; 2008b: 307-308). The settlements recently studied give new and essential meaning to discoveries of individual stone-curbed graves (Fig. 30) identified at the graveyards at Koninko (Blume 1911: 341) and Wierzenica (Kostrzewski 1919-1920), all in the same area of Wielkopolska. Kostrzewski designated those graves as manifestations of the north-western stone-curbed grave culture (Kostrzewski 1923:143). Moreover, Kostrzewski pointed to a similarity existing between pottery forms (Fig. 31) found in graves attributable to this culture and materials of the same date from the lower Elbe River regions of north-western Germany, Mecklenburg, and Brandenburg. As regards parallels for some scarce ornaments, Kostrzewski indicated finds reported from Jutland, Holstein, and eastern Hanover (Kostrzewski 1923:143-145).

As far as metal ornaments and dress elements are concerned, which relate to the Ripdorf horizon of La Tène influences, particularly noteworthy are those which are deeply rooted in the Jastorf tradition. Here undoubtedly belong pins that continued to be present in the Jastorf circle despite the rapidly progressing absorption of La Tène influences, for example the two winged pins discovered at the graveyard at Biała (Fig. 32:4). In the southern part of Schleswig-Holstein, these forms are linked to Phase Id and persist even into Phase IIIb (Behrends 1968:57; Hingst 1983:46). In Brandenburg, they were basically occurring in the first

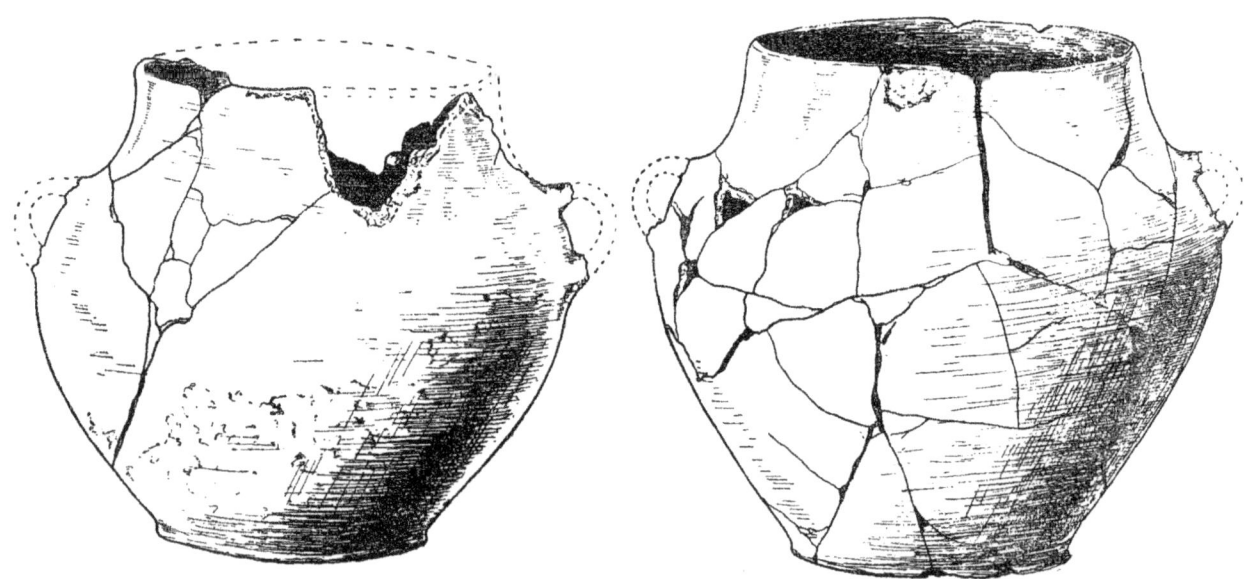

Fig. 31. The pre-Roman Iron Age pottery forms from Wierzenica (after Kostrzewski 1919-1920).

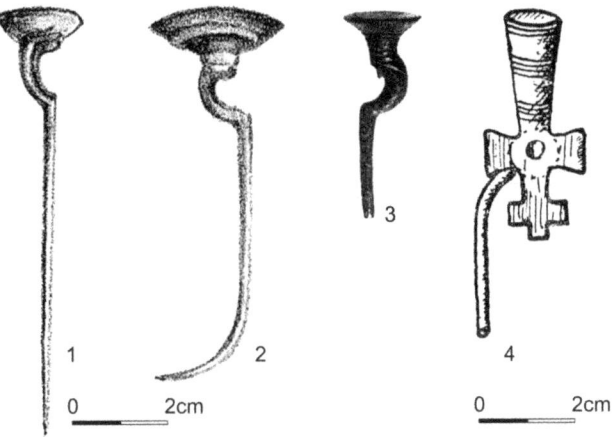

FIG. 32. JASTORF PINS FROM WIELKOPOLSKA: A. ŁUSZCZEWO (ERZEPKI 1890); B. SOBIEJUCHY (ERZEPKI 1890); C. ŻÓŁWIN, SITE 3 (KRES 1965); D. BIAŁA (KOSTRZEWSKI 1914).

half of Phase IIa (Seyer 1982:18). A somewhat similar chronology can be established for Holstein pins present in assemblages of Schleswig-Holstein typical either of Phase IIb, or Phase IIIa, depending on the pin head shape (Behrends 1968:56). Similar pins are reported from four sites in Wielkopolska, i.e. Żółwin, Łuszczewo, Sobiejuchy (Fig. 32:1-3), and probebly from Jutrosin.

Yet another important group of artefacts, which are certainly Jastorf in origin, are fibulae with a pellet-decorated bow of the middle La Tène-type construction (Fig. 33), and fibulae with a step-like bow of the the La Tène-type construction (Fig. 34), primarily from regions on the Noteć River. Four such fibulae were collected from burial contexts: three from Wszedzień I and one from Nowe Miasto on the Warta River. The settlement at Sowinki, although not fully studied yet and roughly linked to the Przework culture, yielded one fibula with three pellets on the bow (Michałowski 2005:167). Most of the seven fibulae with a step-like bow were recovered from northern Wielkopolska, namely the Noteć River area. They were found at graveyards at Biała, Kuźnica Żelichowska, and Wszedzień I. A pit grave at the site of Grotniki, southern Wielopolska, yielded one fibula, while the site of Grodziszcze located in the borderland between Wielkopolska and Land of Lubusz produced one more pin, this also having been deposited in a grave (Michałowski & Żychliński 2011). Metal artefacts manifesting typical Jastorf features undoubtedly include round-shaped jewellery objects, each bound to a different location. These are crown neck rings found at Ćmachów, Milczek, and Staw (Fig. 35:1-3), and enamelled neck rings with budged cylindrical ends from the site at Biała (Fig. 35:4). The scarcity of such objects at Wielkopolska sites may be attributable to almost total and characteristically younger

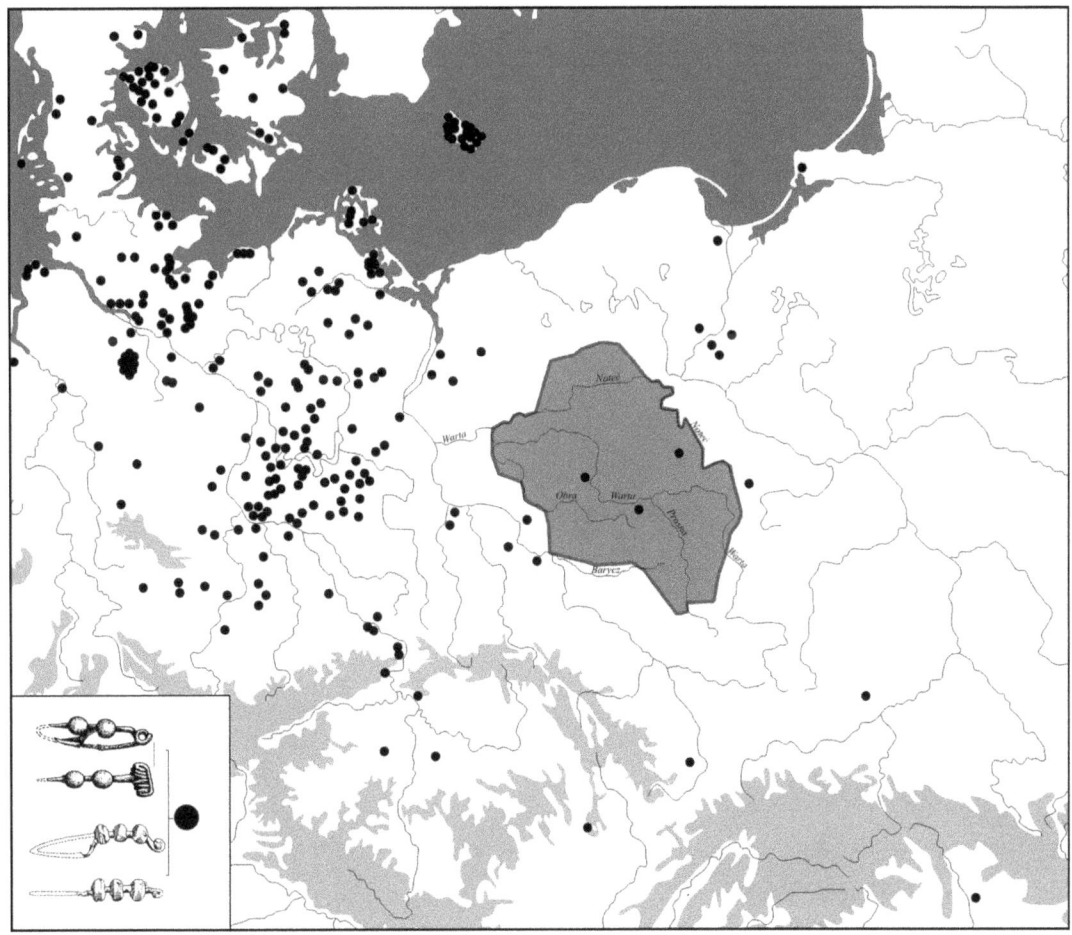

FIG. 33. DISTRIBUTION OF FIBULAE WITH PELLET-DECORATED BOW IN WIELKOPOLSKA.

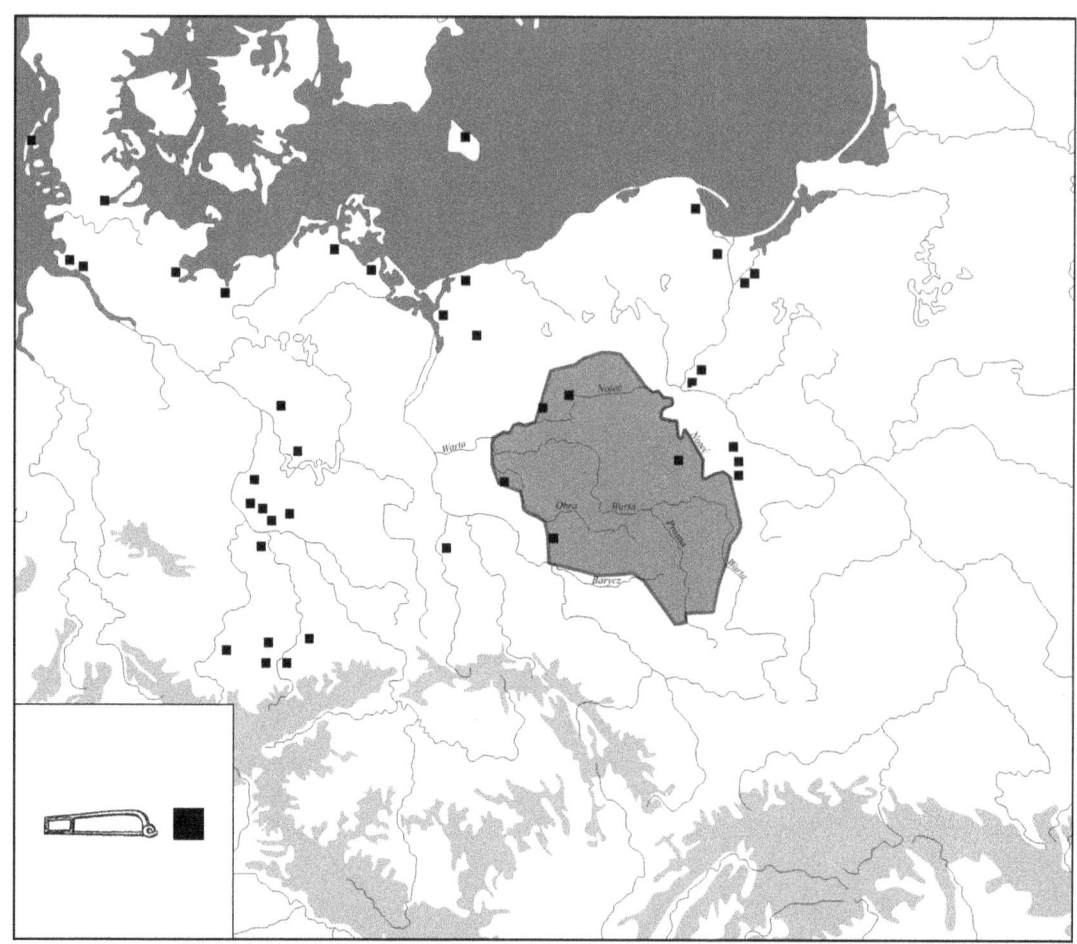

FIG. 34. DISTRIBUTION OF FIBULAE WITH A STEP-LIKE BOW IN WIELKOPOLSKA.

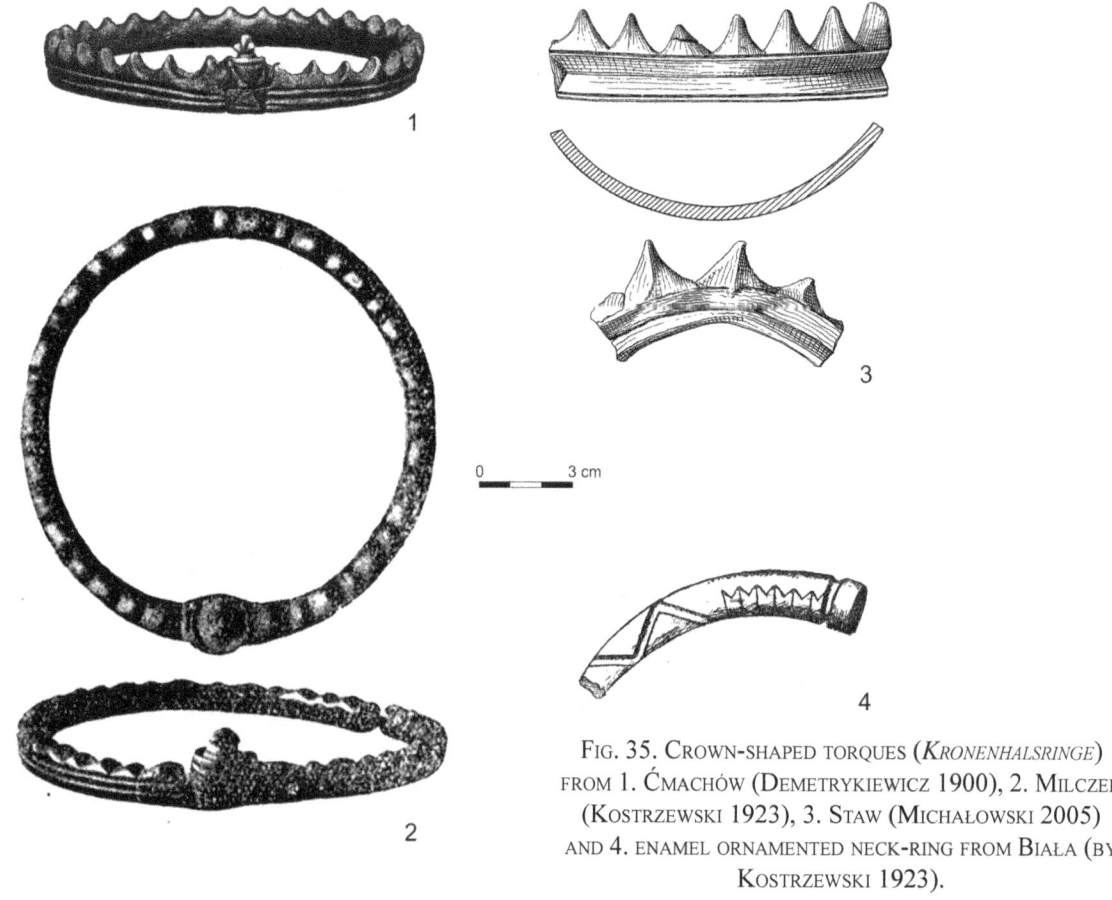

FIG. 35. CROWN-SHAPED TORQUES (*KRONENHALSRINGE*) FROM 1. ĆMACHÓW (DEMETRYKIEWICZ 1900), 2. MILCZEK (KOSTRZEWSKI 1923), 3. STAW (MICHAŁOWSKI 2005) AND 4. ENAMEL ORNAMENTED NECK-RING FROM BIAŁA (BY KOSTRZEWSKI 1923).

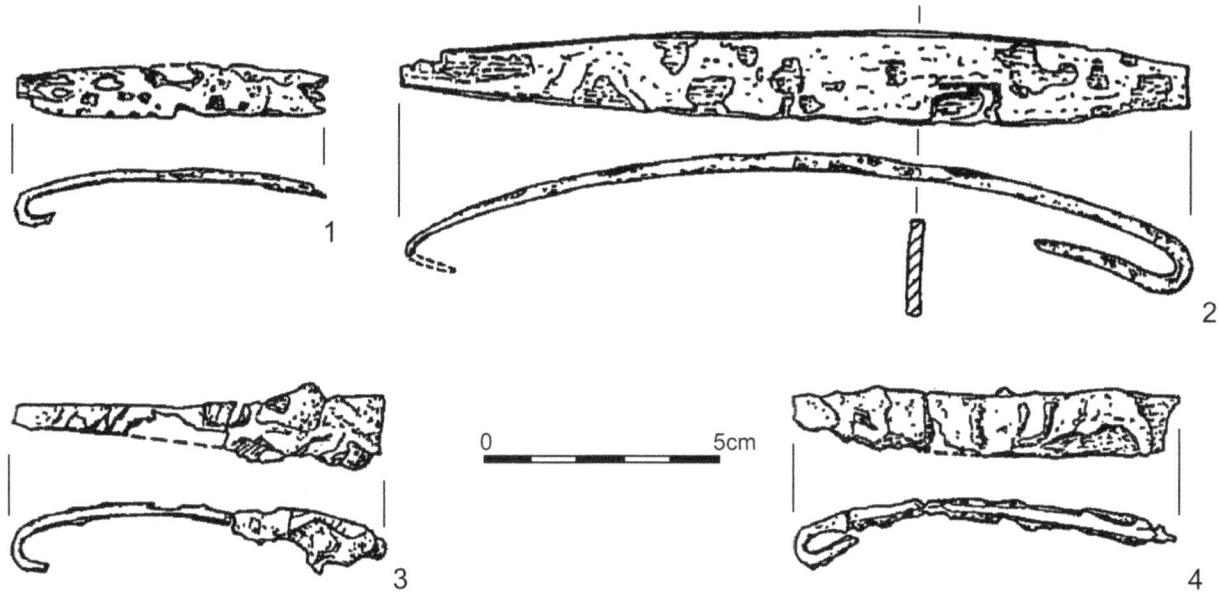

Fig. 36. Kuźnica Żelichowska. Single-partite band belt buckles (after Gałezowska 1996).

Pre-Roman period absence of round-shaped jewellery, such as neck rings or bracelets, starting from Phase IIb in Seyer's chronology, with this kind of jewellery being still quite common at sites dated to Phase IIa (Seyer 1982:79). In Wielkopolska, the Ripdorf phase is also linked to the presence of single-partite band belt buckles (Fig. 36), derived from early tongue forms.

Classified as artefacts of an intercultural nature may be, by contrast, fibulae of La Tène-type construction. Definitely in greater number are middle La Tène fibulae of type A, B, and H in Kostrzewski's classification. Despite being commonly found in various cultural circles, these fibulae are also typical markers of older phases of Jastorf culture under La Tène influences (Hachmann 1961:234; Seyer 1982:18-19, 68). The fibulae of type A are common at Biała where certainly three such pieces from graves are ascertained with "several" more allegedly present; at Wszedzień, five(?) pieces are recorded at Site II and one piece at Site I. Grave 1 at Rosko yielded a double fibula variant, with two pieces connected with chainlets (Fig. 37). The double variant evokes a Kettenschmuck or chainlet jewellery category specific to the Jastrof culture (Behrends 1968:63; Seyer 1982:77-78). It is not unlikely that the same type of Kettengehänge was once among items deposited in destroyed graves at Biała which are roughly described as containing 'several fibulae of type A' and a chainlet fragment (Michałowski 2005:167).

Equally numerous are iron fibulae of Kostrzewski's type B. Four such pieces are identified in funeral assemblages at Biała, Drawsko, Sokołowice, and Świerkówiec. Another six pieces are reported among finds from destroyed graves at Biała, Grzępy, Kuźnica Żelichowska, and Wszedzień (Michałowski 2005:166). In the settlement context, such a fibula form is recorded in Poznań Nowe Miasto 226 (Machajewski & Pietrzak 2008b:307). A long fibula of type B from Grave 5 at Świerkówiec was accompanied by

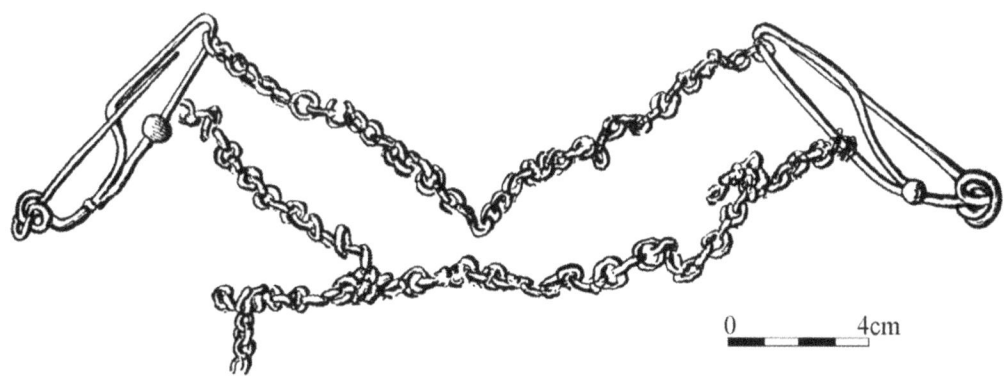

Fig. 37. Chain pendant with two fibulae from Kostrzewski's type A from Rosko, site 7 (After Michałowski 2005).

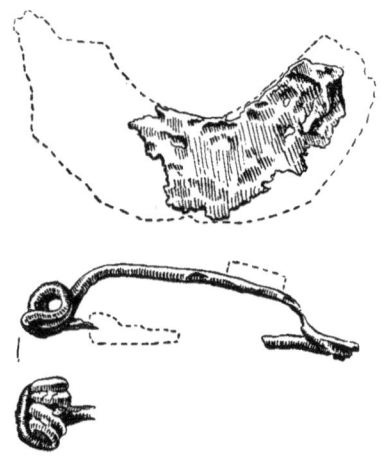

FIG. 38. EQUIPMENT FROM GRAVE 41 IN SOKOŁOWICE (AFTER ŁUKA 1953).

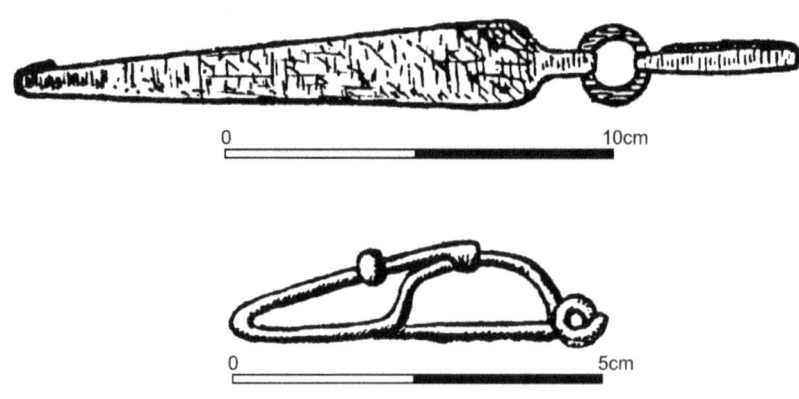

FIG. 39. EQUIPMENT FROM GRAVE 1 IN BIAŁA (AFTER KOSTRZEWSKI 1923).

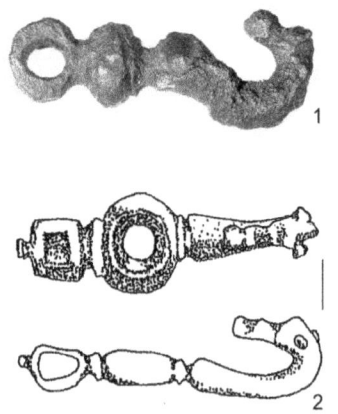

FIG. 40. HORSE-HEADED BUCKLES FROM WIELKOPOLSKA: 1. WSZEDZIEŃ (AFTER MICHAŁOWSKI 2006); 2. ŚWIERKÓWIEC (AFTER BOKINIEC 1999).

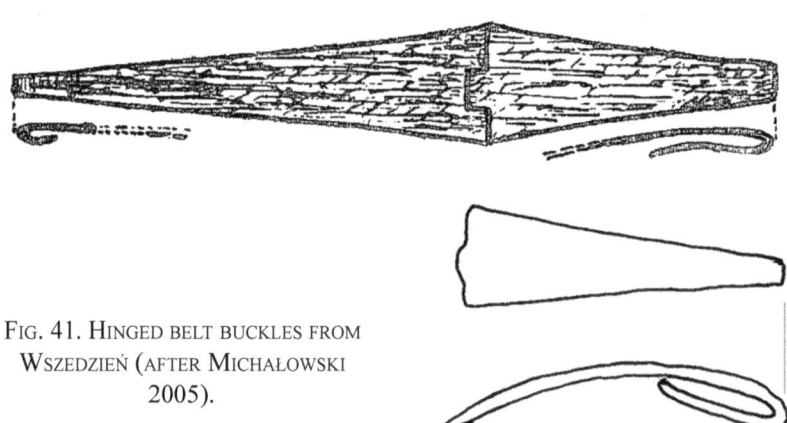

FIG. 41. HINGED BELT BUCKLES FROM WSZEDZIEŃ (AFTER MICHAŁOWSKI 2005).

two fibulae of Kostrzewski's type H. Yet another three such pieces are reported from Graveyards I and II at Wszedzień. These fibulae are present in funeral assemblages together with semi-circular razors (Fig. 38), three-partite belt buckles (Fig. 39), and animal (horse)-headed buckles. The last mentioned objects (Fig. 40) are considered to be imports from the eastern Celtic world. This conclusion is drawn on the fact such buckles' prevalence in the central European Celtic zone which may be thus regarded as the place of their origin (Filip 1956:173). The presence of the animal-headed buckles in the central European Celtic zone is ascertained from LtC1 until late LtD (Filip 1956:173-174; Müller 1985:88; Stanczik & Vaday 1971:26).

Yet another horizon, for which there are typical markers at Wielkopolska sites, is phase A2 corresponding to the early Seedorf horizon in Lower Saxony (Schwantes 1950). In Wielkopolska, these markers constitute a group of rare finds among indigenous material of Jastorf origin. They occur chiefly at graveyards at Wszedzień as hinged belt buckles (Fig. 41) present together with middle La Tène fibulae of type C. Regrettably, none come from a reliable funeral assemblage. However, the co-occurrence of the buckles and fibulae allows confirming a similar set of features that may be then easily distinguishable when compared to, for example, material yielded by the Jastorf Oder group and typical of Phase A2 (Wołągiewicz 1981b:193; Pl. XXVII). Also, some pottery forms unearthed in settlements of Poznań Nowe Miasto evoke designs that, in the Jastorf circle, are characteristic of early younger stages of La Tène influences, corresponding to the Seedorf phase (Machajewski & Pietrzak 2008a:165; 2008b:307).

The picture of how elements rooted in broadly understood Jastorf settlement regions were penetrating into Wielkopolska is far from being homogenous. Certain zones may surely be designated that differ in formal and chronological terms due to the different origin of material occurring there.

Elements connected with older Pre-Roman periods are reported chiefly from southern and central Wielkopolska.

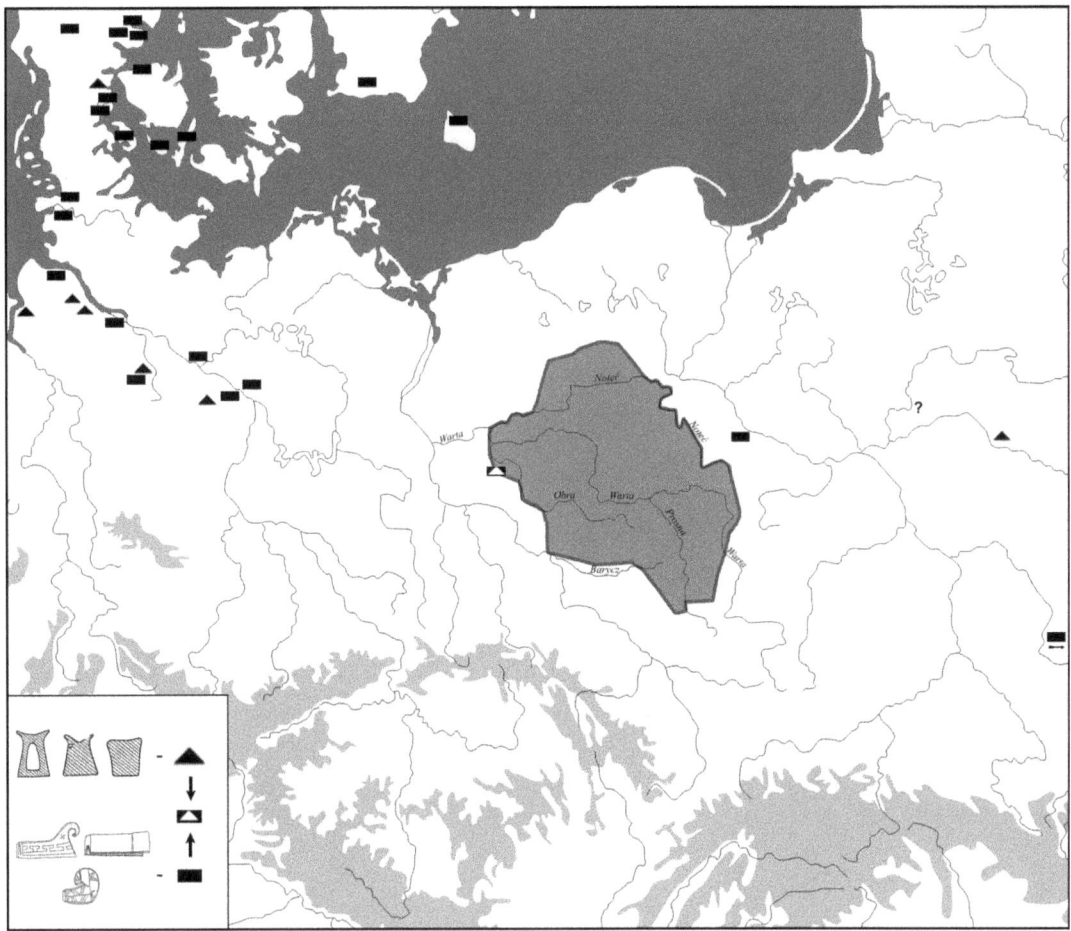

FIG. 42. DISTRIBUTION OF FIRE WOLVES IN WIELKOPOLSKA.

Older ones datable to Jastorf b and Jastorf c are mostly single finds from southern Wielkopolska. Basically, the latter's concentrations are along the Obra River and its tributaries. Their time span can be correlated with contacts between late Lustatian/early Pomerania and early Jastorf circles. All evidence points to objects of such origin present in material from Wielkopolska as having not been connected with any collective settlement activity whatsoever. The objects are most likely to have been a consequence of the process of single foreign forms proliferating into indigenous material.

Jastorf material in central Wielkopolska illustrates a different phenomenon. Already in the twilight of the older Pre-Roman period, i.e. in late Jastorf c and early Ripdorf, a compact settlement centre developed along the middle reach of the Warta River that represented a material culture model characteristic of the Jastorf culture. The region at issue exhibits considerable settlement stability that continued until early Phase A2 of the younger Pre-Roman period. Material from local sites comes either from graveyards (Koniko, Wierzenica) that display cultural homogeneity, or from settlements built on virgin soil (Borzejewo 22; Komorniki 39; Pławce 22; Poznań Nowe Miasto 226, 278, and 284). It clearly shows its prevailing north-western origin as far as Jutland. Linked to regions of Lower Saxony, Schleswig-Holstein, and Jutland are fire wolves (Fig. 42) of types I:2, I:3, and II:1 in M. Babeş' classification (Michałowski, Teska 2012). Genetically linked to these regions seem to be also crown neck rings, although it is just one piece from Milczek (type B) that has its direct parallels in Lower Saxony (Langenmoor) and Lolland (Gallerhøj), while other pieces from Wielkopolska (Babeş, Types E and F) find most of their parallels in Poland, Ukraine, and Moldova (Babeş 1993:108), i.e. outside the genetic area of the Jastorf culture. Jutlandic roots are also acutely evident for pottery retrieved from sites in Wielkopolska (Kasprowicz 2004:227-232; Machajewski & Pietrzak 2008b:307; Żychliński 2004:256). And Brandenburgian provenance is echoed by clay spoons. Such clay spoons collected in the homeland territory of the Jastorf culture were deemed by Seyer to be specific to that territory (1982:46).

In Wielkopolska, clay spoons are reported (Fig. 43) also from another concentration of Jastorf culture sites found in the Pałuki area and Gniezno Lakeland. Curiously enough, also pottery finds include forms known from Brandenburg (Sobucki & Woźniak 2004:211). In addition to those forms and elements typical of the Jutlandic zone, there is also pottery reported which is characteristic of Jastorf cultural groups located in the lower Elbe River area (Sobucki & Woźniak 2004:208) and Mecklenburg (Sobucki & Woźniak 2004:202). In turn, Wszedzień I finds reveal

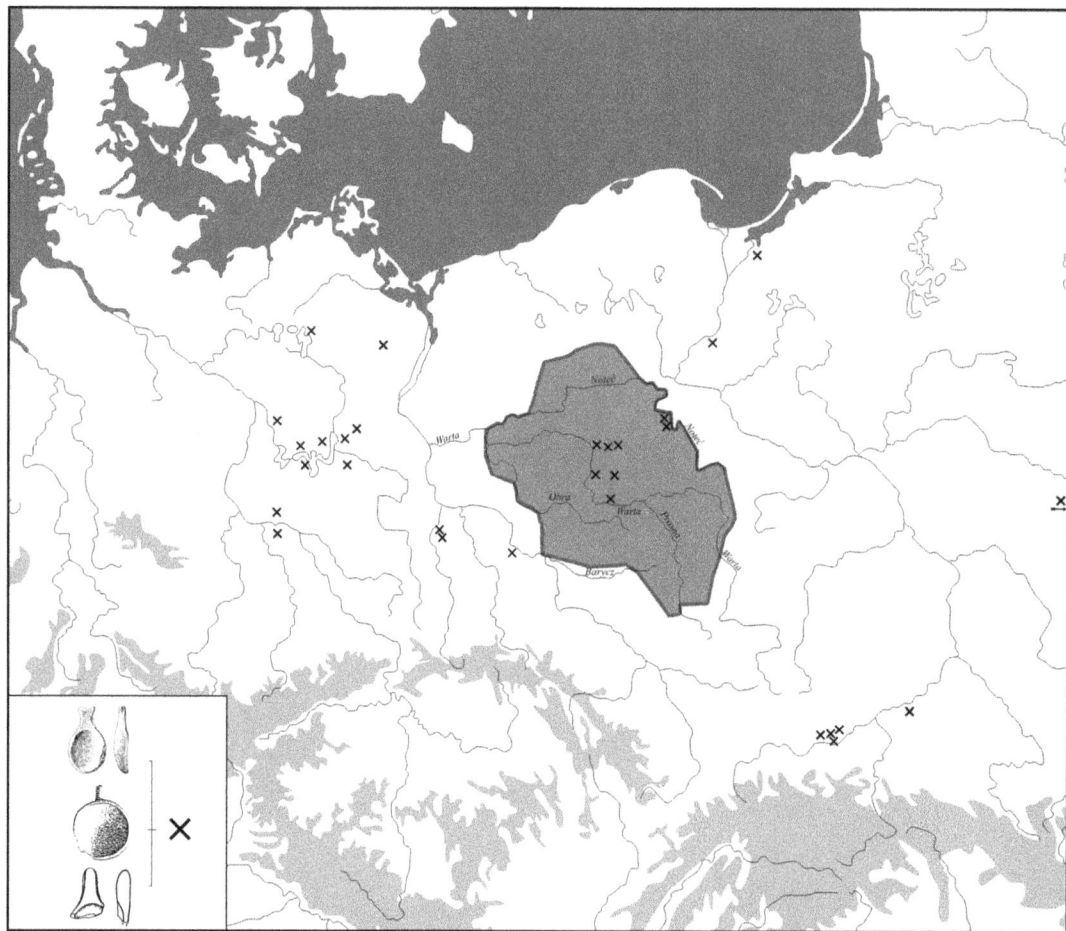

FIG. 43. DISTRIBUTION OF CLAY SPOONS IN WIELKOPOLSKA.

elements clearly associated with the Baltic Sea zone and genetically linked to young Pre-Roman material from the island of Bornholm. Among such finds from Wszedzień I, there is a Bornholm-type fibula (Fig. 44:1) whose very close parallel was found on Bornholm (Vedel 1887: 80, Fig. 122). Bornholm also yielded pellet fibulas decorated in a manner similar to that of objects from Wszedzień (Fig. 44:2), with an engraved cross (Vedel 1887:80, Figs. 122, 118). These artefacts are associated with the Ripdorf horizon; but, as far as the Wszedzień graveyard evidence is concerned, there are grounds to suppose that its Jastorf settlement at Wszedzień might have continued to develop still in Phase A2, i.e. the Seedorf stage, as suggested for the settlement complex of Poznań Nowe Miasto.

As far as the Jastorf component inflow is concerned, a significant settlement zone emerged in the early younger Pre-Roman period on the Noteć River. Material recovered from that region is much more homogenous in terms of dating and manifestly connected with the Ripdrof horizon, i.e. Phase A1 of the younger Pre-Roman period. The research carried out to date suggests that the local settlement pattern was somewhat more mobile than in the Warta River region. Nevertheless, there are some grounds to conclude that a more stable settlement model was also followed. This conclusion is drawn based on the complex that is not yet completely examined but surely comprises a graveyard at Biała 1 and a settlement at Wapniarnia 129, 300m eastwards.

Altogether, the nature of the sites discovered in northern and central Wielkopolska evidently points to their external genesis that was most probably associated with the arrival of population groups bringing their own fully formed cultural model and developing it further based on a continuous inflow of new ideas from their homeland(s). This phenomenon may be linked to the Bastarn and Scirian migration mentioned in written sources that led to the emergence of the Poienești-Lukaševka culture in Dacian territories in the early 2nd.century B.C. (Babeș 1993:168-173). A genetic variety of forms recorded in Wielkopolska may point either to diversified directions migrants were moving from, or to territorial/tribal diversification of an arriving group of newcomers. The latter possibility seems more plausible. We are probably dealing here with some groups, whose homeland was perhaps in northern Jutland, that, on their way, were joined by other tribes searching for a new challenge in moving eastwards. The route of the eastward migration of the Jastorf people led them through Wielkopolska. Occasionally, single burials from the younger Pre-Roman period appear to be simply 'stuck' to older necropolises, as it is the case for Drawsk 1 (Dernoga

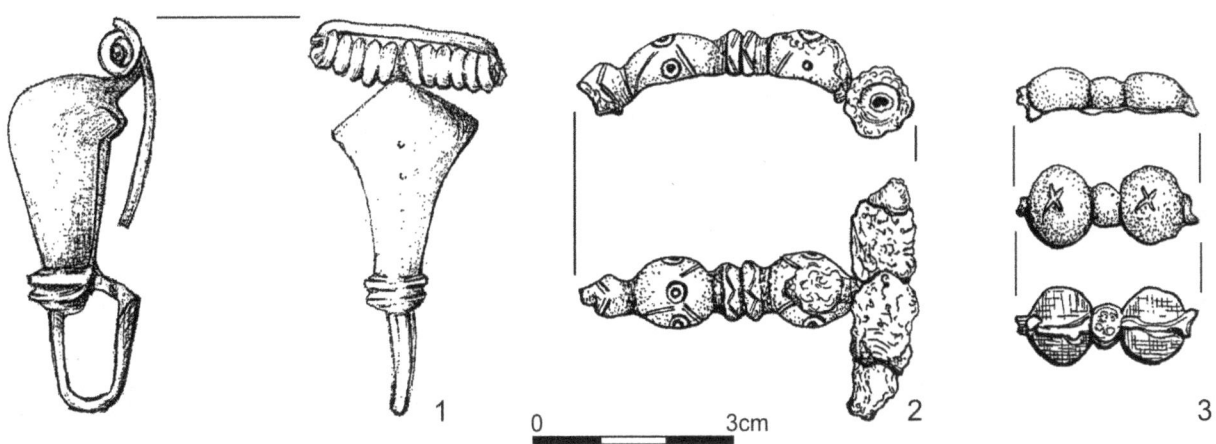

Fig. 44. Wszedzień: 1. Bornholm-type fibula; 2., 3. decorated fibulae with beads (after Michałowski 2008).

& Gajda 2004), Nowe Miasto Nad Wartą 1 (Machajewski & Walkiewicz 1993), or Sokołowice (Łuka 1953). Also the traces of temporary settlements and campsites recovered at Bożejewo (Makiewicz 2004), Rosko (Niedźwiecki 2005), Obórka and Modliszew (Sobucki & Woźniak 2004), or Otorowo (Żychliński 2004) indicate considerable mobility of their founders.

The intensity of the expansion led the migrants to stabilize their settlement patterns in phase A1 of the younger Pre-Roman period; this is reflected in the strong Jastorf influence exerted in the Noteć River region, where larger necropoles such as Kuźnica Żelichowska, Grzępy, and, first and foremost, Biała began to emerge. At that time, at Wapniarnia and Piła-Liksierz, more permanent settlements were established as evidenced by probable traces of long houses combining residential and outbuilding functions. The same process seems to have been occurring also in central Wielkopolska as proved by the development of settlements such as Poznań Nowe Miasto. In Wielkopolska, Jastorf settlements disappeared in early phase A2. This coincides with the intensified settlement activity of the Przeworsk culture people or, basically, with the moment when Wielkopolska was actually inhabited by them. Surely, this was when Przeworsk and Jastorf populations came into contact. This is clearly seen in material recovered from settlements at Dzierżnica or Obórka (Sobucki & Woźniak 2004), and, first and foremost, Poznań Nowe Miasto. Coexistence of the two populations resulted in production of vessels that combined features of the two different styles (Machajewski & Pietrzak 2008b:308). This coexistence is also seen in direct continuity in the use of burial grounds, as observed at the graveyards at Świerkówiec or Kuźnica Żelichowska.

The research work carried out to date does not provide a satisfactory explanation to the discontinuity of material indicators of the Jastorf culture in Wielkopolska. It may be, however, assumed that such discontinuity might have reflected the departure of Jastorf people for the purpose of further migration. It might have been also connected with acculturation of indigenous communities (or at least some of them) and adoption of the Przeworsk cultural model. The latter is far more likely because the Przeworsk culture was rapidly expanding at that time, in order to reach northern Wielkopolska, presumably on its way to Kuyavia, at the end of Phase A1/beginning of PhaseA2 of the younger Pre-Roman period (Grygiel 2004:35). At that time, Przeworsk peoples probably came into larger-scale contacts with Jastorf groups; a consequence of which are intermingled Jastorf and Przeworsk assemblages occurring in the Noteć River and Pałuki areas (Bokiniec 1999:126-127; Gałęzowska 1996:159-162; Machajewski 2002:12-16). Phase A2 marks the commencement of strengthened settlement activities of Przeworsk people, combined with cultural unification in southern and central Wielkopolska. This phenomenon may be linked to the completion of acculturation of the remaining post-Pomerania populations and to the complete absence of Jastorf sites in early Phase A3 (Godłowski 1985:35-37; Machajewski & Pietrzak 2004:101; Michałowski 2008:102), which is further reflected in the absence of Jastorf settlements in the Poznań Nowe Miasto area at that time (Machajewski & Pietrzak 2004:100).

Conclusion

Henryk Machajewski

A quite unprecedented growth in the number of archaeological sources associated with the Jastorf culture on the Polish Lowland in recent years would not be surprising if it were not for the fact that only recently the remains of this culture were recorded only in the drainage basin of the lower and middle Oder River, while east of the river usually single undeterminable elements of this culture were encountered (Dąbrowska 1988:184-185, Map 22–23; Machajewski 2004:7). Publications synthesizing the life of populations settling the lands of present-day Poland in the Pre-Roman period have not answered all the questions raised by the Jastorf culture.

Subsequently a thesis was adopted that the presence of the Jastorf culture on the Polish Lowland, coinciding with the period covering phases Jastorf b through Seedorf I (Lt. A-Lt. D1), illustrated by the Oder and Gubin groups, represented only a small fragment of the culture related to the story of its Middle Elbe and Mecklenburg groups (Dąbrowski 1979:206-208; Wołągiewicz 1981b:192-196; Domański 1981:196-200). Neither fully clarified, the fundamental issues for the Jastorf groups on the Polish Lowland, namely their relationships to the Hallstatt, La Tène and Pre-Roman cultural traditions, were elucidated thanks to later investigations, especially those by Ryszard Wołągiewicz (1979:33-69; 1983:83-106; 1989:307-321) and Zenon Woźniak (1977:269-287; 2007:390-419). They laid foundations for making internal divisions within these groups, based on the conviction that stylistic variability, particularly of pottery and metal dress ornaments, followed from various degrees of adaptation of several cultural trends, and reorganizations precipitated by settlement perturbations.

The elaborate deliberations on the Jastorf culture on the Polish Lowland were always paralleled by extensive discussions of the concept of 'Hallstatt-trait acquisition' (Gedl 1991) and 'La Tène-trait acquisition' in the Polish literature (Wołągiewicz 1979:34-35; Gardawski & Woźniak 1979:29, footnote 1; Hensel [ed.] 1983:124–136). The consequences of these discrepant approaches were noticeable on two planes. On the first, there were difficulties caused by the use of inconsistent chronological systems sequencing the Hallstatt, La Tène and Pre-Roman periods. Attempts to synchronize them, following from the need to correlate various cultural traditions deciding the cultural and settlement character of the Polish Lowland, revealed a relatively clear relationship between Lt. C and Lt. D, on one part, and the younger Pre-Roman period on the other, whereas the relationship between Lt. A and Lt. B, and the Hallstatt and older Pre-Roman periods continued to be shrouded in mystery.

On the other plane, there were taxonomic questions, namely the results of an attempt to systematize the recorded cultural remains. In respect of the Lt. A and Lt. B period, there was considerable debate concerning their systematization, covering, on the one hand, cultures deriving from the decline of the Bronze Age or the Hallstatt period and surviving deep into the La Tène period (Jastorf, Pomerania, Cloche Grave cultures and the decline stages of the Lusatian culture), and on the other, associated with the traditions only of the La Tène period (La Tène culture) (Gardawski 1979:124, Fig. 63). While for the Lt. C and Lt. D period, the set of cultures encompassed only the Przeworsk and Oksywie cultures, both deeply affected by a La Tène impact (Godłowski 1977; Dąbrowska 1988).

This cultural picture of the Polish Lowland, widely considered an arena where two different cultural circles merged – La Tène from the south and Pre-Roman from the north – was painted under a significant influence of the conviction about the pre-eminence of cultural impact emanating from the La Tène circle (Godłowski 1985; Dąbrowska 1988). However, attempts to outline chronological and spatial relationships between these circles failed as a result of not only the state of archaeological sources but above all, the theoretical assumptions and extra-source knowledge.

An attempt to verify the findings concerning the Polish Lowland was made when thorough investigations were undertaken into the chronology and cultural situation in northern Europe in the Pre-Roman period (Martens 1988:159-181; Martens [ed.] 1997). Their results, as it seems, inspired a reflection on the cultural picture on the Polish Lowland as well (Dąbrowska 1994:71-87; Dąbrowska & Woźniak 2005:87-101). These deliberations coincided with the discovery of exceptionally rich settlement remains associated with the Pre-Roman period. Upon preliminary cultural classification, they were tentatively linked to the Jastorf circle, particularly to the Lower Elbe area and Jutland, with, however, clearly marked differences in respect to the materials of this circle hitherto known from the Polish Lowland.

A difficulty in determining the detailed chronology of these finds lies in the fact that they come for the most part from settlements. Nevertheless, attempts based on an inter-regional comparative analysis justified dating these finds to the period from Lt. B2 to Lt. C2/D1, which in the system of Jastorf culture chronology corresponds to the period from the turn of phases Jastorf C and Ripdorf to the turn of phases Ripdorf and Seedorf. Accepting these chronological findings, it can be assumed that this culture's settlement, in terms of archaeological chronology, was relatively brief on the Polish Lowland.

In terms of space, in turn, the elements of this culture are encountered from the drainage basin of the middle Oder, across northern Wielkopolska, Kujawy, Mazovia, as far as the Lublin region. Spatially-speaking, they 'occupied' a vast area attributed earlier to the settlement of the decline phase of the Pomerania and Cloche Grave cultures and later, of the early phase of the Przeworsk culture. An attempt to synchronize the named cultures revealed a peculiar 'crush' taking place generally in Lt. B and Lt. C. In consequence, the area occupied until now by mostly the Przeworsk culture was revised to exclude its northern and north-eastern parts. Changes also took place in the chronology of the earliest horizon of the Przeworsk culture settlement.

The preliminary results of studies of the finds recently discovered on the Polish Lowland and associated with the Jastorf circle have not clarified all the relevant issues. More studies are necessary to determine above all, their chronology. With large sets of pottery being available, stress should be laid on analyzing their style and comparing them with the Lower Elbe, Jutland, Jastorf, Oder and Gubin group, and early Przeworsk culture pottery. The analysis could be supplemented by charting relatively few finds of metal dress ornaments and objects of everyday use.

Another task, potentially helping to trace the dynamics of the Jastorf circle development, could be an attempt to define the cultural dissimilarity of new Jastorf finds vis-à-vis older ones known already from the Polish Lowland, represented by the Oder and Gubin groups. Exhaustive analysis should also be conducted on the question of adaptation of phenomena associated with the process of 'La Tène-trait acquisition' in the Jastorf environment. On the Polish Lowland, this could be an important factor in interpreting dynamic cultural transformations in Lt. C and Lt. D, i.e. in the younger Pre-Roman period.

Finally, an important aspect of research into the Jastorf culture on the Polish Lowland is the need to continue a detailed review of archival resources. This should embrace the introduction of Jastorf finds from areas until now not considered a sphere of Jastorf influence, ever more often into the store of archaeological literature

Catalogue of Jastorf culture sites from the Northwest Poland

Henryk Machajewski and Andrzej Michałowski

Pomerania

1. Babin (Babbin), Pyrzyce district, West Pomerania province
Type: cemetery
Investigations: chance find
Description: cemetery, about 10 cremation graves
Chronology: Ripdorf phase
Collection:
Archives: MNSz, catalogue of H. J. Eggers.
Literature: Bohnsack 1938:156; Dorka 1939: 77, 79-80, 120-121; Eggers & Stary 2001:39, no. 158, Taf. 131: 1-10; Rogalski 2011:312-313.

2. Będarkowo (Mandelkow), Police district, West Pomerania province
Type: cemetery
Investigations: chance find
Description: remains of several urn and pit graves
Chronology: Ripdorf phase
Collections:
Archives: MNSz, catalogue of H. J. Eggers.
Literature: Kunkel 1931:76, Taf. 76: 19; Eggers & Stary 2001:36, no. 142, Taf. 125: 1.

3. Chocielewko (Mackensen), Lębork district, Pomerania province
Type: unattached, possibly from grave (?)
Investigations: chance find
Description: crown neck ring of type I/II according to Kostrzewski
Chronology: Ripdorf phase
Collection:
Archives:
Literature: Bohnsack 1938:36; Maciałowicz 2011, 93-95, Fig. 10.

4. Dębica (Damnitz), Pyrzyce district, West Pomerania province
Type: cemetery
Investigations: chance find
Description: urn grave with a stone structure
Chronology: Ripdorf phase
Collections:
Archives: MNSz, catalogue of H. J. Eggers.
Literature: Dorka 1939:77-79; Eggers & Stary 2001:39, no. 159; Rogalski 2011:331.

5. Długie 3 (Langenhagen). Stargard Szczeciński district, West Pomerania province
Type: cemetery
Investigations: H. J. Eggers 1934-1939
Description: almost completely explored cemetery consisting of 129 urn and pit graves featuring various stone structures and unattached grave goods from several (?) destroyed graves.
Chronology: Jastorf-Ripdorf phase
Collections:
Archives: MNSz, catalogue of H. J. Eggers.
Literature: Eggers 1936:15; Eggers 1964; Wołągiewicz 1959:142-143; Eggers& Stary 2001:42-47, no. 191, Taf. 135-141; Rogalski 2011:331-338.

6. Długołęka (Langkafel), Goleniów district, West Pomerania province
Type: cemetery
Investigations: chance find
Description: urn grave
Chronology: Jastorf phase
Collections:
Archives: MNSz, catalogue of H. J. Eggers
Literature: Eggers & Stary 2001:48, Taf. 146: 7; Rogalski 2011:425, 596.

7. Dobropole Gryfińskie (Dobberphul), Gryfino district, West Pomerania province
Type: cemetery
Investigations: chance find
Description: several urn graves
Chronology: Jastorf-Ripdorf phase
Collections:
Archives: MNSz, catalogue of H. J. Eggers
Literature: Kostrzewski 1919a:58, 69, 71, 81-82; Kunkel 1931, no. 471; Eggers & Stary 2001:38-39; Rogalski 2011:338-339, 596.

8. Dunlewo (Dünow), Kamień Pomorski district, West Pomerania province
Type: cemetery
Investigations: chance find
Description: unattached graves goods
Chronology: Jastorf-Ripdorf phase
Collections:
Archives: MNSz, catalogue of H. J. Eggers
Literature: Kostrzewski 1919b:5-6; Eggers & Stary 2001:48, Taf. 150: 1-14; Rogalski 2011:344-345.

9. Gałowo (Galow), Szczecinek district, West Pomerania province
Type: unattached
Investigations: chance find
Description: metal dress elements in the form of two pins
Chronology: Ripdorf phase
Collections:

Archives: MNSz, catalogue of H. J. Eggers.
Literature: Kunkel 1931:62, Taf. 68; Eggers & Stary 2001:65, Taf. 185: 1; Rogalski 2011:346, 597.

10. Ginawa (Gienow), Stargard Szczeciński district, West Pomerania province
Type: cemetery
Investigations: chance find
Description: cemetery has been only fragmentarily explored. About ten cremation graves were exposed.
Chronology: Ripdorf phase
Collections:
Archives: MNSz, archives of H.J. Eggers
Literature: Eggers & Stary 2001:50, Taf. 155: 3; Rogalski 2011:347

11. Gogolewo (Pegelow), Stargard Szczeciński district, West Pomerania province
Type: cemetery
Investigations: chance find
Description: urn grave and metal dress elements
Chronology: Ripdorf phase
Collections:
Archives: MNSz, catalogue of H. J. Eggers
Literature: Eggers & Stary 2001:47, Taf. 143: 2-3.

12. Goleniów (Gollnow), Goleniów district, West Pomerania province
Type: cemetery
Investigations: chance find
Description: unattached grave goods
Chronology: Ripdorf phase
Collections:
Archives: MNSz, catalogue of H. J. Eggers.
Literature: Eggers & Stary 2001:48, Taf. 146: 1-6; Rogalski 2011:350-351, 596.

13. Golina (Gollin), Stargard Szczeciński district, West Pomerania province
Type: cemetery
Investigations: chance find
Description: destroyed graves yielded ceramic vessels and metal dress elements
Chronology: Ripdorf phase
Collections:
Archives: MNSz, catalogue of H. J. Eggers.
Literature: Wołągiewicz 1959:136, Fig. 3; Eggers & Stary 2001:42, Taf. 142: 2-3; Rogalski 2010:351.

14. Karlino 2 (Körlin), Białogard district, West Pomerania province
Type: cemetery
Investigations: chance find and excavations in 1970, I. Skrzypek (Muzeum Okręgowe in Koszalin)
Description: two cremation graves with metal dress elements
Chronology: Ripdorf phase
Collections: MNSz and Muzeum Okręgowe in Koszalin
Archives: MNSz and Muzeum Okręgowe in Koszalin
Literature: Skrzypek 1973; Machajewski 1999, Fig. 1: 1:4; Eggers & Stary 2001:55

15. Karnice (Karnitz), Gryfice district, West Pomerania province
Type: cemetery
Investigations: chance find
Description: unattached metal grave goods
Chronology: Ripdorf phase
Archives: MNSz, archives of H. J. Eggers
Literature: Eggers & Stary 2001:51, Taf. 155: 7-17; Rogalski 2010:354, 597.

16. Kłęby (Klemmem), Pyrzyce district, West Pomerania province
Type: unattached
Investigations: chance find
Description: fragment of a bronze necklace
Chronology: Jastorf-Ripdorf phase
Collections:
Archives: MNSz, catalogue of H. J. Eggers
Literature: Eggers & Stary 2001, 40, Taf. 133: 1

17. Kopaniewo (Koppenow), Lębork district, Pomerania province
Type: unattached find in aquatic environment(?)
Investigations: chance find
Description: crown neck ring of type I/II according to Kostrzewski
Chronology: Jastorf-Ripdorf phase
Collections:
Archives: MNSz, catalogue of H. J. Eggers.
Literature: Eggers & Stary 2001:73, no 324:a; Rogalski 2011:358; Machajewski, forthcoming.

18. Kozielice (Köselitz), Pyrzyce district, West Pomerania province
Type: unattached
Investigations: chance find
Description: neck ring with thick, cylinder shaped ends
Chronology: Ripdorf phase
Collections:
Archives:
Literature: Dorka 1939:79, 150; Eggers & Stary 2001:40, Taf. 133:2; Rogalski 2010:430.

19. Krzepocin (Lüttenhagen), Kamień Pomorski district, West Pomerania province
Type: unattached
Investigations: chance find
Description: ceramic vessel and metal neck ring
Chronology: Ripdorf phase
Collections:
Archives:
Literature: Kunkel 1931, no. 497; Eggers & Stary 2001:48; Rogalski 2010:431.

20. Kruszyna (Krussen), Słupsk district, Pomerania province

Type: unattached find in aquatic environment
Investigations: chance find
Description: neck ring K. I/II
Chronology: Jastorf-Ripdorf phase
Collections:
Archives:
Literature: Eggers & Stary 2001:72, Taf. 221:4.

21. Kunowo 5 (Kunow), Stargard Szczeciński district, West Pomerania province
Type: cemetery
Investigations: excavations in 1968-1969, R. Wołągiewicz
Description: cemetery preserved in fragments only. There were found 56 cremation graves containing ceramic vessels and metal dress elements as well as 15 hearths.
Chronology: Jastorf-Ripdorf phase
Collections: MNSz
Archives: MNSz
Literature: Łaszkiewicz 1971:17-96

22. Lubień Dolny (Niederhagen), Gryfice district, West Pomerania province
Type: unattached
Investigations: chance find
Description: ceramic vessels and metal dress elements
Chronology: Ripdorf phase
Collections:
Archives: MNSz, catalogue of H. J. Eggers
Literature: Eggers & Stary 2001:51, Taf. 156:8-10; Rogalski 2010:431-432, 596.

23. Lubiszewo 1 (Lübsow), Gryfice district, West Pomerania province
Type: cemetery
Investigations: 1939, H.J. Eggers; 1968-1970, R. Wołągiewicz
Description: a completely explored cemetery, consisting of 149 graves (147 cremation and 2 inhumation ones), including 141 Jastorf culture cremation graves and 6 cremation and 2 inhumation graves of the Gustow group.
Chronology: (a) Jastorf culture: Jastorf-Ripdorf phase, (b) Gustow group: decline of phase A3 MOPR – phase B2 WOR
Collections: MNSz
Archives: MNSz
Literature: Wołągiewicz 1970:103-114; Wołągiewicz 1997; Rogalski 2010:364-372

24. Lubuczewo (Lübzow), Lębork district, Pomerania province
Type: in aquatic environment (?)
Investigations: chance find
Description: necklace fragment
Chronology: Jastorf phase
Collections:
Archives:
Literature: Eggers & Stary 2001:72, Taf. 221:5

25. Łobżany (Labes Tivoli), Łobez district, West Pomerania province
Type: settlement
Investigations: A. Porzeziński (MNSz)
Description: several pits containing ceramic vessels discovered on a multicultural site.
Chronology: Jastorf phase
Collections: MNSz
Archives: MNSz
Literature: Wołągiewicz 1989:316-319, Fig. 8-9.

26. Marianowo (Marienfliesen), Stargard Szczeciński, West Pomerania province
Type: cemetery
Investigations: 1936, H.J. Eggers
Description: almost completely explored cemetery. It consisted of 48 urn graves with few pit ones, mostly stone-lined. Grave goods included ceramic vessels and metal dress elements.
Chronology: Jastorf-Ripdorf phase
Collections:
Archives: MNSz, catalogue of H. J. Eggers
Literature: Eggers & Stary 2001:47, Taf. 142: 4–17; Wołągiewicz 1989:312-313, Fig. 3-4; B. Rogalski 2010, 596.

27. Marszewo (Marsdorf), Goleniów district, West Pomerania province
Type: unattached
Investigations: chance find
Description: bronze fibula
Chronology:
Collections:
Archives: MNSz, catalogue of H. J. Eggers
Literature: Eggers & Stary 2001:48, Taf.146:9; B. Rogalski 2010:596

28. Mosty (Speck), Goleniów district, West Pomerania province
Type: unattached
Investigations: chance find
Description: pottery
Chronology: Ripdorf phase
Collections:
Archives: MNSz, catalogue of H. J. Eggers
Literature: Eggers & Stary 2001:48, Taf. 147:4; Rogalski 2010:433, 596.

29. Obryta (Gross Schönfeld), Pyrzyce district, West Pomerania province
Type: unattached
Investigations: chance find
Description: ceramic vessel
Chronology: Ripdorf phase
Collections:
Archives: MNSz, catalogue of H. J. Eggers
Literature: Eggers & Stary 2001:39; Rogalski 2010:434, 596.

30. Ognica (Stolzenhagen), Stargard Szczeciński district, West Pomerania province
Type: cemetery
Investigations: chance find
Description: cemetery preserved in fragments. There were found about four cremation graves and metal dress elements.
Chronology: Ripdorf phase
Collections:
Archives: MNSz, catalogue of H. J. Eggers
Literature: Eggers & Stary 2001:85, Taf. 144:3-8; Rogalski 2010:382.

31. Piekło (Pieckel), Sztum district, Pomerania province
Type: unattached
Investigations: chance find
Description: necklace in the form of a crown neck ring, K. I/II
Chronology: Ripdorf phase
Collections:
Archives:
Literature: Maciałowicz 2011:91-92, Fig. 8.

32. Pręgowo Dolne, Gdańsk district, Pomerania province
Type: unattached
Investigations: chance find
Description: Zachow-type fibula
Chronology: Jastorf phase
Collections: Muzeum Archeologiczne, Gdańsk
Archives: Muzeum Archeologiczne, Gdańsk
Literature: Prochowicz 2011:237-239, Fig. 1.

33. Redło (Pflugrade), Świdwin district, West Pomerania province
Type: unattached
Investigations: chance find
Description: metal dress elements
Chronology: Ripdorf phase
Collections:
Archives: MNSz, catalogue of H. J. Eggers
Literature: Eggers & Stary 2001:48, Taf. 147:1-3; Rogalski 2010:436.

34. Resko (Regenwalde), Gryfice district, West Pomerania province
Type: cemetery
Investigations: chance find
Description: urn grave and metal dress elements
Chronology: Jastorf-Ripdorf phase
Collections:
Archives MNSz, catalogue of H. J. Eggers
Literature: Eggers & Stary 2001:51, Taf. 157:7-8.

35. Rumia 1, Wejherowo district, Pomerania province
Type: cremation grave
Investigations: in the 1950s and 1960s, a team of archaeologists from Muzeum Archeologiczne, Gdańsk
Description: explored in fragments only, an Oksywie culture cemetery consisted of 343 graves and yielded a Jastorf culture urn grave (grave no. 46)
Chronology: a) Oksywie culture cemetery: phase A1 MOPR – B1 WOR
b) Jastorf culture grave: Ripdorf phase
Collections: MAG
Archives: MAG
Literature: Pietrzak 1987:30, tabl. LXVI:46; Maciałowicz 2011:85, Fig. 4.

36. Rusowo (Rützow), Kołobrzeg district, West Pomerania province
Type: unattached in aquatic environment
Investigations: chance find
Description: crown neck ring, type I/II according to Kostrzewski
Chronology: Ripdorf phase
Collections:
Archives: MNSz, catalogue of H. J. Eggers
Literature: Bohnsack 1938:36; Eggers & Stary 2001:55, Taf. 165:3.

37. Stare Czarnowo (Neumarkt), Gryfino district, West Pomerania province
Type: cemetery
Investigations: chance find
Description: metal dress elements
Chronology: Ripdorf phase
Literature: Rogalski 2010:438-439.

38. Stępnica (Stepenitz), Goleniów district, West Pomerania province
Type: unattached
Investigations: chance find
Description: ceramic vessel
Chronology: Ripdorf phase
Collections:
Archives: MNSz, Archives of H. J. Eggers
Literature: Eggers & Stary 2001:49, Taf. 150: 17; Rogalski 2010:439, 596.

39. Szczecin–Pogodno, Szczecin district, West Pomerania province
Type: cemetery
Investigations: chance find
Description: cemetery preserved in fragments only. There were found about ten urn and pit graves as well as ceramic vessels and metal dress elements.
Chronology: Jastorf–Ripdorf phase
Collections: MNSz
Archives: MNSz, catalogue of H. J. Eggers
Literature: Wołągiewicz 1983:506-509, Fig. 203, Fig. 204: 1-3.

40. Szczecin–Niemierzyn, Szczecin district, West Pomerania province
Type: settlement
Investigations: chance find, the 1930s, rescue investigations, H. J. Eggers.
Description: settlement explored in fragments only, layout

unknown. There were found 6 pits, 1 hearth, four features used for smelting iron and many ceramic vessels.
Chronology: Jastorf–Ripdorf phase
Collections: MNSz
Archives: MNSz
Literature: Wołągiewicz 1983:509-514, Fig. 204: 4-7, Fig. 205

41. Szczecinek (Neustettin), Szczecinek district, West Pomerania province
Type: unattached
Investigations: chance finds
Description: ceramic vessels and metal dress ornaments
Chronology: Ripdorf phase
Collections:
Archives: MNSz, catalogue of H. J. Eggers
Literature: Eggers & Stary 2001:66; Rogalski 2010:440.

42. Tarnówko (Lüttgenhagen), Goleniów district, West Pomerania province
Type: unattached
Investigations: chance find
Description: necklace with stamp-like ends
Chronology: Ripdorf phase
Collections:
Archives: MNSz, catalogue of H. J. Eggers
Literature: Eggers & Stary 2001:48, Taf. 146: 8; Rogalski 2010: 440.

43. Troszyn 10, Kamień Pomorski district, West Pomerania province
Type: cemetery
Investigations: 2005-2006, Henryk Machajewski (IA UG)
Description: an almost completely explored cemetery yielded 158 Jastorf culture pit and urn graves and a cremation grave from phase A3 and an inhumation grave from phase B2a of the Gustow group.
Chronology: a) Jastorf culture graves: Jastorf–Ripdorf
b) Gustow group graves: decline of A3 MOPR phase –B2a WOR phase.
Collections: MNSz
Archives: MNSz
Literature: Machajewski 2006:83-105; Pawlak, (in print).

44. Sąpolnica (Zampelhagen), Nowograd district, West Pomerania province
Type: unattached
Investigations: chance find
Description: fragment of a necklace with stamp-like ends
Chronology: Ripdorf phase
Collections:
Archives: MNSz, Archives of H. J. Eggers
Literature: Eggers & Stary 2001:48, Taf. 148: 5.

45. Stargard Szczeciński 1 (Stargard), Stargard Szczeciński district, West Pomerania province
Type: cemetery
Investigations: chance find
Description: there were found about 8 pit and urn graves, some contained metal dress ornaments
Chronology: Ripdorf phase
Collections:
Archives: MNSz, catalogue of H. J. Eggers
Literature: Eggers & Stary 2001:47, Taf. 143: 4-17; Rogalski 2010: 396.

46. Sulino (Goldbeck), Stargard Szczecinski district, West Pomerania province
Type: cemetery
Investigations: chance find
Description: stone-lined urn grave
Chronology: Jastorf phase
Collections:
Archives: MNSz, catalogue of H. J. Eggers
Literature: Eggers & Stary 2001:42, Taf. 142: 1

47. Święte 22, Stargard Szczeciński district, West Pomerania province
Type: settlement
Investigations: 200; Alina Jaszewska, M.A. and associates (Pracownia Archeologiczno-Konserwatorska mgr A. Jaszewskiej)
Description: in the area of about 2 ha, there were found 354 features and 11,210 pottery shards associated with the Jastorf culture and Gustow group. A Jastorf culture settlement, occupying about 0.6 ha, is associated with 74 features, including dugouts, furnaces for lime burning, household pits, hearths, and postholes. Seen clearly in their layout, the division into economic and residential features is reflected in their location on two different small elevations.
Chronology: Jastorf culture: decline of the Jastorf phase –Seedorf phase
Collections: Muzeum in Świdnica, Zielona Góra district
Archives: Muzeum Archeologiczne Środkowego Nadodrza in Świdnica near Zielona Góra
Literature: Machajewski, Leciejewska, & Wolanin 2011:267-296.

48. Wąwelnica (Wamlitz), Police district, West Pomerania province
Type: cemetery
Investigations: chance find
Description: urn and pit graves containing pottery and metal dress elements
Chronology: Jastorf–Ripdorf phase
Collections: MNSz
Archives: MNSz
Literature: Wołągiewicz 1989:315, Fig. 5; Eggers & Stary 2001:37-38; Rogalski 2010:409, 596.

49. Wójcin (Waitendorf), Pyrzyce district, West Pomerania province
Type: cemetery
Investigations: chance find
Description: cemetery explored in fragments only; it yielded 21 urn and pit graves, containing pottery and metal dress elements

Chronology: Ripdorf phase
Collections:
Archives: MNSz, catalogue of H. J. Eggers
Literature: Dorka 1939:77, 79, 91, 203, Taf. 48; Eggers & Stary 2001:41, Taf. 134: 6-9; B. Rogalski 2010:410, 596.

50. Wygoda 6, Białogard district, West Pomerania province
Type: cremation grave
Investigations: 1980-1981, Henryk Machajewski (IP UAM)
Description: on a fully preserved Oksywie culture cemetery, containing 150 graves, a grave with Jastorf culture pottery was found (grave no. 102)
Chronology: a) Oksywie culture cemetery: A2 MOPR phase – A3/B1 MOPR/WOR phase
                b) grave with Jastorf culture pottery: Seedorf phase
Collections: Muzeum Okręgowe, Koszalin
Archives: Muzeum Okręgowe, Koszalin
Literature: Machajewski 2001.

51. Żeńsko (Schönfeld), Choszczno district, West Pomerania province
Type: unattached
Investigations: chance find
Description: necklace with butt-shaped ends
Chronology: Ripdorf phase
Collections:
Archives:
Literature: Kostrzewski 1919b: 23; Rogalski 2010: 445.

Wielkopolska

52. Biała 1 (Behle), Czarnków-Trzcianka district,. Wielkopolska province
Type: cemetery
Investigations: described for the first time in the chronicle by Fr Jan Ignacy Bocheński (2nd half of the 18th c.); first investigations in 1891 by Specht, Reichert, Schmidt, Kugler, Kühn, Schroeder & Heinrich; field survey in the 1920s by Hessler & Schulc; Excavations: 1965, Łopata; 1976, 1977, 1981, Strzyżewski; 1999-2001, Machajewski (IP UAM)
Description: 70 ares, 18 barrows (14 dug-up ones), a neck ring with thick, cylinder shaped ends, winged pins, fibula with a step-like bow, fibulae K.: A, B, C, one- two- and three-piece belt buckles, hinged belt buckles
Chronology: Ripdorf–Seedorf phase
Collections:
Archives: IP UAM, Archives of Jasnosz
Literature: Szpecht 1892; Kostrzewski 1919a:33; 1919b, 257; Machajewski 2002; Michałowski 2006:185-189; Niedźwiecki 2005:41-43; Petersen 1929:13; Strzyżewski & Żurawski 1979

53. Boruszyn (Boruszin), Czarnków-Trzcianka district, Wielkopolska province
Type: cemetery
Investigations: chance find in 1861
Description: K. I fibula, pottery shards

Chronology: Ripdorf phase
Collections: MfV Berlin
Archives: IP UAM, Archives of Jasnosz
Literature: Sadowski 1877:49; Schwartz 1879,:2; Kostrzewski 1919a,:24, Abb. 10; 1923, 154, Fig. 527; Eggers 1950:150, no. 2004

54. Borzejewo 22, Środa Wlkp. district, Wielkopolska province
Type: settlement
Investigations: rescue excavations preceding the construction of motorway A2, Wierzbicki (IP UAM)
Description: 103,6 ares; 6 features, 284 pottery shards
Chronology: Ripdorf phase
Collections: Centrum Archeologiczne Fundacji UAM in Poznań
Archives:
Literature: Makiewicz 2004; Michałowski 2010:173

55. Broniewice 1, Inowrocław district, Kujawy-Pomerania province
Type: settlement
Investigations: discovered during a field survey by Kostrzewski in 1931; rescue excavations preceding the construction of a water reservoir on Lake Pakość in 1970 and 1971.
Description: 19.5 ares, pottery shards, clay spoon
Chronology: Ripdorf phase
Collections:
Archives:
Literature: Krauze 1973, Tab. XXIX.

56. Bukówiec (Bukowice), Leszno district, Wielkopolska province
Type:
Investigations:
Description: belt buckle
Chronology: Jastorf(?)–Ripdorf phase (?)
Collections: MfV Berlin
Archives:
Literature: Kostrzewski 1925:53; Wołągiewicz 1979:67

57. Czarnków (Czarnikau) – villa Ulmenstein, Czarnków-Trzcianka district, Wielkopolska province
Type: unattached
Investigations: during construction work in 1912-1913
Description: vase-shaped vessel
Chronology: Ripdorf phase
Collections:
Archives: IP UAM, Archives of Jasnosz
Literature: Michałowski 2006:190

58. Czarnków (Czarnikau) – surroundings, Czarnków-Trzcianka district, Wielkopolska province
Type: unattached
Investigations: donated to the Kaiser-Friedrich-Museum in Poznań by the Water Construction Inspectorate in Czarnków in 1909
Description: three-partite vessel

Chronology: Jastorf c-Ripdorf phase (?)
Collections: MAP
Archives: IP UAM, Archives of Jasnosz
Literature: Blume 1909:304, Abb. 8; von Richthofen 1924: 315, Unm. 7; Petersen 1929: 13; Kostrzewski 1923:143; Fig. 494; Michałowski 2006:190, 191.

59. Ćmachowo, Szamotuły district, Wielkopolska province
Type: cemetery(?)
Investigations: 19th-century chance find while excavating a ditch
Description: single cremation grave, fragments of crown neck ring, urn
Chronology: Ripdorf phase
Collections: MAP Poznań
Archives:
Literature: Demetrykiewicz 1900:76-78, Fig. 3; Kohn, Melis 1879:260

60. Dobieszowice 2, Inowrocław district, Kujawy-Pomerania province
Type: settlement
Investigations: rescue excavations preceding the construction of a water reservoir on Lake Pakość in 1970 and 1971; Makiewicz
Description: clay spoon
Chronology: Ripdorf phase
Collections:
Archives:
Literature: Makiewicz 1975, Tabl. LXVI:4

61. Dopiewo 26, 29, 70, Poznań district, Wielkopolska province
Type: settlement
Investigations: excavations preceding the construction of motorway A2
Description: features and pottery shards
Chronology: Ripdorf phase
Collections:
Archives:
Literature: oral communication from Henryk Machajewski

62. Drawsko 1, Czarnków-Trzcianka district, Wielkopolska province
Type: cemetery
Investigations: rescue investigations in 2003, Dernoga (PSOZ), Gajda (Muzeum Ziemi Czarnkowskiej)
Description: 75 sq. m; pit grave[68], fibula K. B, razor, small knife
Chronology: Ripdorf phase
Collections: Muzeum Ziemi Czarnkowskiej
Archives:
Literature: Dernoga & Gajda 2004; Michałowski 2006:190, 191

63. Dzierznica 35, Środa Wlkp. district, Wielkopolska province
Type: settlement

Investigations: discovered in 1985 while making the Archaeological Record of Poland; Investigations: excavations preceding the construction of motorway A2, in 1997, Żychliński (ONK PKZ Poznań) and Sobucki (IP UAM), in 1998-2002, Sobucki
Description: 579 ares; 21 pottery shards, 5 clay spoons and a clay spindle bob[69]
Chronology: Ripdorf-Seedorf phase(?)
Collections: Centrum Archeologiczne Fundacji UAM in Poznań
Archives:
Literature: Sobucki & Woźniak 2004: 207-209; ,Michałowski 2010:173, 174.

64. Grabonóg, Gostyń district, Wielkopolska province
Type:
Investigations:
Description: paddle-shaped pin
Chronology: Ripdorf phase
Collections:
Archives:
Literature: Kostrzewski 1923:137, Fig. 467

65. Grodzieszcze 12, Świebodzin district, Lubuskie province
Type: cemetery
Investigations: rescue excavations preceding the construction of expressway S3, Przybytek (Archeologiczna Pracownia Badawcza „THOR", Niechanowo)
Description: cremation grave
Chronology: Ripdorf phase
Collections: Archeologiczna Pracownia Badawcza „THOR", Niechanowo
Archives:
Literature: Michałowski & Żychliński 2012, Żychliński & Przybytek 2008

66. Grzępy 5, Czarnków-Trzcianka district, Wielkopolska province
Type: cemetery
Investigations: rescue investigations in 1943, Schlicht
Description: destroyed graves; several dozen pottery shards, 2 band-like buckles, fibula K. B
Chronology: Ripdorf phase
Collections: MAP
Archives: IP UAM, Archives of Jasnosz
Literature: Lipińska 1959:247; Michałowski 2006:189

7. Jabłonowo (Jabłkowo), Piła district, Wielkopolska province
Type: cemetery
Investigations: investigated in the early 20th c.
Description: band earring
Chronology: Jastorf b phase
Collections:
Archives:

---

[68] On a cemetery of the Lusatian culture (47graves).

[69] It is possible that some materials preliminarily identified as belonging to the Lusatian or Przeworsk cultures are related to the Jastorf culture settlement (oral communication from Artur Sobucki).

Literature: Wołągiewicz 1979b: 67 ; Malinowski 1981:7; Michałowski 2006:189.

68. Jaromierz 19, Wolsztyn district, Wielkopolska province
Type: settlement
Investigations: rescue excavations preceding the construction of a gas pipeline from Kościan to Zielona Góra
Description: 8 ares, 5 features, 202 pottery shards
Chronology: Jastorf c/Ripdorf phase
Collections: Archeologiczna Pracownia Badawcza „THOR" Niechanowo
Archives:
Literature: Michałowski 2010:174-175; Żychliński 2008

69. Jutrosin, Rawicz district, Wielkopolska province
Type: unattached
Investigations: chance find from 1923, Sievert
Description: tongue buckle; also: bronze pin (with a swan's neck?), iron pin fragment, iron necklace fragment (?), 2 rings (iron and bronze one)
Chronology: Jastorf phase (?)
Collections:
Archives: IP UAM, Archives of Jasnosz
Literature:

70. Komorniki 39, Poznań district, Wielkopolska province
Type: settlement
Investigations: excavations preceding the construction of motorway A2 in 2000-2002, Kabaciński (IAiE PAN, Poznań Branch)
Description: 191.5 ares, 3 features
Chronology: Ripdorf phase
Collections: IAiE PAN, Poznań Branch
Archives:
Literature: Chłodnicki & Pietrzak 2004; Michałowski 2010: 175.

71. Koninko, Poznań district, Wielkopolska province
Type: cemetery
Investigations: graves ploughed up in a field, official investigations on 18 March 1911, Großmann
Description: two stone-lined graves
Chronology: Jastorf (?)-Ripdorf(?) phase
Collections: MAP
Archives:
Literature: Blume 1911:341; Kostrzewski 1923:145, Fig. 491

72. Kuźnica Żelichowska 1(?) (Selchowhammer), Czarnków-Trzcianka district, Wielkopolska province
Type: cemetery
Investigations: first investigations in 1893, Herder; field survey in 1910, Blume; field survey, 1995
Description: urn and pit graves; fibula K. B, step-like bow fibula, belt buckles, pottery
Chronology: Ripdorf phase
Collections: MAP
Archives: Biblioteka Publiczna in Zielona Góra, Archives of Kostrzewski

Literature: Blume 1915:163, no. 64, Abb. 21, 22; Gałęzowska 1996; Michałowski 2006:190-192

73. Łuszczewo, Konin district, Wielkopolska province
Type: unattached find
Investigations: chance find, in peat
Description: Holstein pin
Chronology: Ripdorf phase
Collections:
Archives:
Literature: Erzepki 1890; Wołągiewicz 1979b:68

74. Milczek, Chodzież district, Wielkopolska province
Type:
Investigations:
Description: crown neck ring
Chronology: Ripdorf phase
Collections:
Archives:
Literature: Kostrzewski 1919a:75, Abb. 57; 1923, Fig. 496a-b

75. Młodzikowo 21, Środa Wlkp. district, Wielkopolska province
Type: settlement
Investigations: discovered in 1984 during AZP investigations, excavations in 1988, 1990, Świerkowska-Barańska (MAP); in 1989, drilling and probing, Brzostowicz (MAP)
Description: 4.5 ares; 2 settlement features (56, 60), containing "pottery displaying the traits of the Pomerania-Cloche culture"*, and shards "resembling in form specimens typical of the early phases of the Przeworsk culture"*; 2 clay spoons
Chronology: Ripdorf phase
Collections: MAP
Archives:
Literature: *Świerkowska-Barańska 1992, Michałowski, forthcoming

76. Modliszewo 10, Gniezno district, Wielkopolska province
Type: settlement
Investigations: rescue excavations preceding the construction of the Yamal-Germany gas pipeline in 1995, Sobucki (IP UAM)
Description: 33 vessel fragments, 2 clay spoons
Chronology: Jastorf c/Ripdorf phase
Collections: Muzeum Archeologii Gazociągu Tranzytowego, Szamotuły
Archives:
Literature: Sobucki & Woźniak 2004: 207-209; Michałowski 2010:175.

77. Myszki, Gniezno district, Wielkopolska province
Type: cemetery
Investigations:
Description: cist grave (?)
Chronology: Jastorf c(?)-Ripdorf phase

Collections:
Archives:
Literature: Kostrzewski 1923, Fig. 489; 1925:53, Fig. 23; Petersen 1940, Abb. 200

78. Nowa Wieś 1, 12, Międzyrzecz district, Lubuskie province
Type: settlement; sacrificial place (?)
Investigations: rescue excavations preceding the construction of the Yamal-Germany gas pipeline in 1995. Site 1, Gołub & Mazurek; site 12, Marcinkiewicz; in 1996, Wojtaszek & Nawrocka-Mazurek
Description: 9 ares, 36 settlement features, a pit containing a complete skeleton of a 25-35-year-old man with his hands cut off and placed above his head, vessel fragments[70], 14 *Feuerböcken* figurines
Chronology: Ripdorf-Seedorf phase (?)
Collections: Muzeum Archeologii Gazociągu Tranzytowego, Szamotuły
Archives:
Literature: Dzieduszycki, Makiewicz & Sobucki 1998; Michałowski 2010:175-178; Michałowski & Teska 2012.

79. Nowe Miasto nad Wartą 1, Środa Wielkopolska district, Wielkopolska province
Type: cemetery
Investigations: 1983, Muzeum Regionalne in Jarocin
Description: 3 features[71] (a grave and 2 presumed graves), fibula with two globes on the bow, pottery
Chronology: Ripdorf phase
Collections:
Archives:
Literature: Machajewski & Walkiewicz 1993

80. Obórka 2, Gniezno district, Wielkopolska province
Type: settlement
Investigations: rescue excavations preceding the construction of the Yamal-Germany gas pipeline in 1995, Woźniak (Fundacja UAM)
Description: 55.9 ares, dugout (feature 92), 240 shards[72], spoon
Chronology: Ripdorf phase
Collections: Muzeum Archeologii Gazociągu Tranzytowego, Szamotuły
Archives:
Literature: Sobucki & Woźniak 2004: 199 – 207; Michałowski 2010:178, 179.

81. Otorowo 66, Szamotuły district, Wielkopolska province
Type: settlement
Investigations: rescue excavations preceding the construction of the Yamal-Germany gas pipeline in 1995-1996, Krzyszowski (ONK PKZ, in Poznań)
Description: 5 ares, 13 settlement features, 2,084 vessel fragments
Chronology: Ripdorf phase
Collections: Muzeum Archeologii Gazociągu Tranzytowego, Szamotuły
Archives:
Literature: Żychliński 2004; Michałowski 2010:179.

82. Piła-Lisikierz (Berghorst bei Schneidemühl), Piła district, Wielkopolska province
Type: settlement
Investigations: chance find made in 1936 while building a road from Piły to the border crossing with Poland.
Description: 55 postholes and hearths – a long post house (?)
Chronology: Pre-Roman period
Collections:
Archives:
Literature: Makiewicz 2000; Michałowski 2006:195; 2010:180

83. Pławce 22, Środa Wlkp. district, Wielkopolska province
Type: settlement
Investigations: rescue excavations preceding the construction of motorway A2, Sawicki (MPPP Gniezno)
Description: 107.25 ares, 11 settlement features, 804 vessel fragments
Chronology: Ripdorf phase
Collections: Centrum Archeologiczne Fundacji UAM
Archives:
Literature: Makiewicz 2004; Michałowski 2010:179, 180

84. Podlesie, Oborniki district, Wielkopolska province
Type:
Investigations:
Description:
Chronology:
Collections:
Archives:
Literature: Machajewski 1986:297

85. Poznań-Nowe Miasto 226, Poznań district, Wielkopolska province
Type: settlement
Investigations: discovered in 1987 during AZP investigations, rescue excavations preceding the construction of motorway A2 in 1998-1999, Łastowiecki (MPP on Lednica)
Description: about 0.4 ha, over 108 settlement features, 7,112 shards, 2 clay spoons
Chronology: Ripdorf–Seedorf phase; A2-A3 phase, Przework culture settlement
Collections: Fundacja „Patrimonium" Poznań
Archives:
Literature: Machajewski & Pietrzak 2008b; Michałowski 2010:181

---

[70] Defined by the authors of the publication as belonging to the Przeworsk culture, despite their earlier attribution to the Jastorf culture.
[71] The graves lie 150 m SW of a cemetery of the Lusatian culture from the IV-V period of the Bronze Age.
[72] Fragments of Jastorf culture vessels were found also in features containing Pomerania culture materials (feature 98) and Przeworsk culture ones (features 38 and 110).

86. Poznań-Nowe Miasto 278, Poznań district, Wielkopolska province
Type: settlement
Investigations: discovered in 1987 during AZP investigations, rescue excavations preceding the construction of motorway A2 in 1998-1999, Pietrzak (Fundacja „Patrimonium")
Description: about 3 ha, 38 settlement features, 5,513 shards
Chronology: Ripdorf–Seedorf phase
Collections: Fundacja „Patrimonium", Poznań
Archives:
Literature: Machajewski & Pietrzak 2008a; Michałowski 2010:181

87. Poznań-Nowe Miasto 284, Poznań district, Wielkopolska province
Type: settlement, cemetery
Investigations: discovered in 1987 during AZP investigations, rescue excavations preceding the construction of motorway A2 in 1998-1999, Krzyszowski (MAP)
Description: 206 settlement features, 5 cremation graves
Chronology: Ripdorf–Seedorf phase
Collections: Fundacja „Patrimonium", Poznań
Archives:
Literature: Kasprowicz 2008; Michałowski 2010:181, 182

88. Rosko 4, Czarnków-Trzcianka district, Wielkopolska province
Type: settlement
Investigations: chance find made in the early 20th c., partially destroyed while regulating the Noteć River; amateur work by a teacher named Nowak from Rosko; excavations in 2001-2004, Machajewski (IP UAM)
Description: 5.65 ares, 5 settlement features, shards
Chronology: Ripdorf phase
Collections:
Archives:
Literature: Niedźwiecki 2005:44-46; Michałowski 2006:192, 193; 2010:182

89. Rosko 5, Czarnków-Trzcianka district, Wielkopolska province
Type: settlement
Investigations: known since the early 20th c., owing to the discovery of a hoard of bronze objects on it. Excavations in 2004, Machajewski (IP UAM)
Description: 11.05 ares, 12 shards
Chronology: Ripdorf phase
Collections:
Archives:
Literature: Niedźwiecki 2005:46; Michałowski 2006:193; 2010:182

90. Rosko 7, Czarnków-Trzcianka district, Wielkopolska province
Type: cemetery
Investigations: chance find made in 1897; excavations in 2002, Machajewski (IP UAM)
Description: 5.65 ares, 5 settlement features, shards
Chronology: Ripdorf phase
Collections:
Archives:
Literature: Machajewski, Maciejewski & Niedźwiecki 2004; Michałowski 2006:192

91. Sobiejuchy, Żnin district, Kujawy-Pomerania province
Type: unattached find
Investigations: chance find
Description: Holstein pin
Chronology: Ripdorf phase
Collections:
Archives:
Literature: Erzepki 1890; Kostrzewski 1923, Fig. 498; Wołągiewicz 1979b:68

92. Sokołowice, Wolsztyn district, Wielkopolska province
Type: cemetery
Investigations: known since 1877; excavations in 1949, Dr L. J. Łuka
Description: cremation grave[73], razor, fibula K. B
Chronology: Ripdorf phase
Collections: MAP
Archives:
Literature: Łuka 1953

93. Sowinki 23B, Poznań district, Wielkopolska province
Type: settlement
Investigations: 1989-1990, rescue investigations preceding the construction of a water intake for the city of Poznań, Łaszkiewicz (PA-K PP PKZ)
Description: 61.10 ares[74]; bronze fibula with three globes on the bow
Chronology: Ripdorf phase
Collections:
Archives:
Literature: Makiewicz & Łaszkiewicz 2001

94. Staw, Słupca district, Wielkopolska province
Type: cemetery(?)
Investigations: chance find in the latter half of the 19th c.
Description: fragments of a crown neck ring, urn
Chronology: Ripdorf phase
Collections: MAP Poznań
Archives: IP UAM, Archives of Jasnosz
Literature: Demetrykiewicz 1900:75, 76; Kohn & Mehlis 1879:260; Schwarz 1879:10, Tab. Fig. 15; Undset 1882:101

95. Sulęcin, loco, Lubuskie province
Type: ?

---

[73] The other 83 graves were defined as related to the Pomerania culture; however, some of their grave goods include materials of the Jastorf provenance, typical of those Jastorf stages that did not yield to the La Tène influence. The material from the site calls for another verification!

[74] The site has been preliminarily defined as a settlement of the Pomerania and Przeworsk cultures. The material from the investigations has not been processed yet; a Jastorf culture settlement may be there as well.

Investigations: ?
Description: tongue buckle
Chronology: Jastorf phase
Collections:
Archives:
Literature: Machajewski 1986:298; Wołągiewicz 1979:68

96. Świerkówiec 1, 2, Mogilno district, Kujawy-Pomerania province
Type: cemetery
Investigations: site 2 – 1973; site. 1 – 1978-1979, Janikowski (Muzeum Okręgowe in Toruń)
Description: both sites are part of one extensive cemetery; altogether over 558 sq. m. were investigated, 17 graves, 9 hearths (?); with the Jastorf culture, 4 graves may be associated (nos. 1, 5, 9 & 13), fibulae K. A, B, C, H, zoomorphic belt buckle.
Chronology: a) Jastorf culture graves: Ripdorf phase
  b) Przeworsk culture graves: A_2-A_3 phase
Collections: MO Toruń
Archives:
Literature: Bokiniec 1999

97. Wapniarnia 129, Czarnków-Trzcianka district, Wielkopolska province
Type: settlement
Investigations: discovered in 1998, excavated in 1999, Machajewski (IP UAM)
Description: 6.5 ares, fragment of a hall used for residential and economic purposes(?), shards
Chronology: Ripdorf phase
Collections:
Archives:
Literature: Machajewski 2002:16, 17; 2003:309-312; Michałowski 2006:189; 2010:182, 183

98. Wierzenica, Poznań district, Wielkopolska province
Type: cemetery
Investigations: excavations in 1918, Kostrzewski
Description: 12 cremation graves with stone linings
Chronology: Jastorf(?) phase
Collections:
Archives:
Literature: Kostrzewski 1919-1920

99. Więckowice 20, Poznań district, Wielkopolska province
Type: settlement
Investigations: discovered during AZP investigations, excavations in 1998-1999, Brzostowicz (MAP) & Machajewski (IP UAM)
Description: 9.7 sq. m, household pit, shards
Chronology: Ripdorf–Seedorf phase(?)
Collections:
Archives:
Literature: Brzostowicz & Machajewski 2003; Michałowski 2010:183

100. Wilcza (Wiłcza), Jarocin district, Wielkopolska province
Type: unattached
Investigations:
Description: paddle-shaped pin
Chronology: Ripdorf phase
Collections:
Archives:
Literature: Wołągiewicz 1979b:68

101. Włoszakowice, Leszno district, Wielkopolska province
Type: unattached
Investigations:
Description: paddle-shaped pin
Chronology: Ripdorf phase
Collections:
Archives:
Literature: Kostrzewski 1923, Fig. 467; Wołągiewcz 1979b:68

102. Wojnowo 23, Poznań district, Wielkopolska province
Type: settlement, cemetery(?)
Investigations: rescue excavations preceding the construction of the Yamal-Germany gas pipeline in 1996, Kasprowicz (MAP)
Description: about 27 ares, 3 settlement features, 6 graves(?), 1,848 shards, clay spoon
Chronology: Ripdorf phase
Collections: Muzeum Archeologii Gazociągu Tranzytowego, Szamotuły
Archives:
Literature: Kasprowicz 2004; Michałowski 2010:183

103. Wszedzień I (Wszedzin), Mogilno district, Kujawy-Pomerania province
Type: unattached
Investigations: excavations in 1876 and 1881, Mathes
Description: about 1 ha, over a dozen cremation urn graves, fibulae with globes, fibula with a step-like bow, Bornholm-type fibula, fibulae K. A & B, horse-head clasp, pottery
Chronology: Ripdorf phase
Collections: MAP, Muzeum Okręgowe in Toruń
Archives: IP UAM, Archives of Jasnosz
Literature: Erzepki & Kostrzewski 1914:22, T. LX:4-10; Undset 1882:89, 90, 99, Tabl. XII:22-29, XIII:6

104. Wszedzień II (Wszedzin), Mogilno district, Kujawy-Pomerania province
Type: unattached
Investigations: excavations in 1882
Description: cremation graves, hinged buckle, tweezers, small knives, 2 awls, fibulae K. A, C; K; iron rings, shards
Chronology: Seedorf phase
Collections: MfV Berlin
Archives:
Literature: Kostrzewski 1919a:18, 51, 346, Fig. 3, 39; Beltz 1911:788

105. Wytomyśl, Nowy Tomyśl district, Wielkopolska province
Type: ?
Investigations: ?
Description: disc-head pin
Chronology: Jastorf–Ripdorf phase(?)
Collections: ?
Archives: ?
Literature: Machajewski 1986:298; Wołągiewicz 1979b:68

106. Wybranowo, Inowrocław district, Kujawy-Pomerania province
Type:
Investigations:
Description: crown neck ring
Chronology: Ripdorf phase
Collections:
Archives:
Literature: Kostrzewski 1923, Fig. 497

107. Żółwin 3, Międzyrzecz district, Lubuskie province
Type: settlement
Investigations: rescue investigations by Konserwator Zabytków Archeologicznych in Zielona Góra in 1962 and1963
Description: 3 ares, 20 settlement pits attributed to two settlements: of the Pomerania and Przeworsk cultures; Holstein pin
Chronology: Jastotf c-Ripdorf phase
Collections:
Archives:
Literature: Kres 1965a, 1965b, 1967; Wołągiewicz 1979b: 68; Michałowski 2010:183-184.

108. Żółwin 8, Międzyrzecz district,. Lubuskie province
Type: settlement
Investigations: rescue excavations preceding the construction of the Yamal-Germany gas pipeline in 1995, Kołomański (ONK PKZ Poznań)
Description: 20 ares, 1 settlement pit; 187 shards
Chronology: Pre-Roman period
Collections: Muzeum Archeologii Gazociągu Tranzytowego, Szamotuły
Archives:
Literature: Dzieduszycki 1998:410-412

Bibliography

Written sources

Gajusz Juliusz Cezar, Wojna galijska
Gajusz Juliusz Cezar, Wojna galijska, przełożył i opracował E. Konik, Wrocław-Warszawa-Kraków-
-Gdańsk 1978.
Liwiusz Tytus, Dzieje
Tytus Liwiusz, Dzieje Rzymu od założenia miasta (Ab urbe condita), księgi I – V, przełozył A. Kościółek, Wrocław – Warszawa – Kraków 1968,
Tytus Liwiusz, Dzieje Rzymu od założenia miasta (Ab urbe condita), księgi XLI – CXLII, przełożył M. Brożek, Wrocław 1969.
Plutrach
Żywoty sławnych mężów, przełożył M. Brożek, opracował T. Sinko, Wrocław-Warszawa, Kraków 1955.
Polibiusz, Dzieje
Polibiusz, Dzieje, t. I, przełożył S. Hammer, Wrocław 1957,
Polibiusz, Dzieje, t. II, przełożył S. Hammer, M. Brożek, Wrocław, Warszawa, Kraków 1962.
Tacyt, Germania
Tacyt, Dzieła, przeł. S. Hammer, Warszawa 2004, s. 599 – 619.

References

Abramowicz A.
1956 *Materiały z cmentarzyska w Zadowicach pow. Kalisz (Część I)*, Prace i Materiały Muzeum Archeologicznego i Etnograficznego w Łodzi, Seria Archeologiczna Nr 1, pp. 61 - 95.
Abramowicz A., Lepówna B.
1957 *Materiały z cmentarzyska w Zadowicach pow. Kalisz (Część II)*, Prace i Materiały Muzeum Archeologicznego i Etnograficznego w Łodzi, Seria Archeologiczna Nr 2, pp. 25 – 51.
Albrectsen E.
1954 *Fynske jernaldergrave I. Førromersk jernalder*, Københaven.
1973 *Fynske jernaldergrave V. Nye fund*. Odense.
Andrałojć M.
1986 *Pochówki psów u pradziejowych społeczeństw Europy Środkowej*, Inowrocław.
Andrzejowska M., Andrzejowski J.
1997 *Wyniki ratowniczych badań wykopaliskowych na stanowisku 6 w Starych Koczargach, gmina Stare Babice, województwo warszawskie*, Wiadomości Archeologiczne, t. LIII/2 (1993-1994), pp. 85 – 99.
Babeş M.
1973 *Germanische latènezeitliche Einwanderungen im Raum östlich der Karpaten (Zum heutigen Stand der Forschung über die Poieneşti – Lukaševka – Kulturgruppe)*, [In:] Actes du Congrès International des Sciences Préhistoriques et Protohistoriques 3, Belgrad, pp. 207-213.
1988 *Die Frühgermannen im östlichen Dakien in den letzten Jahrhunderten v. u.Z. Archäologische und historische Belege*, [In:] Frühe Völker in Mitteleuropa, ed. F. Horst, F. Schlette, Berlin, pp. 129 – 156.
1993 *Die Poieneşti – Lukaševka – Kultur. Ein Beitrag zur Kulturgeschichte im Raum östlich der Karpaten in den letzten Jahrhunderten vor Christi Geburt*, Saarbrücker Beiträge zur Altertumskunde, Bd. 30, Bonn.
Babeş M., Untaru I.
1969 *Der früheste latènezeitliche germanischische Funde aus der Moldau der Kronenhalsring von Davideni*, Dacia, 13, pp. 283-290.
Becker C.-J.
1951 *Førromersk jernalder I Danmark. Aktuelle problemer*, Finsk Fornminnesforenings Tidskraft LIII, pp. 29 – 50.
1961 *Førromersk jernalder I Syd – og Mitdtjylland*, Nationalmuseets Skrifter VI, København.
1965 *Ein früheisenzeitliches Dorf bei Grøntoft, Westjütland*, Acta Archaeologica, vol. XXXVI, København, pp. 209 - 222.
Bech J.-H.
1975 *Nordjyske fibler fra per. IIIa af førromersk jernalder – et bidrag til diskussionen vedrørende kulturforbindelserne i yngre førromersk jernalder*, Hikuin 2, pp. 75 – 88.
1987 *Lerkarskår i tusindvis. Om betydningen af oltidskeramik fra arkæologiske udgravningen*, [In:] Danmarks længste udgravning. Arkæologi på naturgassens vej 1979-86, København, pp. 94 – 100.
Bednarczyk J., Sujecka A.
2004 *Młodszy okres przedrzymski*, [In:] Od długiego domu najstarszych rolników do dworu staropolskiego. Wyniki badań archeologicznych na trasach gazociągu Mogilno – Włocławek i Mogilno – Wydartowo, ed. J. Bednarczyk, A. Kośko, Poznań, pp. 399 – 451.
Bednarek M.
1994 *Celtycki grób ciałopalny z czworobocznym obiektem rowkowym w Nowej Cerekwi, gm. Kietrz, woj. opolskie*, Śląskie Sprawozdania Archeologiczne, t. 35, pp. 495 – 506.
1996 *Die Latènekultur in Oberschlesien im Lichte der neuesten Forschungen*, [In:] Kontakte längs der Bernsteinstrasse (zwischen Caput Adriae und den

Ostseegebieten) in der Zeit um Christi Geburt, ed. Z. Woźniak, Kraków, pp. 267 – 272.
2009   *Nowa Cerekwia – celtyckie numizmatyczne El Dorado na Górnym Śląsku,* Wrocławskie Zapiski Numizmatyczne, nr 2/2009, pp. 6 – 13.

Behrends R.-H.
1968   *Schwissel. Ein Urnengräberfeld der vorrömiaschen Eisenzeit aus Holstein,* Neumünster.

Beltz R.
1911   *Die Latènefibeln,* Zeitschrift für Ethnologie 43, pp. 664 – 817.

Bernat W.
1955   *Cmentarzysko ciałopalne z okresu rzymskiego we wsi Drozdowo, powiat Płońsk,* Wiadomości Archeologiczne, t. XXII/2, pp. 212 – 214.

Bezzenberger A.
1904   *Analysen vorgeschichtlichen Bronzer Ostpreussens,* Königsberg.

Biborski M., Kaczanowski P.
2010   *Celtycki miecz z Mazowsza,* [In:] Terra Barbaria, red. A. Urbaniak, R. Prochowicz, I. Jakubczyk, M. Levada, J. Schuster, Warszawa – Łódź, pp. 155 – 165.

Biegier A.
2003   *Kugelfibeln. Eine typologiach-Chronologische Untersuchung zu den Varianten F, N und O von Beltz,* Bonn.

Bienia M., Żółkowski S.
1994   *Badania ratownicze na stanowisku z młodszego okresu przedrzymskiego w Dobryniu Małym stan. VII, gm. Zalesie, woj. Biała Podlaska,* [In:] Najważniejsze odkrycia archeologiczne w Polsce środkowo – wschodniej w 1993 roku, Biała Podlaska, pp. 70 – 79.

Binding U.
1993   *Studien zu den figürlichen Fibeln der Frühlatènezeit,* Universitätsforschungen zur prähistorischen Archäologie, 16, Bonn.

Birkhan H.
1997   *Kelten. Versuch einer Gesamtdarstellung ihrer Kultur,* Wien.

Blume E.
1909a *Vor – und frühgeschichtliche Altertümer aus dem Gebiet der Provinz Posen. Ausstellung im Kaiser Friedrich – Museum,* Posen.
1909b *Aus der Provinz Posen. Erwerbungen des Kaiser – Friedrich – Museums zu Posen vom Januar bis Juni 1909,* Mannus, Bd. I, pp. 303 – 305.
1911   *Kaiser – Friedrich – Museum in Posen. Aus dem Posener Lande,* Monatsblat für Heimatkunde, Bd. 6, H. 7, pp. 340 – 342.
1915   *Aus der Provinz Posen. Erwerbungen der Kaiser – Friedrich – Museums zu Posen im Jahre 1910,* Mannus, Bd. VII, pp. 147 – 168.

Bochnak T.
2004a *Rola kultury puchowskiej i grupy tynieckiej w kształtowaniu się modelu uzbrojenia kultury przeworskiej w fazie A3 młodszego okresu przedrzymskiego,* [In:] Okres lateński i rzymski w Karpatach polskich, ed. J. Gancarski, Krosno, pp. 263 – 287.
2004b *Zróżnicowanie typologiczne ostróg oraz bojowe zastosowanie konia w kulturze przeworskiej w młodszym okresie przedrzymskim,* Zeszyty Naukowe Uniwersytetu Rzeszowskiego, 1, pp. 9 – 61.
2005   *Uzbrojenie ludności kultury przeworskiej w młodszym okresie przedrzymskim,* Rzeszów.
2006   *Early Circular Umbones of the Przeworsk Culture. The Role of Tradition and Celtic Influences on the Diversity of Metal Parts of Shields at the Beginning of the Pre-Roman Period,* Analecta Archaeologica Ressoviensia, I, pp. 161-194.
2011   *Kierunki napływu celtyckich kotłów z żelaznym brzegiem jako odbicie oddziaływań latenizacyjnych,* (In:] Między kulturą pomorska a kulturą oksywską, ed. M. Fudziński, H. Paner, Gdańsk, pp. 57 – 77.

Bockius R.
1990   *Eine „pommersche" Fibel aus Ungarn ?,* Archäaologisches Korrespondenzblatt, 20/1, pp. 101 – 112.
1996   *Zu einigen Schildbeschlägen der jüngeren vorrömischen Eisenzeit aus Fundkomplexen der Przeworsk – Kultur,* [In:] Kontakte längs der Bernsteinstrasse (zwischen Caput Adriae und den Ostseegebieten) in der Zeit um Christi Geburt, ed. Z. Woźniak, Kraków, pp. 143 – 155.

Bohnsack D.
1938   *Die Burgunden in Ostdeutschland und Polen wahrend des letzten Jahrhunderts v. Chr. .* Quellenschriften zur ostdeutschen Vor – und Fruhgeschichte, Bd. 4, Leipzig.

Bokiniec E.
1999   *Cmentarzysko z młodszego okresu przedrzymskiego w Świerkówcu, gm. Mogilno,* [In:] COMHLAN. Studia z archeologii okresu przedrzymskiego i rzymskiego w Europie Środkowej dedykowane Teresie Dąbrowskiej w 65. rocznicę urodzin, ed. J. Andrzejowski, Warszawa, pp. 115-140.
2001   *Uwagi na temat powiązań kultury oksywskiej z kręgiem jastorfskim i Europa północną w świetle materiałów z cmentarzyska w Podwiesku, stanowisko 2, pow. Chełmno, woj. kujawsko – pomorskie,* Wiadomości Archeologiczne, t. LIV (1995 – 1998), pp. 37 – 48.
2005   *Podwiesk, Fundstelle 2. Ein Gräberfeld der Oksywie – Kultur im Kulmem Land,* Monumenta Archaeologica Barbaria XI, Warszawa – Toruń.
2008   *Kultura oksywska na ziemi chełmińskiej w świetle materiałów sepulkralnych,* Toruń.

Bokiniec E., Chudziak W., Cyrek K., Gackowski J.
2003   *Sprawozdanie z ratowniczych prac wykopaliskowych przeprowadzonych w 2000 roku w strefie planowanej budowy autostrady A-1 na odcinku województwa kujawsko – pomorskiego (b. woj. toruńskie),* [In:] Raport 2000, wstępne wyniki konserwatorskich badań archeologicznych w strefie budowy autostrad w Polsce za rok 2000,

Zeszyt OODA, Seria B: Materiały Archeologiczne, ed. Zb. Bukowski, M. Gierlach, Warszawa, pp. 29 – 59.

Bouzek J.
2005 *Celtic campaigns In southern Thrace and the Tylis Kingom. The Duchcov fibula in Bulgaria and the destruction of Pistiros in 279/8 B.C.,* [In:] Celts on the Margin. Studies in European Cultural Interaction 7th Century BC – 1st Century AD Dedicated to Zenon Woźniak, ed. H. Dobrzańska, V. Megaw, P. Poleska, Kraków, pp. 93 – 101.

Böhme – Schönberger A.
2002 *Neue Forschungen zu den Schwertscheiden mit opus interrasile Zierblechen,* [In:] Bewaffung der Germanen und ihrer Nachbarn in den letzten Jahrhunderten von hristi Geburt, ed. C. von Carnap Bornheim, J. Ilkjær, A. Kokowski, P. Łuczkiewicz, Lublin, pp. 199 – 209.

Brandt J.
2001 *Jastorf und Latène. Kultureller Austausch und seine Auswirkungen auf soziopolitische Entwiklungen in der vorrömischen Eisenzeit,* Internationale Archäologie, Bd. 66, Rahden/Westf.

Brzostowicz M., Machajewski H.
2003 *Wyniki badań archeologicznych na osadzie z młodszego okresu przedrzymskiego w Więckowicach, powiat Poznań, stanowisko 20,* Wielkopolskie Sprawozdania Archeologiczne, 6, pp. 300 – 307.

Březinová G.
2009 *Neskorolatenske osidleni Nitry,* [In:] Archeologia Barbarzyńców 2008: powiązania i kontakty w świecie barbarzyńców, ed. M. Karwowski, E. Droberjar, Rzeszów, s. 55 – 70.

Budinský P., Walhauser J.
2004 *Druhé keltiské pohřebiště z Radovesic v severozápadních Čechách,* Archeologický vyzkum v severnich Čechách, t. 31, Teplice.

Bujna J.
1982 *Spiegelung der Sozialstruktur auf latènezeitlichen Gräberfeldern im Karpatenbecken,* Pamiátky Archeologické, t. 71, pp. 312 – 431.
1993 *Malé Kosihy. Latènezeitliches Gräberfeld. Katalog,* Archaeologica Slovaca monographie, Nitra.
1994 *Mladšia doba železná – laténska na Slovensku (prehlad stavu bádania za posledné dve dasatročia),* Studia Historica Nitrensia, t. II, pp. 7 – 39.
2003 *Spony z keltských hrobov bez vyzbroje z územia Slovenska (Typovo-chronologické tredenie LTB – a C1 – spôn),* Slovenská archeólogia, t. LI/1, pp. 39 – 108.

Bukowski Zb.
1978 *Bemerkungen zum Charakter der sog. Skythischen Funde im Grenzgebiet von ČSSR, DDR und Polen,* Arbeits – und Forschungsberichte zur sächsischen Bodendenkmalpflege, Bd. 22 (1977), pp. 247 – 268.

Byrska – Fudali M., Przybyła M. M., Rudnicki M.
2009 *Celtic coins fund At site 2 in Modlniczka, dist. Cracow,* Sprawozdania Archeologiczne, t. 61, pp. 273 – 295.

Čebotarenko G. F., Ščerbakova T. A, Ščukin M. B.
1987 *Dve nachodzi latenskogo i rimskogo vremeni v Moldavii,* Sovetskaja Archeologia, nr 4, pp. 242 – 248.

Chłodnicki M., Pietrzak R.
2004 *Ratownicze badania archeologiczne na trasie autostrady A-2 w 2001 i 2002 roku realizowane przez Ekspedycję Archeostrada Muzeum Archeologicznego w Poznaniu i Poznańskiego Towarzystwa Prehistorycznego.* [In:] Raport 2001 – 2002. Wstępne wyniki konserwatorskich badań archeologicznych w strefie budowy autostrad w Polsce za lata 2001 – 2002, ed. Zb. Bukowski, M. Gierlach,Warszawa, pp. 165 – 200.

Chmielewski et al. (Chmielewski B. J., Okoński J., Suchorska – Rola M.)
2006 *Sprawozdanie z ratowniczych badań wykopaliskowych na stanowisku 2 w Zagórzu, Gm. Niepołomice w latach 2003 – 2004,* [In:] Raport 2003 – 2004. Wstępne wyniki konserwatorskich badań archeologicznych w strefiebudowy autostrad w Polsce za lata 2003 – 2004, ed. Zb. Bukowski, M. Gierlach, Warszawa, s. 497 – 612.

Ciesielski M.
1980 *Osada kultury przeworskiej w Gniewowie,* Poznań (unpublished dissertation).

Cofta – Broniewska A.
1979 *Grupa kruszańska kultury przeworskiej. Z badań nad rozwojem regionalizmu społeczeństw Kujaw,* Poznań

Cumberpatch C. G.
1993 *The circulation of Late La Tène slip decorated pottery in Slovakia, suthern Poland and Transdanubian Hangary,* Slovenská Archeológia, t. 41, pp. 59 – 81.

Czarnecka K.
2002 *Schwertscheiden mit dem Gittermuster in Mitteleuropa an der Zeitwende,* [In:] Bewaffung der Germanen und ihrer Nachbarn in den letzten Jahrhunderten vor Christi Geburt, ed. C. von Carnap Bornheim, J. Ilkjær, A. Kokowski, P. Łuczkiewicz, Lublin, pp. 89 – 100.

Czerska B.
1959 *Osada z okresu późnolateńskiego koło Nowej Cerekwi w powiecie Głubczyce,* Archeologia Śląska, t. III, pp. 25 – 68.
1963a *Wyniki badań późnolateńskiej osady kultury celtyckiej koło Nowej Cerekwi, pow. Głubczyce w latach 1958 – 1960,* Wiadomości Archeologiczne, t. XXIX/3, pp. 289 – 311.
1963b *Badania archeologiczne późnolateńskiej osady celtyckiej pod Nowa Cerekwią, pow. Głubczyce, w 1961 roku,* Sprawozdania Archeologiczne, t. XV, pp. 136 – 143.

1968 *Ceramika późnolateńskiej kultury przeworskiej z Mierzyc w powiecie Legnica*, Śląskie Sprawozdania Archeologiczne, t. XI, pp. 22 – 24.

1974 *Badania w Nowej Cerekwi w powiecie głubczyckim, w 1973 roku*, Śląskie Sprawozdania Archeologiczne, t. XVII, pp. 33 – 36.

1976 *Osada celtycka koło wsi Nowa Cerekwia w powiecie głubczyckim w świetle najnowszych badań*, Studia Archeologiczne, t. VII, pp. 95 – 137.

1983 *Osada celtycka z okresu późnolateńskiego w Łanach, gm. Cisek*, Studia Archeologiczne, t. XIII, pp. 57 – 93.

Czopek S.

1981 *Problem kultury zarubinieckiej na Lubelszczyźnie*, [In:] Problemy Studenckiego Ruchu Naukowego, nr 2/54, Warszawa, pp. 40 - 44.

1985 *Kultura pomorska a kultura zarubiniecka. Z badan nad schyłkową fazą kultury pomorskiej we wschodniej Lubelszczyźnie*, [In:] Memoire Archeologiques, ed. A. Kokowski, Lublin, pp. 93 – 107.

1986 *Die Keramik mit skytischen und skytisch-thrakischen Einflüssen aus der Fundstelle 8 in Przeworsk*, Acta Archaeologica Carpathica, t. 25, pp. 105 – 129.

1991a *Grupa czerniczyńska jako wynik latenizacji wschodniej Lubelszczyzny*, Archeologia Polski, t. 36, pp. 93 – 111.

1991b *Grupa czerniczyńska – prezentacja i analiza źródeł*, Prace i Materiały Zamojskie, t. 3, pp. 45 – 143.

1992a *Południowo – wschodnia strefa kultury pomorskiej*, Rzeszów.

1992b *Uwagi o chronologii względnej i periodyzacji materiałów z okresu halsztackiego i starszego okresu przedrzymskiego w świetle analizy ceramiki kultury pomorskiej*, [In:] Ziemie polskie we wczesnej epoce żelaza i ich powiązania z innymi terenami, ed. S. Czopek, Rzeszów, pp.81 - 89.

1993 *Die älteste Drehscheibenkeramik aus Südostpolen – Probleme der Kulturverhältnisse in jüngeren Hallstatt – und frühen Latènezeit*, Bericht derRömische – Germanischen Kommission, Bd. 74, pp. 487 - 502.

1999 *W kwestii tzw. grupy czerniczyńskiej*, [In:] Kultura przeworska, t. IV, ed. J. Gurba, A. Kokowski, Lublin, pp. 201 – 204.

2007 *Związki dorzecza Wisły z terenami lasostepu ukraińskiego w epoce brązu i wczesnej epoce żelaza*, [In:] Wspólnota dziedzictwa archeologicznego ziem Ukrainy i Polski (Łańcut 2005), Warszawa, pp. 213 – 225.

Čambal R. et. al. (Čambal R., Gregor M., Harmadynová K., Halásová E., Hlavatá – Hudáčkova N).

2009 *Dácka keramika z bratislavskéhooppida a Devína*, [In:] Archeologia Barbarzyńców 2008: powiązania i kontakty w świecie barbarzyńskim,ed. M. Karwowski, E. Droberjar, Rzeszów, pp. 77 – 99.

Čižmář M.

1970 *Relativi chronologie keltiských pohřebišt na Moravě*, Pamiátky Archeologické, t. 66, pp. 417 – 436.

1993 *Keltská okupace Moravy (doba laténska)*, [In:] Pravěké dějiny Moravy, red. V. Podborsky, Brno, pp. 380 – 423.

Čižmář M., Kolníkova E.

2006 *Němečice – obchodní a industriálni centrum doby laténske na Moravě*, Archeologické Rozhledy, t. 58, pp. 261 – 283.

Dąbrowska T.

1973 *Cmentarzysko kultury przeworskiej w Karczewu, pow. Węgrów*, Materiały Starożytne i Wczesnośredniowieczne, t. II, pp. 383 – 531.

1988 *Wczesne fazy kultury przeworskiej. Chronologia – zasięg – powiązania*, Warszawa.

1994 *Wpływy jastorfskie na kulturę przeworska w młodszym okresie przedrzymskim*, [In:] Kultura przeworska, t. I, ed. J. Gurba, A. Kokowski, Lublin,pp. 71 – 87.

1996 *Frühe Stufen der Przeworsk – Kultur. Bemerkungen zu den Kontaktem mit Südosteuropa*, [In:]Kontakte längs der Bernsteinstrasse (zwischen Caput Adriae und den Ostseegebieten) in der zeit um Christi Gebert, ed. Z. Woźniak, Kraków, pp. 127 – 142.

1997 *Kamieńczyk. Ein Gräberfeld der Przeworsk – Kultur in Ostmasowien*, Munumenta Archaeologica Barbarica III, Kraków – Warszawa.

2001 *Wschodnie tereny kultury przeworskiej w młodszym okresie przedrzymskim*, Wiadomości Archeologiczne, t. 54, pp. 25 – 36.

2004 *Materiały kultury zarubinieckiej z ziem polskich*, [In:] Wspólnota dziedzictwa kulturowego ziem Białorusi i Polski, ed. A. Kośko, Warszawa, pp. 209-226.

2005 *Bransolety z młodszego okresu przedrzymskiego w kulturach przeworskiej i oksywskiej*, [In:] Monumenta Studia Gothica, t. IV, Europa Barbaria, ed. A. Kokowski, pp. 79 – 90.

2008 *Młodszy okres przedrzymski na Mazowszu i zachodnim Podlasiu*, Materiały Starożytne i Wczesnośredniowieczne, t. VII, pp. 5 - 246.

Dąbrowska T. (Piętka – Dąbrowska T.), Liana T.

1962 *Sprawozdanie z badań ratowniczych przeprowadzonych w 1959 r. na stanowisku I w Werbkowicach – Kotorowie, pow. Hrubieszów*, Wiadomości Archeologiczne, t. XXVIII/2, pp. 142 – 173.

1963 *Sprawozdanie z prac wykopaliskowych w Werbkowicach – Kotorowie, pow. Hrubieszów*, Wiadomości Archeologiczne, t. XXIX/1, pp. 44 – 60.

Dąbrowska T., Woźniak Z.

2005 *Problem genezy kultury przeworskiej i oksywskiej*, [In:] Archeologia o początkach Słowian, ed. P. Kaczanowski, M. Parczewski, Kraków, pp. 87 – 101.

Dehn W., Stöllner T.
1996 *Fusspaukenfibel und Drahtfibel (Marzabottofibel). Beitrag zum kulturhistorischen Verständnis des 5. Jahrhundert in Mitteleuropa*, [In:] Europa celtica. Untersuchungen zur Halstatt – und Latènekultur, ed. T. Stöllner, Veröffebtlichungen des Vorgeschichtlichen Seminars Marburg, Marburg, Sonderband 10, pp. 1 – 54.

Dementrykiewicz W.
1900 *Korony bronzowe przedhistorycznezanlezione na obszarze ziem dawnej Polski*, Materiały Antropologiczno – Archeologiczne I Etnograficzne, t. IV, pp. 70 – 91.

Dernoga M., Gajda E.
2004 *Grób z młodszego okresu przedrzymskiego w Drawsku, gm. Drawsko, woj. wielkopolskie*, [In:] Kultura jastorfska na Nizinie Wielkopolsko – Kujawskiej, ed. H. Machajewski, Poznań, s. 259 – 263.

Dobesch G.
1982 *Die Kimber in den Ostalpen und die Schlacht bei Noria*, Mitteilungen der Österreichischen Arbeitsgmeinschaft fürUr – undFrühgeschichte 32, pp. 51 – 68.
1996 *Überlegungen zum Heerwesen und Sozialstruktur der Keltern*, [In:] Die Kelten in den Alpen und an der Donau, Archaeolinqua, t. I, ed. E. Jerem, Budapest – Wien, pp. 13 – 71.

Domański G.
1975 *Studia z dziejów środkowego Nadodrza w III – I w. p.n.e.*, Wrocław.
1981 *Grupa gubińska*, [In:] Prahistoria ziem polskich, t. V, ed. J. Wielowiejski, Wrocław-Watrszaw-Kraków-Gdańsk, pp. 191 - 196
1996 *Die Jastorf – Kultur in Polen*, [In:] Kontakte langs der Bernsteinstrasse (zwischen Caput Adriae und den Ostseegebieten) in der Zeit um Cristi Geburt, ed. Z. Woźniak, Kraków, pp. 293 – 299.
1999 *Szlak czarnomorski*, [In:] COMHLAN. Studia z archeologii okresu przedrzymskiego i rzymskiego w Europie Środkowej dedykowane Teresie Dąbrowskiej w 65. rocznicę urodzin, ed. J. Andrzejowski, Warszawa, pp. 179 – 188.

Domański G., Lodowski J.
1984 *Osada z okresu lateńskiego w Starym Zamku*, woj. Wrocław, Silesia Antiqua, t. XXVI, pp. 35 – 43.

Domaradzka S., Waluś A.
2011 *Izdebno Kościelne, st. I, woj. mazowieckie. Badania w latach 2008 – 2009*, Warszawa (in print)

Dorka G.
1939 *Urgeschichte des Weizackreises Pyritz*, Pyritz.

Drda P., Rybova J.
1995 *Les Celtes de Bohême*, Paris.

Dulęba P.
2006 *Importowane celtyckie miecze z odciskami stempli z terytorium kultury przeworskiej*, [In:] Nowe znaleziska importów rzymskich z ziem Polski I, Suplement, t. III, ed. A. Bursche, R. Ciołek, Warszawa, pp. 177 – 206.
2009 *Przemiany kulturowe w Małopolsce Zachodniej w okresie od III do I wieku przed Chr. Przyczynek do kontaktów między Celtami a Germanami*, [In:] Archeologia Barbarzyńców 2008: powiązania i kontakty w świecie barbarzyńskim, ed. M. Karwowski, E. Droberjar, Rzeszów, pp. 11 – 35.

Dymaczewski A.
1958 *Cmentarzysko w Żrenicy, pow. Środa*, Zeszyty Naukowe Uniwersytetu im. Adama Mickiewicza w Poznaniu, nr 15, Archeologia, Etnografia, zeszyt I, pp. 3 – 34.

Dzembas O.
1995 *Doslidžennja kel'tskoho poselennja Hališ – Lovačka bilja Mukačeva (1986-1989 r.)*, [In:] Problemy archeologii Schidnych Karpat, Užhorod, pp. 104 – 110.

Dzieduszycki W.
1998 *Żółwin, st.8, gmina Międzyrzecz (GAZ nr 66, AZP 51 – 15: 100*, [In:] Archeologiczne badania ratownicze wzdłuż trasy gazociągu tranzytowego. Tom 1, Ziemia Lubuska, ed. R. Mazurowski, Poznan, pp. 403 – 419.

Dzieduszycki W., Makiewicz T., Sobucki A.
1998 *Nowa Wieś, st. 1 i 12, gmina Bledzew, GAZ nr 43/43a, AZP 51 – 12: 7 i 55*, [In:] Archeologiczne badania ratownicze wzdłuż trasy gazociągu tranzytowego. Tom I. Ziemia Lubuska, ed. R. Mazurowski, Poznań, pp. 117 – 181.

Dzieńkowski T., Gołub I.
1999 *Wyniki badań w roku 1988 w Chełmie – Biełwinie*, Archeologia Polski Środkowowschodniej, t. IV, pp. 176 – 180.

Dzięgielewska M.
2006 *Osada grupy wyciąsko – złotnickiej oraz ze środkowego okresu lateńskiego i wczesnego okresu rzymskiego w Podłężu (stan. 17), pow. Wieliczka, w świetle badań w latach 2003 - 2004*, [In:] Raport 2003 – 2004. Wstępne wyniki konserwatorskich badań archeologicznych w strefie budowy autostrad w Polsce za lata 2003 – 2004, ed. Zb. Bukowski, M. Gierlach, Warszawa, pp. 638 – 672.

Dzięgielewski K.
2010 *Expansion of the Pomerania Culture In Poland during the Early Iron Age: Rearks on the Mechanizm and Possibile Causes*, [In:] Migration in Bronze and Early Iron Age Europe, ed. K. Dziegielewski, M.S. Przybyła, A. Gawlik, Prace Archeologiczne, Nr 63, Kraków, pp. 173 – 196.

Dzięgielewski K., Purowski T.
2011 *Uwagi o datowaniu i technikach wykonania celtyckich ozdób szklanych z osady w Podłężu koło Krakowa (stanowisko 17)*, Przegląd Archeologiczny, 59, pp. 77 – 135.

Eggers H. J.
1936 *Das Gräberfeld von Langenhagen, Kr. Saatzig*, Monatsblätter der Gesellschaft für pommersche Geschichte und Altertumskunde, 50, pp. 128 – 129.
1955 *Die Mittel – Latènezeit in Mittelpommern*, Baltische Studien, N.F., 43, pp.13 – 16.

1964 *Die Kunst der Germanen in der Eisenzeit*,[In:] Kelten und Germanen in heidnischer Zeit. Kunst der Welt, ed. H.J. Eggers, R. Joffroy, Baden-Baden, pp. 5 – 87.

Eggers H. J., Stary P. F.
2001 *Funde der Vorrömischen Eisenzeit, der Römischen Kaiserzeit und der Völkerwanderungszeit in Pommern*. Beiträge zur Ur – und Frühgeschichte Mecklenburg – Vorpommerns, Bd. 38, Lübstorf.

Emilov J.
2005 *Changing paradigms: Modem interpretations of Celtic raids in Thrace reconsidered*, [In:] Celts on the Margin. Studies in European Cultural Interaction 7th Century BC – 1st Century AD Dedicated to Zenon Woźniak, ed. H. Dobrzańska, V. Megaw, P. Poleska, Kraków, pp. 103 – 108.

Erzepki B.
1890 *Przedhistoryczne bronzy z Łuszczewa*, [In:] Zapiski Archeologiczne Poznańskie, tom I, ed. W. Jażdżewski, B. Erzepki, Poznań, pp. 53 – 54.

Erzepki B, Kostrzewski J.
1914 *Album zabytków przedhistorycznych Wielkiego Księstwa Poznańskiego zebranych w Muzeum Towarzystwa Przyjaciół Nauk w Poznaniu*, Zeszyt III, Poznań.

Fedorov G. B.
1960 *Naselenie prusko – dnestrovskogo meždureč'ja v I tysjačeletii n.n.* Materialy i Issledovanija po archeologii SSSR, t. 89, Moskva.

Felczak O.
1985 *Cmentarzysko kultury wschodniopomorskiej w Sychowie, gm. Luzino oraz kwestia popielnic z wyobrażeniem rąk*, Pomorania Antiqua, t. XII, pp. 121 – 148.

Filip J.
1956 *Keltové ve středni Evropĕ*, Praha.

Forkiewicz I.
2009 *Monety geto – dackie z obszaru Polski – nowedane*, [In:] Archeologia barbarzyńców 2008: powiązania i kontakty w świecie barbarzyńskim, red. M. Karwowski, E. Droberjar, Rzeszów, pp. 101 – 121.

Gaerte W.
1929 *Urgeschichte Ostpreussen*, Königsberg.
1938 *Bericht über die Tätigkeit des Prussia – Museums im Jahre 1937*, Nachrichtenblatt für Deutsche Vorzeit, 14/5, pp. 113 – 116.

Galewski T., Michalak K.
2011 *Nowy Drzewicz, stanowisko 5. Opracowanie ceramiki osadowej z okresu przedrzymskiego*, Gdańsk (unpublished dissertation).

Gałęzowska A.
1996 *Materiały z młodszego okresu przedrzymskiego i okresu wpływów rzymskich z Kuźnicy Żelichowskiej, w woj. pilskim*, Wielkopolskie Sprawozdania Archeologiczne, t. IV, pp. 155 – 184.

Gancarski J. (ed.)
2004 *Okres lateński i rzymski w Karpatach polskich*, Krosno.

Gawlik A.
2010 *Interpretation of the cultural transformations in the Early Iron Age In South – Eastern Poland and Western Ukraine*, [In:] Migration in Bronze and Early Iron Age Europe, ed. K. Dzięgielewski, M. S. Przybyła, A. Gawlik, Prace Archeologiczne, nr 63, Kraków, pp. 153 – 172.

Gebhard R.
1991 *Die Fibel aus dem Oppidum von Manching*, Die Ausgrabungen in Manching, Bd. 14, Stuttgard.

Gediga B.
2002 *W kręgu kultury Celtów*, [In:] U źródeł Polski. Polska dzieje cywilizacji i narodu do roku 1038, ed. M. Derwich, A. Żurek, Warszawa – Wrocław, pp. 86 – 91.

Gedl M.
1972 *Ze studiów nad schyłkową fazą kultury łużyckiej*, Archeologia Polski, t. XVII, pp. 309 - 348.
1978 *Gräber der Latènekultur in Kietrz, Bezik Opole*, [In:] Beiträge zum Randbereich derLatènekultur, Prace Archeologiczne, nr 26, Kraków.
1985 *Schyłek kultury łużyckiej w Polsce południowo - zachodniej*, Prace Archeologiczne, nr 37, Kraków.
1991 *Die Hallstatteinflüsse auf den polnischen Gebiet in der Früheisenzeit*, Warszawa – Kraków.
2004 *Die Fibeln in Polen*, Prähistorische Bronzefunde, Abteilung XIV, Bd. 10, Stuttgart.

Gensen R.
1963 *Typengruppen in der jungbronzezeitlichen und eisenzeitlichen Keramik zwischen Niederrhein und Wesser*, Germania, 41, pp. 243 – 259.

Ginalski J., Muzyczuk A.
1999 *Stan badań nad osadnictwem celtyckim na Podkarpaciu*, [In:] Na granicach antycznego świata, ed. S. Czopek, A, Kokowski, Rzeszów, pp. 9 – 14.

Godłowski K.
1977 *Okres lateński w Europie*, Archeologia pierwotna i wczesnośredniowieczna, cz. IV, Kraków.
1978 *Zur Besiedlungsveränderungen in Schlesien und die Nachbarräumen während der jüngeren vorrömischen Eisenzeit*, Prace Archeologiczne, nr 26, Kraków, pp. 107 – 133.
1981 *Kultura przeworska*, [In:] Prahistoria ziem polskich, t. V, ed. J. Wielowiejski, Wrocław-Warszawa-Kraków-Gdańsk, pp. 57 – 135.
1985 *Przemiany kulturowe i osadnicze w południowej i środkowej Polsce w młodszym okresie przedrzymskim i w okresie rzymskim*, Wrocław-Warszawa-Kraków-Gdańsk-Łódź.
1992 *Germanische Wanderungen im 3. Jh. v. Chr. – 6. Jh. n. Chr. und ihre Wiederspiegelung in den historischen und archäologischen Quellen*, [In:] Peregrinatio Gothica III, Universitetets Olsaksamlings Skrifter, Nyrekke, 14, Oslo, pp. 53 – 75.
1995 *Die ältere Kaiserzeit in der Umgebung von Kraków*, [In:] Kelten, Germanen, Römer im Mitteldonaugebiet vom Ausklang der Latène –

Zivilisation bis zum 2. Jahrhundert, Brno – Nitra, pp. 83 – 102.

Godłowski K., Woźniak Z.
1981 *Chronologia – późny okres przedrzymski*, [In:] Prahistoria ziem polskich, t. V, ed. J. Wielowiejski, Wrocław-Warszawa-Kraków-Gdańsk, pp. 52 – 53.

Grabarek A.
2011 *Grób jastorfski z młodszego okresu przedrzymskiego z miejscowości Wilcza Wólka, pow. piaseczyński*, Światowit VIII(XLIX)/B, pp. 69-75.

Griesa S.
1982 *Die Göritzer Gruppe*, Berlin.

Grygiel M.
2004 *Problem chronologii i przynależności kulturowej materiałów o charakterze jastorfskim z Brześcia Kujawskiego, woj. kujawsko – pomorskie, w świetle ostatnich badań nad problematyką okresu przedrzymskiego w Polsce*, [In:] Kultura jastorfska na Nizinie Wielkopolsko – Kujawskiej, ed. H. Machajewski, Poznań, pp. 13 – 82.
2012 *Chronologia przemian kulturowych na Nizu Polskim na przełomie starszego i młodszego okresu przedrzymskiego*, Kraków (unpublished dissertation)

Grygiel M., Pikulski J.
2006 *Archäologische Forschungen von 2001 – 2002 an der multikulturellen Fundstelle 1 in Zagórzyce, Gde. Kazimierza Wielka, Wiow. Świętokrzyskie*, [In:] Recherches Archéologiques de 1992 – 2003, Kraków, pp. 136 – 159.

Grygiel M., Pikulski J., Trojan M.
2009 *The research on the multicultural site no. 1 in Zagórzyce, com. And distr. Kazimierza Wielka, voiv. Świętokrzyskie during the years 2003 – to 2004*, [In:] Recherches Archéologiques, Kraków, pp. 199 – 275.

Grygiel R.
1995 *Sytuacja kulturowa w późnym okresie halsztackim i wczesnym lateńskim w rejonie Brześcia Kujawskiego*, [In:] Kultura pomorska i kultura grobów kloszowych. Razem czy osobno ?, ed. T. Węgrzynowicz, M. Andrzejowska, J. Andrzejowski, E. Radziszewska, Warszawa, pp. 319 – 359.

Hachmann R.
1956/1957 *Ostgermanische Funde der Spätlatènezeit in Mittel – und Westdeutschland*, Archaeologia Geographica, 5 - 6 , pp. 55 – 68.
1957 *Jastorf – Funde ausserhalb der Jastrof – Kultur*, Die Kunde, NF 8, pp. 7 – 24.
1961 *Die Chronologie der jüngeren vorrömischen Eisenzeit. Studien zum Stand der Forschung im nördlichen Mitteleuropa und in Skandinavien*, Bericht der Römisch – Germanische Komission, 41, (1960), pp. 1 – 276.
1970 *Die Goten und Skandinavien*, Berlin.

Haevernick Th. – E.
1960 *Die Glasarmringe und Glasperlen der Mittel – und Spätlatènezeit auf dem europäischen Festland*, Bonn.

Harasim P.
2011 *Problematyka importowanych fibul proweniencji lateńskiej w kulturze oksywskiej*, [In:] Między kulturą pomorską a kultura oksywską, ed. M. Fudziński, H. Paner, Gdańsk, pp. 221 – 264.

Hânceanu G. D.
2008 *Ceramica bastarnă din aşezarea de la Roşiori – Dulceşti (jud. Neamţ)*, Archeologia Moldavei, t. XXX (2007), pp. 277 – 286.

Hatt G.
1958 *Nørre Fjand an Early Iron Age Village Site in West Jutland*, Arkæeologisk – kunsthistoriske skrifter, skr. B. 2. 2. København.

Hellebrandt M.
1971 *Előzetes jelentés a Vác-Kavicsbányai Kelta temető 1969 – 1970. Évi feltárásáról*, Archeologiai Értesitő, vol. 98, pp. 176 – 185.

Hingst H.
1959 *Vorgeschichte des Kreises Stormarn*, Die vor – undfrühgeschichtlichen Denkmäler und Funden Schleswig – Holstein 5, Neumünster.
1974 *Jevenstedt. Ein Urnenfriedhöf der älteren vorrömischen Eisenzeit im Kreis Rendsburg-Eckernforde*, Urnenfriedhofe Schleswig-Holstein, 4, Offa-Bücher, 27, Neumünster.
1983 *Die vorrömische Eisenzeit Westholsteins*, Offa – Bücher 49, Neumünster.
1986 *Urnenfriedhöfe der vorrömischen Eisenzeit aus dem östlischen Holstein und Schwansen*, Offa-Bücher 58, Neumünster.
1989 *Urnenfriedhöfe der vorrömischen Eisenzeit aus Südostholstein*, Neumünster.

Holodňak P., Waldhauser J.
1984 *Předduchcovský horizont (fáze LT B1a) v Čechách*, Archeologické Rozhledy, t. 63, pp. 31 – 48.

Horvath L.
1987 *The Surroundings of Keszthely*, [In:] Corpus of Celtic Finds in Hungary, vol. 1, Transdanubia 1, Budapest, pp. 62 – 178.

Hvass S.
1985 *Hodde. Et vestjysk landsbysamfund fra ældre jernalder*, Arkæologiske Studier, vol. VII, København.

Jahn M.
1931 *Die Kelten in Schlesien*, Quellenschriften zur ostdeutschen Vor – und Frühgeschichte, Bd. I, Leipzig.

Jakimowicz R.
1925 *Sprawozdanie z działalności Państwowego Konserwatora Zabytków Przedhistorycznych Okręgu Warszawskiego za rok 1923*, Wiadomości Archeologiczne, t. IX, z.3 - 4, pp. 306 – 331.

Jakimowiczowa Z.
1930 *Miecz celtycki z Żerania w powiecie warszawskim*, [In:] Księga pamiątkowa ku uczczeniu 70 rocznicy urodzin prof. W. Demetrykiewicza, ed. J. Kostrzewski, Poznań, pp. 291 – 300.

Jarosz P., Rodak T.
2006 *Sprawozdanie z ratowniczych badań wykopaliskowych na stanowisku 6 i 7 w Zakrzowcu, gm. Niepołomice, woj. małopolskie*, [In:] Raport 2003 – 2004. Wstępne wyniki badań archeologicznych w strefie budowy autostrad w Polsce za lata 2003-2004, ed. Zb. Bukowski, M. Gierlach, Warszawa, pp. 619 – 634.

Jarysz R.
1999 *Grób kultury przeworskiej z Brodna, stan. 1, gm. Środa Śląska*, Śląskie Sprawozdania Archeologiczne, t. 41, pp. 469 – 474.

Jasnosz St.
1951 *Cmentarzysko z okresu późnolateńskiego i rzymskiego w Wymysłowie, pow. Gostyń*, Fontes Archaeologici Posnanienses, vol. 2, pp. 1 - 282.

Jażdżewska M.
1992 *Cimetière de la Tène III et de la période romaine á Śmiechów (suite)*, [w:] Inventaria Archaeologica Pologne, fasc. LXIV: PL 386 – 392, Warszawa – Łódź.
1994 *Nowe spojrzenie na hełm z Siemiechowa*, Łódzkie Sprawozdania Archeologiczne, t. 1, pp. 63 – 74.
1986 *Ein römischer Legionärshelm aus Polen*, Germania, 64, pp. 61 – 73.

Jażdżewski K.
1939 *Kujawskie przyczynki do zagadnienia tubylczości Słowian na ziemiach polskich*, Wiadomości Archeologiczne, t. XVI, pp. 107 – 161.

Jensen C.-K.
1996 *Chronologische Probleme und ihre Bedeutung fur das Verständnis der vorrömischen Eisenzeit in Süd-/Mitteljütland*, Praehistorische Zeitschrift, Bd. 71, H. 2, pp. 194 – 216.
1997 *Kronologiske problemer og deres betydning for forståelsen af førrmersk jernalder i Syd – og Midtjylland*, [In:] Chronological problems of the Pre-Roman Iron Age in Northeren Europe, ed. J. Martens, Arkæologiske Studier, vol. 7, København, pp. 91 – 106.
2005 *Kontekstuel kronologi: en revision af det kronologiske grundlag for førromersk jernalder i Sydskandinivien*, Aarhus.

Jerem E.
1996 *Zur Ethnogenese der Ostkelten – Späthallstatt – und frühlatènezeitliche Gräberfelder zwischen Traisental und Donauknie*, [In:] Die Kelten in den Alpen und an der Donau Archaeololingua, t. 1, Budapest – Wien, pp. 91 – 110.

Jurkiewicz B., Machajewski H.
2008 *Osada wielokulturowa w Łękach Górnych, gm. Krzyżanów, woj. łódzkie. Osada z okresu przedrzymskiego*, [In:] Via Archaeologica Pultuskiensis, vol. II, pp. 61 – 175.

Kaczanowski P.
1992 *Bemerkungen zur Chronologie des Zustroms romischer Waffenimporte in das Europäischen Barbaricum*, [In:] Probleme der relativen und absoluten Chronologie ab Latènezeit bis zum Frühmittelalter, ed. K. Godłowski, R. Madyda – Legutko, Kraków, pp. 171 – 186.
1996 *Złota moneta celtycka z osady kultury przeworskiej w Kryspinowie, woj. Kraków*, Sprawozdania Archeologiczne, t. 48, pp. 119-133.

Kaczanowski P., Kozłowski J. K.
1998 *Najdawniejsze dzieje ziem polskich (do VII w.)*, Wielka Historia Polski, t. 1, Kraków.

Kaczmarek M.
1995 *Kwestia wydzielenia kultury grobów kloszowych w Wielkopolsce*, [In:] Kultura pomorska i kultura grobów kloszowych. Razem czy osobno, ed. T. Węgrzynowicz, M. Andrzejowska, J. Andrzejowski, E. Radziszewska, Warszawa, pp. 111 – 125.
1999 *Aktualne problemy badań nad kulturą pomorska w Wielkopolsce*, Folia Praehistorica Posnaniensia, t. IX, pp. 135 – 172.

Kamiński L., Kosicki A.
1992 *Wyniki badań ratowniczych przeprowadzonych na birytualnym cmentarzysku kultury celtyckiej w Tyńcu nad Ślężą*, Śląskie Sprawozdania Archeologiczne, t. XXXIII, pp. 51 – 55.

Karwowski M.
1997 *Keltische Glasfunde im polnischen Gebiet*, Przegląd Archeologiczny, t. 45, pp. 33 – 71.
2004a *Latènzeitlicher Glasringschmuck aus Österreich*, Mitteilungen der Prähistorischen Kommision, Bd. 55, Wien.
2004b *Początki osadnictwa kultury lateńskiej na Podkarpaci w świetle szklanych importów celtyckich*, [In:] Okres lateński i rzymski w Karpatach polskich, ed. J. Gancarski, Krosno, pp. 153 – 162.
2005 *The earliest types of eastern Celtic glass ornaments*, [In:] Celts on the Margin. Studies in European Cultural Interaction 7th Century BC – 1[st]Century AD Dedicated to Zenon Woźniak, ed. H. Dobrzańska, V. Megaw, P. Poleska, Kraków, pp. 163 – 171.

Karwowski M., Ginalski J.
2002 *Fragment szklanej bransolety celtyckiej z grodziska "Horodyszcze" koło Sanoka*, Acta Archaeologica Carpathica, t. 37, pp. 67 – 83.

Kasparowa K. V.
1981 *R'jugozapadnych svjazej v processe formirovanija zarubineckoj kul'tury*, Sovetskaja Archeologija (1981/1982), pp. 57 – 79.
1992 *O chronologii i svjazach zarubineckoj kul'tury*, [In:] Ziemie polskie we wczesnej epoce żelaza i ich powiązania z innymi terenami, ed. S. Czopek, Rzeszów, pp. 289 – 302.

Kasprowicz T.
2004 *Stanowisko kultury jastorfskiej w Wojnowie, stan. 23, Gm. Murowana Goślina, woj. wielkopolskie*, [In:] Kultura jastorfska na Nizinie Wielkopolsko – Kujawskiej, ed. H. Machajewski, Poznań, pp. 215 – 233.
2008 *Osada i cmentarzysko ludnościz okresu przedrzymskiego na stanowisku 284 (AUT 192) Poznań – Nowe Miasto*, [In:] Poznań – Nowe

Miasto. Źródła archeologiczne do studiów nad pradziejami i wczesnym średniowieczem dorzecza środkowej Warty, ed. H. Machajewski, R. Pietrzak, Poznań, pp. 225 – 298.

Kaszewska E.

1961 *Materiały z cmentarzyska w Zadowicach, pow. Kalisz (część III)*, Prace i Materiały Muzeum Archeologicznego i Etnograficznego w Łodzi, Seria Archeologiczna, Nr 6, pp. 191-290.

1962 *Cmentarzysko kultury wenedzkiej w Piotrkowie Kujawskim, pow. Radziejów*, Prace i Materiały Muzeum Archeologicznego i Etnograficznego w Łodzi, Seria Archeologiczna, Nr 8, pp. 5 – 78.

1967 *Fibule z późnego okresu lateńskiego i z początku okresu rzymskiego między Prosną a Pilicą*, Prace i Materiały Muzeum Archeologicznego i Etnograficznego w Łodzi, Seria Archeologiczna, Nr 14, pp. 231 – 248.

1969 *Cmentarzysko kultury wenedzkiej w Nowym Młynie, pow. Włocławek*, Prace i Materiały Muzeum Archeologicznego i Etnograficznego wŁodzi, Seria Archeologiczna, Nr 16, pp. 107 – 134.

1975 *Wielookresowe cmentarzysko ciałopalne w Zadowicach, pow. Kalisz*, Sprawozdania Archeologiczne, t. XXVII, pp. 141 – 164.

1977a *Cmentarzysko kultury przeworskiej w Gledzianówku (st. 1), woj. płockie*, Prace i Materiały Muzeum Archeologicznego i Etnograficznego w Łodzi, Seria Archeologiczna, Nr 24, pp. 63 – 232.

1977b *Problem der keltischen Besiedlung in Mittel – und Nordpolen*, [In:] Symposium Ausklang der Latène – Zivilisation und Anfänge der Germanischen Besiedlung im mittleren Donaugebiet, ed. B. Chropovský, Bratislava, pp. 107 – 122.

Kaszewski Z.

1979 *Materiały starożytne z Kałdusa, woj. toruńskie*, Pomorania Antiqua, t. VIII, pp. 155 – 227.

Kaul F., Martens J.

1995 *Southeast european influences in the early iron age in Scandinavia*, Acta Archaeologica, pp. 111 – 160.

Keiling H.

1968 *Die formenkreise der vorrömische Eisenzeit im Norddeutschland und das Problem der Enstehung der Jastorf – Kultur*, Zeitschrift für Archäologie, 2, pp. 161 – 177.

1969 *Die vorrömische Eisenzeit im Elde – Karthane – Gebiet (Kreis Perleberg und Kreis Ludwigslust)*, Beiträge zur Ur – und Frühgeschichte der Bezierke Rostock, Schwerin und Neubrandenburg 3, Schwerin.

1970 *Fundgut von einem Urnenfriedhof der vorrömischen Eisenzeit bei Granzow, Kreis Neustrelitz*, Bodendenkmalpflege in Mecklenburg Jahrbuch (1969), pp. 165 – 230.

Kelemen M.-H.

1987 *Komárom county*, [In:] Corpus of Celtic Finds in Hungary, vol. 1, Transdanubia 1, Budapest, pp. 179 – 230.

Kendelewicz T.

2006 *Sprawozdanie z badań wykopaliskowych stanowiska Wierzchowice 2, pow. Jawor*, [In:] Raport 2003 – 2004. Wstępne wyniki konserwatorskich badań archeologicznych w strefie budowy autostrad w Polsce za lata 2003 – 2004, ed. Zb. Bukowski, M. Gierlach, Warszawa, pp. 317 – 328.

Klindt – Jansen O.

1949 *Foreign influence in Denmark's Early Iron Age*, Acta Archaeologica, vol. XX, pp. 1 – 229.

1953 *Bronzekedelen fra Brå*, Jysk Arkæologisk Selskabs Skrifter, Bd. III, Aarhus.

Kłosińska E. M.

2007 *Lubelszczyzna I Ukraina w młodszych okresach epoki brązu i we wczesnej epoce żelaza – pytania o losy wspólne i niewspólne*, [In:] Wspólnota dziedzictwa archeologicznego ziem Ukrainy i Polski (Łańcut 2005), Warszawa, pp. 213 – 225.

Kobal J.V.

1995/1996 *Manche Probleme der La Tène – Kultur des oberen Theissgebietes (Karpatoukraine)*, Acta Archaeologica Carpathica, t. 33, pp. 139 – 184.

Kobyliński Z., Szymański W.

2005 *Pradziejowe i wczesnośredniowieczne osadnictwo w zespole kemów w Haćkach*, [In:] Haćki. Zespół przyrodniczo – archeologiczny na Równinie Bielskiej, ed. J. B. Faliński, A. Bera, Z. Kobyliński, A. J. Kwiatkowska – Falińska, Białowieża – Warszawa, pp. 43 – 74.

Kohn A., Melis C.

1879 *Materialien zur Vorgesichichte des Menschen im ostlichen Europa, 1 – 2*, Jena.

Kokowski A.

1983 *Stosunki kulturowe na Lubelszczyźnie od II w. p.n.e. do schyłku starożytności (w młodszym okresie przedrzymskim i wpływów rzymskich)*, Archeologiczne Listy, nr 4, pp. 1 – 7.

1986 *Stan i potrzeby badań nad młodszym okresem przedrzymskim i okresem wpływów rzymskich na Lubelszczyźnie*, [In:] Stan i potrzeby badań nad młodszym okresem przedrzymskim i okresem wpływów rzymskich w Polsce, ed. K. Godłowski, R. Madyda-Legutko, Kraków, pp. 181 – 200.

1989 *Krusza Zamkowa. Strefa sepulkralna cmentarzyska z późnego podokresu lateńskiego*, [In:] Miejsce pradziejowych i średniowiecznych praktyk kultowych w Kruszy Zamkowej, województwo bydgoskie, stanowisko 13. Studia i Materiały do Dziejów Kujaw, ed. A. Cofta – Broniewska, Poznań, pp. 65 – 124.

1991a *Lubelszczyzna w młodszym okresie przedrzymskim i w okresie rzymskim*, [In:] Lubelskie Materiały Archeologiczne, t. IV, Lublin..

1991b *Udział elementów celtyckich w strukturze cmentarzyska birytualnego w Kruszy Zamkowej, woj. Bydgoszcz, st. 13*, Archeologia Polski, t. 36, pp. 115 – 149.

2006 *Hrubieszowskie w dobie późnej epoki brązu i w epoce żelaza*, [In:] Dzieje Hrubieszowa, t. I.

Od pradziejów do 1918 roku, ed. R. Szczygieł, Hrubieszów, pp. 49 – 69.

Kolendo J.
1998 *Lugius – człowiek z plemienia Lugiów z inskrypcjami z Narbo (CIL XII 4466)*, [In:] Świat antyczny i barbarzyńcy. Teksty, zabytki, refleksja nad przeszłością, t. I, Warszawa, pp. 213 – 220.
2004 *Karpaty w koncepcjach geograficznych świata antycznego*, [In:] Okres lateński i rzymski e Karpatach polskich, ed. J. Gancarski, Krosno, pp. 13 – 27.

Kolnikova E.
2006 *Význam minci z moravského laténskeho centra Němčice nad Hanou pre keltskú numizmatyku*, Numismatický Sborník, t. 21, pp. 3 – 56.

Kołacz M.
1995 *Osada kultury przeworskiej w Izdebnie Kościelnym, stanowisko 1, gmina Grodzisk Mazowiecki*, Barbaricum, t. 5, pp. 3 – 63.

Kontny B.
1998 *Próba odtworzenia technik walki mieczem w młodszym okresie przedrzymskim. Wpływ formy broni na jej zastosowanie*, Światowit, t. 41/B, pp. 388 – 406.

Kosicki A.
1996 *Der Forschungsstand über die Latènekultur in Niederschlesien*, [In:] Kontakte längs der Bernsteinstrasse (zwischen Caput Adriae den Ostseegebieten) in der Zeit um Christi Geburt, ed. Z. Woźniak, Kraków, pp. 273 – 279.

Kostrzewski J.
1914 *Wielkopolska w czasach przedhistorycznych*, Poznań
1919a *Die Ostgermanische Kultur der Spätlatènezeit*, Teil I – II, Mannus – Bibiothek, Nr 19, Leipzig – Würzburg.
1919b *Kultura lateńska (La Tène) na obszarze b. Królestwa Polskiego*, Przegląd Archeologiczny, nr 1 -2, pp. 2 – 27.
1919-1920 *Badania archeologiczne w Wierzenicy w powiecie poznańskim wschodnim*, Zapiski Muzealne, z. IV – V, pp. 30 – 40.
1921 *Jeszcze o kulturze lateńskiej na obszarze b. Królestwa Polskiego*, Przegląd Archeologiczny, nr 3 – 4 (1920-1921), pp. 114 – 122.
1923 *Wielkopolska w czasach przedhistorycznych*, Poznań.
1926 *Kronenhalsringe*, [In:] Reallexikon der Vorgeschichte, Bd. 7, ed. M. Ebert, Berlin, pp. 106 – 108.
1939 *Kilka osad kultury grobów skrzynkowych i zagadnienie przynależności etnicznej tej kultury*, Przegląd Archeologiczny, t. VI, pp. 273 – 292.
1955 *Wielkopolska w pradziejach*, Warszawa – Wrocław.
1966 *Pradzieje Pomorza*, Wrocław.

Krämer W.
1985 *Die Grabfunde von Manching und die latènezeitlichen Flachgräber von Südbayern*, Die Ausgrabungen in Manching, Bd. 9, Stuttgard.

Krause E.
1973 *Badania archeologiczne na stanowisku 1 w Broniewicach, pow. Mogilno*, Poznań (unpublished dissertation).

Kres B.
1965a *Tymczasowe sprawozdanie z wykopalisk w Żółwinie, pow. Międzyrzecz Wlkp. w 1962 roku*, Materiały Komisji Archeologicznej, nr 1, pp. 44 – 54.
1965b *Osada lateńska w Żółwinie, pow. Międzyrzecz Wlkp.*, [In:] Z badań nad przeszłością Ziemi Lubuskiej. Informator, Zielona Góra.

Krušel'nickaja L. I.
1963 *Kel'tskij pamjatnik v verchnem Podnestrov'e*, Kratkie Soobščenija Instituta Archeologii SSSR, nr 105, pp. 119-122.

Kubicha J.
1997 *Okres lateński i młodszy okres przedrzymski*, [In:] Z archeologii Małopolski. Historia i stan badań zachodniomałopolskiej wyżyny lessowej, ed. K. Tunia, Kraków, pp. 287 – 329.

Kunkel O.
1931 *Pommersche Urgeschichte in Bildern*, Stettin.

Kurnatowski St.
1983 *Paleodemograficzny aspekt przełomu kulturowego w I tyś p.n.e.*, [In:] Przemiany ludnościowe i kulturowe I tysiąclecia p.n.e. na ziemiach między Odrą i Dnieprem, ed. W. Hensel, Wrocław, pp. 21 – 28.
1992 *Próba oceny zmian zaludnienia ziem polskich miedzy XIII w. p.n.e. a IV w. n.e.*, [In:] Zaludnienie ziem polskich miedzy XIII w. p.n.e. a IV w. n.e.. Materiały źródłowe, próba oceny, ed. K. Kaczanowski. Monografie i opracowania SGH, nr 342, Warszawa, pp. 15 – 111.

Langenhan A.
1890 *Fibelfunde in Schlesien*, Schlesiens Vorzeit in Bild Schrift, Bd. V, Nr 4, pp. 95 – 112.

Lasota A., Pawlikowski S.
2009 *Osadnictwo kultury puchowskiej w rejonie podkrakowskim na przykładzie osady w Wieliczce, stan. XI*, [In:] Archeologia Barbarzyńców 2008: powiązania i kontakty w świecie barbarzyńskim, ed. M. Karwowski, E. Droberjar, Rzeszów, pp. 363 – 375.

Laursen J.
1984 *Danske kuglefibler*, Hikuin, 10, pp. 127 – 136.

Leńczyk G.
1956 *Wyniki dotychczasowych badań na Tyńcu, pow. Kraków*, Materiały Starożytne, t. 1, pp. 7 – 49.

Lewczuk J.
1997 *Kultura przeworska na środkowym Nadodrzu w okresie lateńskim*, Poznań.

Lipińska A.

1959 *Wykaz nabytków Muzeum Archeologicznego w Poznaniu w latach 1943 – 1944*, Fontes Archaeologici Posnanienses, t. 10, pp. 243 – 255.

Lorentzen A.

1-1993 *Fibelformen der älteren vorrömischen Eisenzeit nördliche und südlich der Mittelgebirge*, Offa, Bd. 49/50, pp. 57 – 126.

Łaszkiewicz T.

1971 *Cmentarzysko ludności kultury jastorfskiej w Kunowie, pow. Stargard Szczeciński*, Materiały Zachodniopomorskie, t. XVII, pp. 17 – 75.

Łowmiański H.

1962 *Początki Polski*, t. I, Warszawa.

Łuczkiewicz P.

1997 *Miecze lateńskie z obszaru kultury przeworskiej*, [In:] Kultura przeworska, t. III, ed. J. Gurba, A. Kokowski, Lublin, pp. 169 – 225.

2006 *Uzbrojenie ludności ziem Polski w młodszym okresie przedrzymskim*, Lublin.

Łuczkiewicz P., Schönfelder M.

2009 *Gelschaftsstruktur und Zentralorte – auf der Suche nach strukturellen Gemeinsamkeiten in Latène – und Przeworsk – Kultur*, [In:] Archeologia Barbarzyńców 2008: powiązania i kontakty w świecie barbarzyńców, ed. M. Karwowski, E. Droberjar, Rzeszów, pp. 77 – 99.

Łuka L.

1953 *Cmentarzysko z wczesnego i środkowego okresu lateńskiego w Sokołowicach w pow. kościańskim*, Fontes Archaeologici Posnanienses, vol. 3, pp. 98 – 149.

Machajewski H.

1986 *Stan badań nad młodszym okresem przedrzymskim i okresem rzymskim w Wielkopolsce*, [In:] Stan i potrzeby badań nad młodszym okresem przedrzymskim i okresem wpływów rzymskich w Polsce, ed. K. Godłowski, R. Madyda – Legutko, Kraków, pp. 269 – 298.

1999 *Stosunki kulturowe w dorzeczu Parsęty w młodszym okresie przedrzymskim*, [In:] COMHLAN. Studia z archeologii okresu przedrzymskiego i rzymskiego w Europie Środkowej dedykowane Teresie Dąbrowskiej w 65. rocznicę urodzin, ed. J. Andrzejowski, Warszawa, pp. 233 – 245.

2001 *Wygoda. Ein Gräberfeld der Oksywie – Kultur in Westpommern*, Monumenta Archaeologica Barbarica IX, Warszawa.

2002 *Ze studiów nad relacjami kulturowymi na przełomie epoki brązu i żelaza w dorzeczu środkowej Noteci*, Wielkopolski Biuletyn Konserwatorski, t. 1, pp. 7 – 25.

2003 *Wapniarnia, wielokulturowe stanowisko nr 129, gmina Trzcianka, pow. trzcianecko – czarnkowski, woj. wielkopolskie*, Wielkopolskie Sprawozdania Archeologiczne, t. 6, pp. 308 – 323.

2004 *Kilka uwag wprowadzenia*, [In:] Kultura jastorfska na Nizinie Wielkopolsko – Kujawskiej, ed. H. Machajewski, Poznań, pp. 7 – 11.

2006 *Cmentarzysko ludności kultury jastorfskiej z fazy marianowickiej oraz grób z młodszego okresu przedrzymskiego w Troszynie, pow. Kamień Pomorski, stan. 10*, [In:] Goci i ich sąsiedzi na Pomorzu, ed. W. Nowakowski, Koszalin, pp. 83 – 105.

2010 *Studien zur Besiedlung Norgosspolens zur Vorrömischen Eisenzeit. Das Problem der Siedlungen vom Typ Posen – Nowe Miasto*, [In:] Haus – Gehöft – Weiler – Dorf, ed. M. Meyer, Berliner Archäologische Forschungen 8, Berlin, pp. 199 – 216.

2011 *Ze studiów nad okresem przedrzymskim na Pomorzu Zachodnim*, [In:] Między kulturą pomorska a kulturą oksywską, ed. M. Fudziński, H. Paner, Gdańsk, pp. 209 – 219.

Machajewski H., Leciejewska A., Wolanin P.

2011 *Osada ludności z okresu przedrzymskiego i wczesnorzymskiego w Świętym, gmina Stargard Szczeciński, stan. 10*, [In:] XVII Sesja Pomorzoznawcza, vol. 1, Od epoki kamienia do wczesnego średniowiecza, ed. M. Fudziński, H. Paner, Gdańsk, pp.267 – 296.

Machajewski H., Maciejewski M., Niedźwiecki R.

2004 *Wyniki badań na cmentarzysku kultury jastorfskiej w Rosku, gm. Wieleń, woj. wielkopolskie*, [In:] Kultura jastorfska na Nizinie Wielkopolsko – Kujawskiej, ed. H. Machajewski, Poznań, pp. 267 – 271.

Machajewski H., Pietrzak R.

2004 *Z badań nad ceramiką naczyniową z okresu przedrzymskiego w Wielkopolsce*, [In:] Kultura jastorfska na Nizinie Wielkopolsko – Kujawskiej, ed. H. Machajewski, Poznań, pp. 83 – 121.

2008a *Osada ludności z okresu przedrzymskiego na stanowisku 278 (AUT 191) Poznań – Nowe Miasto*, [In:] Poznań – Nowe Miasto. Źródła archeologiczne do studiów nad pradziejami i wczesnym średniowieczem dorzecza środkowej Warty, ed. H. Machajewski, R. Pietrzak, Poznań, pp.153 – 223.

2008b *Osada ludności z okresu przedrzymskiego na stanowisku 226 (AUT 194) Poznań – Nowe Miasto*, [In:] Poznań – Nowe Miasto. Źródła archeologiczne do studiów nad pradziejami i wczesnym średniowieczem dorzecza środkowej Warty, ed. H. Machajewski, R. Pietrzak, Poznań, pp. 299 – 350.

Machajewski H., Rozen J.

2011 *Wielokulturowa osada w Izdebnie Kościelnym, stanowisko 1, gmina Grodzisk Mazowiecki*, Warszawa (unpublished dissertation).

Machajewski H., Wakiewicz B,

1993 *Wyniki archeologicznej penetracji terenowej przeprowadzonej w okolicy Nowego Miasta nad Wartą, woj. poznańskie*, Wielkopolskie Sprawozdania Archeologiczne, t.2, pp. 103 – 113.

Maciałowicz A.
2004 *Dwie interesujące misy z cmentarzyska kultury przeworskiej w Suchowole, powiat sochaczewski – ślad kontaktów wzdłuż tzw. „szlaku bastarneńskiego?*, Barbaricum, t. 7, pp. 43 – 60.
2009 *Nowe spojrzenie na grób nr 94 z Równiny Dolnej (d. Unterplehnen) jako przyczynek do interpretacji wybranych znalezisk z okresu przedrzymskiego w południowo – wschodniej strefie Bałtyku*, [In:] Bałtowie i ich sąsiedzi. Marian Kaczyński in memoriał, ed. A. Bitner – Wróblewska, G. Iwanowska, Warszawa, pp. 183 – 217.
2011 *Pomorze Gdańskie na przełomie starszego i młodszego okresu przedrzymskiego w świetle analizy zewnętrznych oddziaływań kulturowych*, [In:] Między kulturą pomorska a kulturą oksywską, ed. M. Fudziński, H. Paner, Gdańsk, pp. 79 – 120.

Maciałowicz A., Nowakowska M.
2006 *Naszyjniki tzw. koronowane z Kluczowa i Lochstadt. Przyczynek do badań kontaktów Sambii i północnego Mazowsza w młodszym okresie przedrzymskim*, [In:] Pogranicze trzech światów. Kontakty kultur przeworskiej, wielbarskiej i bogaczewskiej, ed. W. Nowakowski, A. Szela, Warszawa, pp. 321 – 334.

Mačinskij D. A.
1973 *Kelty na zemljach k vostoku ot Karpat*, Archeologičeskij Sbornik Ermitaža, t. 15, pp. 52 – 64.

Madsen A.-P., Neergaard C.
1894 *Jydske gravpladser fra den førromerske jernalder*, Aarbøger, Bd. 9, pp. 165 – 212.

Madyda – Legutko R.
1995 *Zróżnicowanie kulturowe polskiej strefy beskidzkiej w okresie lateńskim i rzymskim. Katalog stanowisk*, Kraków.
1996 *Zróżnicowanie kulturowe polskiej strefy beskidzkiej w okresie lateńskim i rzymskim. Tekst*, Kraków.
2004 *Polskie Karpaty w okresie późnolateńskim i okresie wpływów rzymskich. Uwagi dotyczące zróżnicowania kulturowego*, [In:] Okres lateński i rzymski w Karpatach polskich, ed. J. Gancarski, Krosno, pp. 71 – 92.

Makiewicz T.
1975 *Osadnictwo kultury przeworskiej w rejonie Jeziora Pakowskiego*, Poznań (unpublished dissertation).
1976 *Ołtarze i „paleniska" ornamentowane z epoki żelaza w Europie*, Przegląd Archeologiczny, t. 24, pp. 103 – 183.
1977 *W sprawie genezy trackich i dackich ołtarzy i palenisk kultowych*, Przegląd Archeologiczny, t. 25, pp. 179 – 187.
1987 *Znaczenie sakralne tak zwanych „pochówków" psów na terenie środkowoeuropejskiego Barbaricum*, Folia Praehistorica Posnaniensia, t. 2, pp. 239 – 277.
1992 *Odkrycie tzw. grobów psów w Polsce i ich sakralne znaczenie*, [In:] Wierzenia przedchrześcijańskie na ziemiach polskich, ed. M. Kwapiński, H. Paner, Gdańsk, pp. 110 – 117.
2000 *Nieznane odkrycie wielkiego domu halowego z późnego okresu przedrzymskiego w Pile*, Archeologia Historia Polona, t. 8, pp. 297 – 305.
2004 *Osada kultury jastorfskiej na stan. 22 w Pławcach, woj. wielkopolskie*, [In:] Kultura jastorfska na Nizinie Wielkopolsko – Kujawskiej, ed. H. Machajewski, Poznań, pp. 235 – 244.

Makiewicz T., Łaszkiewicz T.
2001 *Znalezisko zapinki kultury jastorfskiej z osady w Sowinkach koło Poznania*, [In:] Instatntia est mater doctrinae. Księga jubileuszowa prof. Władysława Filipowiaka, ed. E. Wilgocki, Szczecin, pp. 71 – 76.

Maksymov E. V.
1999 *Evropejski vplyvy v zarubenec'kij kul'turi*, Archeologia (Kiev), nr 1999/4, pp. 41 – 48.

Malinowski T.
1956 *Nabytki b. Działu Przedhistorycznego Muzeum Wielkopolskiego w Poznaniu w latach 1929 – 1932*, Fontes Archaeologici Posnanienses, vol. VI, pp. 104 – 161.
1979(ed.) *Problemy kultury pomorskiej*, Koszalin.
1981 *Katalog cmentarzysk ludności kultury pomorskiej, t. 2*, Słupsk.
1989 *Kultura pomorska*. Pradzieje ziem polskich, t.1 – 2, Warszaw – Łódź, pp. 716-752.

Marciniak J.
1957 *Cmentarzysko ciałopalne z okresu późnolateńskiego w Wilanowie koło Warszawy*, Materiały Starożytne, t. II, pp. 7 – 174.

Marshall K.
1882 *Heidnische Funde im Weichsel – Nogat Delta*, Schriften der Naturforschenden Gesellschaft in Danzig, N.F. Bd. V, Hf. 3, pp. 1 – 7.

Martens J.
1988 *Borremose Reconsidered. The Date and Development of a Fortified Settlement of the Early Iron Age*, Journal of Danish Archeology, vol. 7, pp. 159 – 181.
1992a *Borremose in North Jutland – a Fortified Settlement of the Early Iron Age*, Barbaricum, t. 2, pp. 102 – 113.
1992b *The Pre-Roman Iron Age Cementary at Kraghede*, Barbaricum, t. 2, pp. 114 – 136.
1994a *On the so-called Kraghede – group – the Pre – Roman Iron Age in North Jutland and its connections with the Przeworsk Culture*, [In:] Kultura przeworska, t. 1, ed. J. Gurba, A. Kokowski, Lublin, pp. 37 – 69.
1994b *Refuge Fort-Fortified Settlement – Central Place? Three years of archaeological investigations in the Borremose Stronghold*, Ethnograpisch – Archäologische Zeitschrift (1994/2), pp. 177 – 198.
1996 *Die vorrömische Eisenzeit in Südskandinavien. Probleme und Perspektiven*, Praehistorische Zeitschrift, Bd. 71, H. 2, pp. 217 – 243.
1997 *The Pre – Roman Iron Age in North Jutland*, [In:] Chronological problems of the Pre – Roman Iron Age in Nortern Europe (1992), ed. J. Martens, København, pp. 107 – 136.

1998 *Local Devlopment or Foreign Influemces. On the Late Pre-Roman Iron Age of North Juthland*, [In:] 20 lat archeologii w Masłomęczu, t. II Goście, ed. J. Illkjær, A. Kokowski, Lublin, pp. 157 – 201.

Martyniak G., Pastwiński R., Pazda S.
1997 *Cmentarzysko kultury przeworskiej w Ciecierzynie, gmina Byczyna, woj. opolskie*, Wrocław.

Maute M.
1993 *Fibeln. Letènezeit. Fibel – Typen und Verbreitung*, [In:] Reallexikon der Germanischen Altertumskunde, Bd. 8, Berlin – New York, pp. 458 – 462.

Mazurek W.
1994 *Badania ratownicze na stanowisku z okresu przedrzymskiego w Wytycznie, stan. 5, woj. Chełm*, [In:] Najważniejsze odkrycia archeologiczne w Polsce środkowo – wschodniej w 1993 roku, Biała Podlaska, pp. 80 - 85.

1995a *Materiały grupy czerniczyńskiej w województwie chełmskim*, [In:] Kultura pomorska i kultura grobów podkoszowych. Razem czy osobno ?, ed. T. Węgrzynowicz, M. Andrzejowska, J. Andrzejowski, E. Radziszewska, Warszawa, pp. 229 – 264.

1995b *Badania sondażowe na osadzie z okresu przedrzymskiego w Leszczynach, stan. 3, gm. Żmudź*, [In:] Informator o badaniach archeologicznych w województwie chełmskim w 1992 – 1993 roku, nr 7, Chełm, pp. 9 – 16.

1995c *Wyniki badań ratowniczych na stanowisku z okresu przedrzymskiego w Wytycznie, stan. 5, gm. Urszulin*, [In:] Informator o badaniach archeologicznych w województwie chełmskim w 1992 – 1993 roku, nr 7, Chełm, pp. 17 – 34.

2001 *Materiały typu jastorfskiego ze stanowiska 5 w Wytycznie, gm. Urszulin, woj. lubelskie*, Wiadomości Archeologiczne, t. LIV (1995 – 1998), pp. 49-57.

Mazurek T., Mazurek W.
1996 *Wyniki badań osady z okresu przedrzymskiego w Wytycznie, stan. 5, gm. Urszulin, woj. chełmskie*, Archeologia Polski Środkowowschodniej, t.1, pp. 75 – 81.

1997a *Kilka uwag na temat tzw. grupy czerniczyńskiej*, [In:] 20 lat archeologii w Masłomęczu, ed. J. Illkjær, A. Kokowski, Lublin, pp. 135 – 148.

1997b *Wyniki badań wykopaliskowych w Wytycznie, stan. 5 i nadzorow archeologicznych na stanowiskach wokół jeziora Wytyckiego w woj. chełmskim*, Archeologia Polski Środkowowschodniej, t. 2, pp. 86 – 94.

2006 *Plemiona barbarzyńskie wśród poleskich błot*, [In:] Badania archeologiczne na Polesiu Lubelskim, ed. E. Banasiewicz – Szykuła, Lublin, pp. 87 – 104.

Meduna J.
1964 *K otázce počátku pohřbivani na plochých keltských pohřebištich na Moravě*, Archeologické Rozhledy, t. 17, pp. 795 – 825.

1980 *Die latènezeitliche Siedlungen in Mären*, Praha.

Megaw J.V.S.
2005 *Notes on two belt-plates of Early La Tène type from Northern Poland*, Pomorania Antiqua, t. 20, pp. 257 – 275.

Merkbuch für Ausgarbungen
1914 *Merkbuch für Ausgrabungen. Eine Anleitung zum Ausgraben und Aufbewahren von Altertümern*, Berlin.

Meyer H.
1897 *Hügelgräber auf dem Bromberge in derHeide des Hofbesitzers Gross-Hahn, Wessenstedt, Kr. Uelzen, Hannover*, Nachrichten über deutsche Altertumskunde, Bd. 8.

Meyer M.
1994 *Funde vom Charakter der Przeworsk – Kultur aus Hessen*, [In:] Kultura przeworska, t. 1, ed. J. Gurba, A. Kokowski, Lublin, pp. 183 – 192.

Michałowski A.
2003 *Powiat wrzesiński w okresie przedrzymskim, wpływów rzymskich i wędrówek ludów*, [In:] Archeologia powiatu wrzesińskiego, ed. M. Brzostowicz, Poznań-Września, pp. 63 – 87.

2004 *Łyżki gliniane z okresu przedrzymskiego z terenów Europy środkowej*, [In:] Kultura jastorfska na Nizinie Wielkopolsko – Kujawskiej, ed. H. Machajewski, Poznań, pp. 123 – 159.

2005 *Przedmioty osobiste jako dar w grobach kultury jastorfskiej z Wielkopolski*, [In:] Do, ut des – dar , pochówek, tradycja. Funeralna Lednickie, Spotkanie 7, ed. J. Wrzesiński, W. Dzieduszycki, Poznań, pp. 163 – 180.

2006 *Kultura jastorfska w Wielkopolsce północnej*, [In:] Pradolina Noteci na tle pradziejowych i wczesnośredniowiecznych szlaków handlowych, ed. H. Machajewski, J. Rola, Poznań, pp. 183 – 199.

2008 *Okres przedrzymski w Wielkopolsce*, [In:] Wielkopolska w dziejach. Archeologia o regionie, ed. H. Machajewski, Poznań, pp. 87 – 105.

2010 *Die Siedlungen der Jastorf – Kultur in Grosspolen*, [In:] Haus – Gehöft- Weiler-Dorf, ed. M. Meyer, Berliner Archäologische Forschungen, 8, Berlin, pp. 169 – 198.

forthcoming *Element sof the Jastorf culture In Wielkopolska. Import of ideas or migration of peoples?*, Veröffentlichungen des Helms – Museums.

Michałowski A., Teska M.
2012 *Nowe odkrycia figurek Feuerbocke z terenów ziem polskich*, Folia Praehistorica Posnaniensia, t. XVI, pp. 331-344

Michałowski A., Rożański A., Wierzbicki J.
2012 *Osady ze stan. 7 w Grabkowie, gm. Kowal, pow. włocławski, woj. kujawsko – pomorskie*, Poznań (unpublished dissertation).

Michałowski A., Żychliński D.
2012 *Zapinka o konstrukcji późnolateńskiej ze schodkowatym kabłąkiem z Grodziszcza, pow. Świebodzin, woj. lubuskie, stan. 12. Przyczynek do poznania rozprzestrzenienia*

się „zachodniogermańskich" form zapinek na obszarach współczesnej Polski, [In:] Z najdawniejszych dziejów. Grzegorzowi Domańskiemu na pięćdziesięciolecie pracy naukowej, ed. A. Jaszewska, Zielona Góra, pp. 365 – 382.

Mielczarek M.
1988 *O monetach greckich wybitych przed końcem I w. p.n.e. znalezionych na obszarze Polski*, Wiadomości Numizmatyczne, XXXII, z.3-4, pp.129 – 159.

Mikołajczak A.
1982 *Północne znaleziska monet geto – dackich*, Prace i Materiały Muzeum Archeologicznego i Etnograficznego w Łodzi, Seria Numizmatyczno – Konserwatorska, t. 2, pp. 5 – 30.

Miroššayová E., Tomášová B.
2004 *Povodie Torysy a Tople v dobe latènskej*, [In:] Okres lateński i rzymski w Karpatach polskich, ed. J. Gancarski, Krosno, pp. 181 – 196.

Montelisu O.
1896 *Den nordiska jernålders kronologi*, Svenska Fornminnesföreningens Tidskrift, 9, pp. 155 – 274.

Muzolf B.
2012 *Zapinka celtycka w Polsce środkowej*, [In:] Z najdawniejszych dziejów. Grzegorzowi Domańskiemu w pięćdziesięciolecie pracy naukowej, ed. A. Jaszewska, Zielona Góra, pp. 181 – 184.

Müller R.
1985 *Grabfunde der Jastorf – und Latènezeit an unterer Saale und Mittelelbe*, Berlin.
2000 *Jastorf-Kultur*, [In:] Reallexikon der Germanischen Altertumskunde, Bd. XVI, ed. R. Müller, Berlin – New York, pp. 43 – 55.

Müller S.
1912 *Vendsyssel – studier III. Jernalderens og fund*, Aarbøger, Bd. 2, pp. 83 – 142.

Mycielska R., Woźniak Z.
1988 *Cmentarzysko wielokulturowe w Błoniu. Część I*, Materiały Archeologiczne, t. XXIV, pp. 5 – 326.

Natuniewicz M.
2006 *Osady z okresu rzymskiego w Kołozębiu i Poświętnem. Studium krytyczne wyników wykopalisk*, [In:] Pogranicze trzech światów. Kontakty kultur przeworskiej, wielbarskiej i bogaczewskiej, ed. W. Nowakowski, A. Szela, Warszawa, pp. 115 – 144.

de Nawarro J.-M.
1959 *Zu einigen Schwertscheiden aus La Tène*, Bericht der Römisch – Germanische Kommision, Bd. 40, pp. 79 – 119.

Neergaard C.
1931 *Nogle sønderjyske fund fra den ælder jœrnalder*, Fra Nationalsmuseet Arbejdsmark, pp. 63 – 80.

Niedźwiecki R.
2005 *Społeczności okresu przedrzymskiego w dorzeczu środkowej Noteci*, Poznań (unpubliched dissertation).

Nowakowski Z.
2006 *Nowe znaleziska z Kamieńczyka, pow. wyszkowski*, Wiadomości Archeologiczne, t. LVIII, pp. 388 – 390.

Oblomskij A. M., Terpilovskij R. V.
1994 *O svjazach nasielenija central'noj Europy i vostoka dneprovskogo levoberež'ja v latenskoe i rannerimskoe vremia*, Kultura przeworska, t. 1,ed. J. Gurba, A. Kokowski, Lublin, pp. 159 – 181.

Okoński J.
2004 *Wyniki ratowniczych badań archeologicznych na stanowisku 2 w Zagórzu, gm. Niepołomice*, [In:] Raport 2001 – 2002. Wstępne wyniki konserwatorskich badań archeologicznych w strefie budowy autostrad w Polsce za lata 2003 – 2004, ed. Zb. Bukowski, M. Gierlach, Warszawa, pp. 257 – 268.

Okulicz J. (Okulicz – Kozaryn J.)
1973 *Pradzieje ziem pruskich od późnego paleolitu do VII w. n.e.*, Wrocław.

Okulicz – Kozaryn J., Nowakowski W.
1996 *In Serch of the Amber Router. Traces of Contacts between South-Eastern Coasts of the Baltic Sea and the Celto-Illyrian and Dacian Territories*, [In:] Kontakte langs der Bernsteinstrasse (zwischen Caput Adriae und den Ostseegebieten) in der Zeit um Christi Geburt, ed. Z. Woźniak, Kraków, pp. 157 – 172.

Olędzki M.
2004 *Transkarpackie powiazania kulturowo – osadnicze w epoce La Tène. Zarys problematyki*, [In:] Okres lateński i rzymski w Karpatach polskich, ed. J. Gancarski, Krosno, pp. 123 – 135.

Pačkova S. P.
1983 *Archeologičeskie issledovanija mnogoslojnogo poselenija Goroševa ternopol'skoj obl.*, Archeologičeskije pamjatniki Srednego Podnestrov'ja, pp. 4 – 63.
1999 *Učast'pryšlogo komponentu u formuvanni zarubynec'koj kul'tury*, Archeologia, nr 1999/4, pp. 24 – 41.
2002 *Pochoval'nyj obrjad zarubinec'koï kul'turi na seredn'omu Podniprov'ï*, Archeologia, nr 2002/3, pp. 27 – 39.

Pačkova S. P., Romanovskaja M. A.
1983 *Pamjatniki karpato – dnestrovskogo regiona konca I tys. do n. e.*, [In:] Slavjane na Dnestre i Dunae, Kijev, pp. 48 – 77.

Parczewski M.
1978 *Denkmäler der Latènekultur von Bachórz Am Mittellauf des San (Südostpolen)*, [In:] Beiträge zum Randbereich der Latènekultur, Prace Archeologiczne Uniwersytetu Jagiellońskiego nr 26, Kraków, pp. 135 – 151.
2000 *Piętnasty sezon badań wykopaliskowych na stanowisku 16 w Bachórzu, pow. Rzeszów*, Materiały i Sprawozdania Rzeszowskiego Ośrodka Archeologicznego, t. 21, pp. 271 – 283.

Parczewski M., Pohorska – Kleja E.
1995 *Najdawniejsze dzieje Sanoka*, [In:] Sanok. Dzieje miasta, Kraków, pp. 45 – 88.

Pare Ch.

2003 *Zur Bewaffnung*, [In:] Bevor die Romer Kamen. Kelten im Alzeyer Land. Katalog zur Sonderausstellung im Museum der Stadt Alzey, 17, November 2003 bis 25. Januar 2004, Alzeyer Geschichtsblatter, Sonderheft 17, ed. Chr. Pare, Mainz, pp. 63 – 68.

Parzinger H.

1993 *Zum Ende der westlichen Lausitzer Kultur – Kulturverhältnisse zwischen Elbe und Warthe während des 5. vorchristlichen Jahrhunderts*, Bericht der Römische – Germanischen Kommission, Bd. 74, pp. 503 – 528.

Pasternak J.

1944 *Der Kronenhalsring von Ulwiwok*, Posener Jahrbuch für Vorgeschichte, Erster Jahrgang, Posen, pp. 103 – 110.

Pastwinski J.

1970 *Wyniki badań wykopaliskowych na cmentarzysku kultury przeworskiej w Ciecierzynie, pow. Kluczbork w latach 1965 – 1968*, Sprawozdania Archeologiczne, t. XXII, pp. 117 – 130.

Pawlak T.

2009 *Cmentarzysko ludności kultury jastorfskiej w Troszynie, stanowisko 10, powiat Kamień Pomorski*, Materiały Zachodniopomorskie (in print).

Pazda S.

1992 *Osada kultury lateńskiej w Radłowicach, gm. Domaniów, woj. Wrocław, w świetle badań w latach 1964 – 1968*, Studia Archeologiczne, t. XXII, pp. 85 – 127.

Pescheck Ch.

1939 *Die frühwandalische Kultur in Mittelschlesien (100 vor bis 200 nach Christus)*, Leipzig.

Peschel K.

1978 *Kelten und Germanen während der jüngeren vorrömischen Eisenzeit (2. – 1. Jh. v.u.Z.*, [In:] Frühe Völker in Mitteleuropa, ed. F. Horst, F. Schlette, Berlin, pp. 167 – 200.

1992 *Zu Bewegungen im Mittelgebirgsraum vor den Kimbern (Belgen – Bastarnen – Sueben)*, [In:] Beträgre zur keltisch-germanischen Besiedlumg im Mittelgebirgsraum, Weimarer Monographien zur Ur – und Frühgeschichte, Bd. 28, pp. 113 – 128.

Petersen E.

1928 *Eine Spätletènezeitliche Siedlung aus Niederschlesien*, Mannus, VI, Ergänzungsband, pp. 59 – 66.

1929a *Die frühgermanische Kultur in Ostdeutschland und Polen*, Berlin.

1929b *Westgermanische Einflüsse in der vorrömischen Eisenzeit Ostdeutschlands und ihre Bedeutung*, Blätter für deutsche Vorgeschichte, H. 6, pp. 10 – 17.

1940 *Bastarnen und Skiren*, [In:] Vorgeschochte der deutschen Stamme. Germanische Tat und Kultur auf deutschen Boden. Dritte Band. Ostgermanen und Nordgermanen, ed. H. Reinerth, Leipzig, pp. 867 – 1489.

Pfutzenreiter F.

1933 *Die vor – und frühgeschichtetliche Besiedlung des Kreises Fraustadt. 2*, Sonderheft der Grenzmärkischen Heimatblätter, Jhrg. 1933, Fraustadt.

Pieta K.

1982 *Die Púchov – Kultur*, Nitra.

1986 *Stand und Notwendigkeit der Erforschung der Púchov – Kultur*, [In:] Stan i potrzeby badań nad młodszym okresem przedrzymskim i okresem wpływów rzymskich w Polsce, ed. K. Godłowski, R. Madyda – Legutko, Kraków, pp. 25 – 49.

2010 *Die keltische Besiedlung der Slowakai. Jüngere Latènezeit*, Archaeologica Slovaca, t. XII, Nitra.

Pieta K., Zachar L.

1993 *Mladšia doba železna (latènska)*, [In:] Najstaršie dejiny Bratislavy, ed. K. Štefaničová, Bratislava, pp. 143 – 209.

Pietraszewski J.

1925 *Notatki archeologiczne z ziemi sandomierskiej. 3. Znalezisko z okresu lateńskiego we wsi Dwikozy, pow. sandomierski*, Wiadomości Archeologiczne, t. IX (1924-25), pp. 122 – 124.

Pietrzak M.

1987 *Rumia. Cmentarzysko z młodszego okresu przedrzymskiego i wpływow rzymskich*, Gdańsk.

Pilarski B., Cyganiewicz P.

2011 *Kruszyn st. 13. Analiza osadnictwa z okresu przedrzymskiego o cechach kultury jastorfskiej*, Warszawa (unpoblished dissertation).

Polenz H.

1971 Mittel – und Spätlatènezeitliche Brandgräber aus Dietzenbach, Landkreis Offenbach am Main, Studien und Forschungen, NF., 4, Langen, pp. 1 – 115.

1978 *Gedanken zu einer Fibel von Mittellatèneschema aus Káysevi in Anatolien*, Bonner Jahrbücher, 178, pp. 181-216.

Poleska P.

2000 *Celtycki warsztat garncarski na osadzie w Krakowie – Pleszowie (stan. 20)*, Materiały Archeologiczne Nowej Huty, t. 22, pp. 75 – 93.

2006 *Celtycki mikroregion osadniczy w rejonie podkrakowskim*, Kraków.

Poleska P., Toboła G.

1987 *Osada grupy tynieckiej kultury lateńskiej na stan. 41 w Krakowie – Krzesławicach, część I*, Materiały Archeologiczne Nowej Huty, t. 11, pp. 8 -119.

Poleska P., Woźniak Z.

1999 *Zabytki typu jastorfskiego z zachodniej Małopolski*, [w:] COMHLAN. Studia z archeologii okresu przedrzymskiego i rzymskiego w Europie Środkowej dedykowane Teresie Dąbrowskiej w 65. rocznicę urodzin, ed. J. Andrzejowski,Warszawa, pp. 379 – 394.

Popko O.O.

1965 *Znichidky bronzovych lenen'skych koronopodibnych prykras v men'skomu rajoni černigivs'koï oblasti*, Archeologia, t. 19, pp. 179 – 182.

Poradyło W.

1997 *Wyniki badań ratowniczych na stanowisku 62 w Medyce, woj. przemyskie na tle zagadnień okresu lateńskiego w górnym i środkowym dorzeczu Sanu*, Rocznik Przemyski, t. XXXVIII/5, pp. 69-92.

Preda V.
1979 *Mondele Geto – Dacilor*, Bucureşti.

Prochowicz R. J.
2006a *Szpila holsztyńska ze stanowiska 4 w Tomaszach, pow. ostrołęcki*, Wiadomości Archeologiczne, t. LVIII, pp. 384 – 388.
2006b *Osada z młodszego okresu przedrzymskiego i okresu rzymskiego w Strzyżowie, pow. hrubieszowski, w świetle badań z lat 1935 – 1937 i 1939*, Wiadomości Archeologiczne, t. LVIII, pp. 265 – 281.
2011 *Zapinka typy Zachow z Pręgowa Dolnego w powiecie Gdańskim*, Wiadomości Archeologiczne, t. LXII, pp. 237 – 241.

Przyborowski J.
1873 *Kilka wycieczek archeologicznych po prawym brzegu Wisły*, Wiadomości Archeologiczne, t. I, pp. 39 – 96.

Przybyła M. J.
2004 *Nowe znaleziska kultury lateńskiej z obszaru Podgórza Rzeszowskiego*, [In:] Okres lateński i rzymski w Karpatach polskich, ed. J. Gancarski, Krosno, pp. 219 – 235.
2009 *Bericht von den Rettungsgrabungen In Lipniki, Fst. 3, Gde. Kańczuga, Kr. Przeworsk, Woiw. Podkarpacie. Saison 2003 – 2004*, Recherches Archeologiques SN., 1, pp. 171 – 198.

von Richthofen B.
1924 *Auf den Spuren alten Siedlungen*, Altschlesien, Bd. 1., Nr 2, pp. 59 – 65.
1927 *Einfuhrungin die Ur – und fruhgeschichtliche Abteilung des Museums Ratibor*, Ratibor.
1931 *Herkunft der Wandelen*, Altschlesien, Bd. 3, pp. 21 – 36.

Rindel P. – O.
1997 *Den keramiske udvikling i sen forromersk og ældre romersk jernalder i Sønderjylland*, [In:] Chronological Problems of the Pre-Roman Iron Age of Northern Europe, ed. J. Martens, Copenhagen, pp. 159 – 167.

Roczniki TN w Toruniu
1905 Roczniki Towarzystwa Naukowego w Toruniu, t. XII, Toruń.

Rogalski B.
2010 *Przemiany kulturowe na Pomorzu Zachodnim i Przednim w młodszym okresie przedrzymskim (III – I w. p. n. e.)*, Szczecin.

Rosen – Przeworska J.
1948 *Zabytki celtyckie na ziemiach polskich*, Światowit, t. XIX (1946-1947), pp. 179 – 322.

Rudnicki M.
1996 *Celtic Settlement at Pełczyńska near Złota*, [In:] Kontakte längs der Bernsteinstrasse (zwischen Caput Adriae und den Ostseegebieten) in der Zeit um Christi Geburt, ed. Z. Woźniak, Kraków, pp. 243 – 256.
2003 *Celtic coin finds from a settlement of La Tène period at Pełczyska*, Wiadomosci Numizmatyczne, R. XLVII/1, pp. 1 – 24.
2005 *Złota moneta celtycka z osady w Pełczyskach, woj. świętokrzyskie*, [In:] Europa Barbaria. Ćwierć wieku archeologii w Masłomęczu, ed. P. Łuczkiewicz, M. Gładysz-Juścińska, M. Juściński, B. Niezabitowska, S. Sadowski,, Lublin, pp. 391 – 404.

Rudnicki et al. (Rudnicki M., Miłek S., Ziąbka L., Kędzierski A)
2009 *Mennica celtycka pod Kaliszem*, Wiadomości Numizmatyczne, R. LIII/ 2, pp. 103 – 145.

Rustoiu A.
1993 *Observaţii privind ceramica Latène cu grafit în pastă din România*, Thraco – Dacica, t. XIV, pp. 131 – 142.

Sadowski J. N.
1877 *Wykaz zabytków prehistorycznych na ziemiach polskich, I, Porzecze Warty i Baryczy*, Kraków.

Schoknecht U.
1991 *Zislow. Ergebnisse archäologischer Untersuchungen*, Beiträge zur Ur – und Frühgeschichte der Mecklenburg – Vorpommerns, 25, Schwerin.

Schubart H.
1953 *Fibeln der älteren Eisenzeit von Quitzenow Kreis Teterow*, Bodendenkmalpflege in Mecklenburg Jahrbuch 1953, pp. 57 –68.
1957 *Zachower Fibeln in Berliner Museum*, Berliner Blatter fur Vor – und Fruhgeschichte, Bd. 6, pp. 81 – 96.

Schwantes G.
1904 *Der Urnenfriedhof bei Jastorf im Kr. Uelzen*, Jahrbuch des Provinzialmuseums, pp. 13 – 26.
1909 *Die Gräber der ältesten Eisenzeit im östlichen Hannover*, Praehistorische Zeitschrift, Bd. I, Heft 2, pp. 140 – 162.
1911 *Die ältesten Urnenfriedhöfe bei Uelzen und Lünenburg*, Urnenfriedhöfe Niedersachsen I, Heft 1-2, Hannower.
1950 *Die Jastorfzivilisation*, [In:] Reinecke Festschrift zum 75. Geburtstag von Paul Reinecke am 25. September 1947, ed. G. Behrens, J. Werner, Mainz, pp. 119 – 130.
1958 *Die Gruppen der Ripdorf – Stufe*, Jahresschrift fur mitteldeutsche Vorgeschichte, Bd. 41/42, pp. 334 – 388.

Schwarz F.
1879 *Nachtrag zu den Materialien zur prahistorischen Kartographie der Provinz Posen*, Posen.

Seidel M.
1996 *Frühe Germanen am unteren Main. Bemerkungen zu neuen Zeugnissen der Przeworsk – Kultur aus Oberhessen*, Germania, Bd. 74, pp. 238 – 247.

Seger H.
1899 *Schlesische Fundchronis*, Schlesiens Vorzeit in Bild und Schrift, Bd. VII, Nr 4, pp. 531 – 558.

1902 Ein *Begräbnisplatz der mittleren La Tènezeit. Beiträge zur Urgeschichte Schlesiens*, Schlesiens Vorzeit in Bild und Schrift, N.F., Bd. II, pp. 31 - 44.

Seroczyński Z., Wysocka M.
2006 *Osadnictwo pradziejowe, wczesnośredniowieczne I nowożytne na stanowisku nr 5 (AUT 27) w Powodowie II, gm. Wartkowice, pow.poddębicki, woj. Łódź*, Poznań (unpublished dissertation).

Seyer H.
1976 *Die regionale Gliederung der Kulturę der vorröomischen Eisenzeit – Stammesgebiete – ersted Wanderungen*, [In:] Die Germanen. Geschichte und Kultur der germanischen Stämmein Mitteleuropa, Bd. I, ed. J. Hermann, Berlin, pp. 186 – 198.

1982 *Siedlung und archaologische Kultur der Germanen im Havel – Spree-Gebietin den Jahrhunderten vor Beginn u. Z.*, Berlin.

Shchukin M. B.
1989 *Rome and the Barbarians in Central and Eastern Europe 1st Century B.C. – 1st Century A. D. part I*, BAR International Series 542, Oxford.

Shchukin M. B., Val'kova T. P., Schevchenko Y.Y.
1992 *New findes of "kronenhalsringe" in the Chernigow region, Ukraine and some problems of their interpretation*, Acta Archaeologica, vol. 63, pp. 39 – 56.

Ščukin M. B., Eremenko V.
1991 *Frage der Datierung keltischer Altertümer in Transkarpatengebiet der Ukraina und einige Probleme der Latène – Chronologie*, Acta Archaeologica Carpathica, t. 30, pp. 115 – 140.

Skowron J.
2002a *Tynki wapienne I naczynia z "polewą" wapienną z osady kulturyprzeworskiej w Antoniewie, stan. 1, woj. mazowieckie. Przyczynek do badań nad wykorzystaniem wapna w młodszym okresie przedrzymskim*, Archeologia Polski, t. XLVII, z.1 - 2, pp. 229 – 244.

2002b *Ausgrabungen auf der Siedlung der Przeworsk – Kultur in Antoniew, Masowien*, Ethnographisch – Archäologische Zeitschrift, 43, pp. 23 – 45.

2006 *Kultura przeworska w dorzeczu środkowej i dolnej Bzury. Monografia osadnictwa*, Poznań.

2008 *Cmentarzysko ludności kultury przeworskiej w Kunach na stanowisku 4, w Wielkopolsce wschodniej*, [In:] Kultura przeworska. Odkrycia – interpretacje – hipotezy, t. 2, ed. J. Skowron, M. Olędzki, Łódź, pp. 11 – 210.

Skrzypek I.
1973 *Archeologiczne badania ratowniczo – zabezpieczające na stanowisku 2 w Karlinie, powiat Białogard*, Koszalińskie Zeszyty Muzealne, t. 3, pp. 70-78.

Sobucki A., Woźniak Zb.
2004 *Nowe materiały kultury jastorfskiej w Wielkopolsce*, [In:] Kultura jastorfska na Nizinie Wielkopolsko – Kujawskiej, ed. H. Machajewski, Poznań, pp. 199 – 214.

Stanczik I., Vaday A.
1971 *Keltische Bronzegürtel „ungarischen" Typs im Karpaten*, Folia Archaeologica, t. 22, pp. 7 – 27.

Stąporek M.
1995 *Najstarsza faza kultury oksywskiej*, Kraków (unpubliched dissertation).

Stöckli W. – E.
1980 *Chronologie der jüngeren Eisenzeit im Tessin*, Veröffentlichungen der Schweizerischen Gesellschaft für Ur – und Frühgeschichte, Antiqua 2, Basel.

Strobin H.
2011 *Ceramika naczyniowa kultury oksywskiej*, Gdańskie Studia Archeologiczne. Monografie nr 2, Gdańsk.

Strzyżewski Cz., Żurawski Zb.
1979 *Sprawozdanie z badań archeologicznych przeprowadzonych w rejonie Trzcianki, woj. pilskie w 1976 r.*, Fontes Archaeologici Posnanienses, vol. 28, pp. 76 – 83.

Szabo M.
1992 *Les Celtes de l'est. Le second âge du fer dans la cuvette des Karpates*, Paris.

1997 *Die Wanderung der Kelten nach Ost – und Südosteuropa*, [In:] Die Welt derKelten, Eberdingen, pp. 147 – 150.

Szenicowa W.
1983 *Badania archeologiczne w Łagiewnikach w woj. bydgoskim*, Komunikaty Archeologiczne, [w:] Badania wykopaliskowe na terenie województwa bydgoskiego w latach 1973 – 1979, Bydgoszcz, pp. 81 – 99.

Szpunar A.
1988 *Cmentarzysko w Łętowicach, gm. Wierzchosławice, woj. Tarnów*, Sprawozdania Archeologiczne, t. 39, pp. 179 – 192.

Świerkowska – Barańska E.
1992 *Sprawozdanie z badań wykopaliskowych osady z okresu lateńskiego i wpływów rzymskich w Młodzikowie, Gm. Krzykosy, woj. poznańskie, stan. 21*, Wielkopolskie Sprawozdania Archeologiczne, t. I, pp. 31 –44.

Tackenberg K.
1925 *Die Wandalen in Niederschlesien*, Vorgesichtliche Forschung, Bd. 1, Heft 2, Berlin.

1926 *Diefrühgermanische Kultur in Schlesien*, Altschlesien, Bd. 1, Heft ¾, pp. 121 – 156.

1930 *Zu den Wanderungen der Ostgermanen*, Mannus, Bd. 22,pp. 268 – 295.

1934 *Die kulturen in Eisenzeit in Mittelss und Wresthannover*, Hildesheim - Leipzig

1963a *Zu den Funden von Lukaschewka im Bezirk Kischinew Moldau Republik*, Alt – Thüringen, Bd. VI, (1962/1963), pp. 403 – 427.

1963b *Eine Fibel südrussischer Firm mit Mittellatèneschema von der Elbemündung*, Die Kunde, N.F., Bd. 14, pp. 169 – 171.

Tankó K.
2005 *"Horn-handled" bowls of the Central Europe Iron Age*, [In:] Celts on the Margin. Studies in

European Cultural Interaction 7th Century BC – 1st Century AD Dedicated to Zenon Woźniak, ed. H. Dobrzańska, V. Megaw, P. Poleska, Kraków, pp. 153 – 162.

Teleagâ E.
2008 *Die La-Tène-zeitliche Nekropole von Curtuiuşeni/Érkőrtvélys (Bihor, Rumänien). Der Forschungsstand*, Dacia N. S., t. 52, pp. 85 – 165.

Teodor S.
1988 *Elemente celtice pe peritoriul est – carpatic al României*, Archeologia Moldovei, t. 12, pp. 33 – 51.

Tezlaff W.
1963 *Sprawozdanie z prac wykopaliskowych w Zarębowie, pow. Aleksandrów Kujawski, i Nowinach, pow. Inowrocław, przeprowadzonych w 1959 roku*, Sprawozdania Archeologiczne, t. XIV, pp. 146 – 153.
1967 *Cmentarzysko z okresu lateńskiego w Zarębowie, pow. Aleksandrów Kujawski*, Slavia Antiqua, t. XIV, pp. 253 – 306.

Tkaciuk M.
1994 *Manifestări culturale din sec. V – Ia Chr.*, Thraco-Dacica, t. XV, pp. 215 – 256.

Tomaszewska I.
1997 *Uwagi na temat celtyckiej pochwy miecza z Warszawy – Żerania*, Archeologia Polski, t. 42, pp. 141 – 154.
1998 *Młodszy okres przedrzymski i okres wpływów rzymskich. Rezultaty ostatnich badań*, [In:] Osadnictwo pradziejowe i wczesnośredniowieczne w dorzeczu Słupianki pod Płockiem. Archeologia Mazowsza i Podlasia, Studia i materiały, t. I, ed. W. Szymański, Warszawa, pp. 65 – 93.

Trachsel M.
2004 *Untersuchungen zur relativen und absoluten Chronologie der Hallstattzeit*, [In:] Universitätsforschungen zur prähistorischen Archäologie, t. 104, Bonn.

Undset I.
1882 *Das erste Auftreten des Eisens in Nordeuropa*, Deutsche Ausgabe von J. Mestorf, Hamburg.

Uzarowiczowa A.
1970 *Nowe znaleziska archeologiczne z powiatu Puławy*, Wiadomości Archeologiczne, t. XXXV/3, pp. 422 – 423.

Venclova N.
1990 *Prehistoric Glass in Bohemia*, Praha.

Vendel E.
1887 *Bornholms Oldtidsminder og Oldsager*, Kjøbenhavn

Venskus R.
1976 *Bastarnen*, [In:] Realleksikon der Germanischen Altertumskunde, Bd. II/1, Berlin – New York, pp. 88 – 90.

Voss A. (ed.)
1880 *Photographisches Album der Ausstellung Praehistorischer und Anthropologischer Funde Deutschlands*, Berlin.

Vulpe R.
1953 *Săpăturile Dela Poieneşti din 1949*, Materiale şi Cercetări Archeologice, t. 1, pp. 213 – 506.
1955 *Le problème des Bastarnes à la lumière des découvertes archéologiques en Moldavie*, [In:] Nouvelles études d'histoire présentees au X-me Congrèş des Sciences Historiques Rome 1950, Bucureşti, pp. 103 – 119.

Waluś A.
1991 *Zabytki metalowe kultury lateńskiej z Rembielina, woj. ostrołęckie*, Barbaricum, t. 2, pp. 89 – 101.

Waluś A., Domaradzka S., Brzóska A.
2010 *Via Archaeologica Masoviensis. Badania archeologiczne na mazowieckim odcinku autostrady A-2*, Warszawa (unpublished dissertation).

Wendowski-Schünemann A.
2000 *Fibeln mit Spatlateneschema vom Typ „Cuxhaven" – Bemerkungen zum Typenkonzept „Hornbek 3a2"*, Nachrichten aus Niedersachsens Urgeschichte, Bd. 59, pp. 105 – 120.

Węgrzynowicz T. (ed.)
1995 *Kultura pomorska i kultura grobów kloszowych. Razem czy osobno ?*, Warszawa.

Wielowiejski J.
1986 *Die spätkeltischen und römischen Bronzegefässe in Polen*, Bericht der Römisch-Germanischen Kommission, Bd. 66, pp. 123 – 320.
1991 *Chronologie und Zustrom von Bronzegefässen aus der späten römischen Republik nach Mitteleuropa*, Acta Archaeologica Carpathica, t. XXX, pp. 141 – 166.

Wiklak H.
1960 *Grób ciałopalny z późnego okresu lateńskiego odkryty w miejscowości Widawa, pow. Łask*, Wiadomości Archeologiczne, t. XXVI/3 - 4 (1959-1960), pp. 392 – 393.

Wiślański T.
1959 *Wynikii prac wykopaliskowych w Strzelcach w pow. mogileńskim w latach 1952 i 1954*, Fontes Archaeologici Posnanienses, t. X, pp. 1 – 95.

Wołągiewicz R.
1959 *Uwagi do zagadnienia stosunków kulturowych w okresie lateńskim na Pomorzu Zachodnim*, Materiały Zachodniopomorskie, t. V, pp. 121 – 143.
1963 *Oblicze kulturowe Pomorza Zachodniego u progu naszej ery*, [In:] Munera Archaeologica Iosepho Kostrzewski oblata, ed. K. Jażdżewski, Poznań, pp. 291 – 311.
1968 *Der östliche Ausdehungsbereich der Jastorf – Kultur und sein siedlungsgeschichtliches Verhältnis zur pommerschen Gesichtsurnenkultur und der jüngeren vorrömischen Unterweicheelsgruppe*, Zeitschrift für Archäologie, Bd. 2, pp. 178 – 191.
1970 *Kultura jastorfska na Pomorzu Zachodnim*, [In:] Materiały do prahistorii ziem polskich, cz. V, Epoka żelaza, ed. W. Hensel, Warszawa, pp. 43 – 66.
1979 *Kultura pomorska a kultura oksywska*, [In:] Problemy kultury pomorskiej, ed. T. Malinowski, Koszalin, pp. 33 – 69.

1981a *Kultura oksywska*, [In:] Prahistoria ziem polskich, t. V, ed. J. Wielowiejski, Wrocław- Warszawa- Kraków-Gdańsk, pp. 156 – 165.

1981b *Grupa nadodrzańska*, [In:] Prahistoria ziem polskich, t. V, ed. J. Wielowiejski, Wrocław- Warszawa-Krakow-Gdańsk, pp. 192 – 196.

1989 *Cmentarzysko w Marianowie i problem schyłkowej fazy kultury łużyckiej na Pomorzu*, [In:] Problemy kultury łużyckiej na Pomorzu, ed. T. Malinowski, Słupsk, pp. 307-321.

1997 *Lubieszewo. Materiały do studiów nad kulturą społeczności Pomorza Zachodniego w okresie od IV w. p.n.e. do I w.n.e.*, Szczecin.

Woźniak Z.

1970 *Osadnictwo celtyckie w Polsce*, Wrocław-Warszawa-Kraków.

1971 *Die jüngste Phase der keltischen Kultur in Polen*, Archeologicke Rozhledy, 23, pp. 504 – 519.

1974 *Wschodnie pogranicze kultury lateńskiej*, Wrocław-Warszawa-Kraków.

1977 *Kulturelle Beziehungen zwischen den Gebieten Polen und der DDR während der Latène – und der frühen römischer Kaiserzeit*, Arbeits- und Forschungsberichte zur sächsischen Bodendenkmalpflege, Bd. 22, pp. 269 – 287.

1979a *Starsza faza kultury lateńskiej*, [In:] Prahistoria ziem polskich, t. IV, ed. A. Gardawski, Wrocław-Warszawa-Kraków-Gdańsk, pp. 209 - 220.

1979b *Chronologia młodszej fazy kultury pomorskiej w świetle importów i naśladownictw pochodzenia południowego*, [In:] Problemy kultury pomorskiej, ed. T. Malinowski, Koszalin, pp. 125 – 148.

1981 *Młodsza faza kultury lateńskiej i grupa tyniecka*, [In:] Prahistoria ziem polskich, t. V, ed. J. Wielowiejski, Wrocław-Warszawa-Kraków-Gdańsk, pp. 248 – 263.

1983 *Przemiany struktur społeczno – gospodarczych plemion celtyckich i ich wpływ na społeczności nad Odrą i Wisłą*, [In:] Przemiany ludnościowe i kulturowe I tysiąclecia p.n.e. na ziemiach polskich między Odrą a Dnieprem, ed. W. Hensel, Wrocław, pp. 69 – 81.

1984 *Keltische Münzen und Münzprägung in Polen*, [In:] Keltische Numismatik und Archäologie, BAR, IS 206, Oxford, pp. 478 – 483.

1986 *Stan i potrzeby badan nad kulturą lateńską w Polsce*, [In:] Stan i potrzeby badań nad młodszym okresem przedrzymskim i okresem rzymskim w Polsce, ed. K. Godłowski, R. Madyda – Legutko, Kraków, pp. 11 – 24.

1988 *Kulturelle und ethnische Veränderungen während der zweiten helfe der 1. Jahrtausends v.u.Z. im Südpolnischen Raum*, [In:] Frühe Völker in Mitteleuropa, ed. F. Horst, F. Schlette, Berlin, pp. 235 – 245.

1990 *Osada grupy tynieckiej w Podłężu, woj. krakowskie*, Wrocław.

1992 *Zur Chronologie der keltischen Siedlungsmaterialien aus Schlesien und Kleinpolen*, [In:] Probleme der relativen und absoluten Chronologie ab Letènezeit bis zum Frühmittelalter, ed. K. Godłowski, R. Madyda – Legutko, Kraków, pp. 9 – 17.

1994 *Wczesna faza kultury przeworskiej na Wyżynie Sandomierskiej*, [In:] Kultura przeworska, t. 1, ed. J. Gurba, A. Kokowski, Lublin, pp. 127 – 145.

1995 *Kultura pomorska a kultura lateńska*, [In:] Kultura pomorska a kultura grobów kloszowych. Rzem czy osobno ?, ed. T. Węgrzynowicz, M. Andrzejowski, J. Andrzejowski, E. Radziszewska, Warszawa, pp. 201 – 212.

1996a *Neue Forschungsergebnisse über die jüngere Latènezeit in Südpolen*, Arheološki Vestnik, t. 47, pp. 165 – 172.

1996b (ed.) *Kontakte längs der Bernsteinstrasse (zwischen Caput Adriae und den Ostseegebieten) in der Zeit um Christi Geburt*, Kraków.

1996c *Kontakte längs der Bernsteinstrasse un der Zeit um Christi Geburt. Vorbemerkungen*, [In:] Kontakte längs der Bernsteinstrasse (zwischen Caput Adriae und den Ostseegebieten) in der Zeit um Christi Beburt, ed. Z. Woźniak, Kraków, pp. 7 – 14.

2000 *Lateńskie dolia z Krakowa – Mogiły*, [In:] Superiores Barbari. Księga ku czci Profesora Kazimierza Godłowskiego, ed. R. Madyda – Legutko, T. Bochnak, Kraków, pp. 301 – 311.

2004a *Rola Karpat zachodnich w okresie lateńskim*, [In:] Okres lateński i rzymskim a Karpatach polskich, ed. J. Gancarski, Krosno, pp. 43 – 70.

2004b *Wędrówki Celtów i ich odbicie w źródłach archeologicznych*, [In:] Wędrówka i etnogeneza w starożytności i średniowieczu, ed. M. Salamon, J. Strzelczyk, Kraków, pp. 123 – 144.

2004c *Problem istnienia celtyckiego nemetonu na Ślęży*, Przegląd Archeologiczny, t. 52, pp. 131 – 183.

2007a *Rola Celtów i kultury jastorfskiej w przemianach kulturowych i etnicznych na ziemiach Polski w 2. połowie I tysiąclecia p.n.e.*, [In:] Wspólnota dziedzictwa archeologicznego ziem Ukrainy i Polski, Warszawa, pp. 390 – 419.

2007b *Zarys problematyki badań nad okresem przedrzymskim (lateńskim) w Polsce i aspekty ich rozwoju w okresie powojennym*, [In:] Pół wieku z dziejów archeologii polskiej, ed. J. Lech, Warszawa, pp. 285 – 322.

2010 *Kontakty mieszkańców ziem polskich ze światem celtyckim u schyłku okresuhalstackiego i we wczesnym okresie lateńskim*, Przegląd Archeologiczny, t. 58, pp. 39 – 104.

2011 *Wybrane problemy badań nad schyłkiem okresu halsztackiego oraz nad okresami lateńskim i rzymskim w Polsce,* [In:] Między kulturą pomorską a kulturą oksywską, ed. M. Fudziński, H. Paner, Gdańsk, pp. 11 – 44.

Woźniak Z., Poleska P.

1999 *Zabytki typu jastorfskiego z zachodniej Małopolski*, [In:] COMHLAN. Studia z archeologii okresu przedrzymskiego i rzymskiego w Europie Środkowej dedykowane Teresie Dąbrowskiej w 65.

rocznicę urodzin, ed. J. Andrzejowski, Warszawa, pp. 379 – 394.

Wróbel M.
1995 *Znalezisko żelaznej zapinki o konstrukcji starolateńskiej z miejscowości Ziemnice, gm. Osieczna, woj. leszczyńskie*, Wielkopolskie Sprawozdania Archeologiczne, t. 3, pp. 159 – 161.

Wydra F.
1939 *Niestronno. Nowe wykopaliska*, Z Otchłani Wieków, R.XIV, z.7 – 8, pp. 100 – 101.

Zielonka B.
1969/1970 *Rejon Gopła w okresie późnolateńskim i rzymskim*, Fontes Archaeologici Posnanienses, vol. 20, pp. 147 – 217.

Zirra V. V.
1991 *Les plus anciennes fibule laténiennes en Romanie*, Dacia, N.S., t. 35, pp. 177 – 184.
1997 *Contribuţii la cronologia relativă a cimitirul de la Pişcolt. Analiză combinatorie şi stratigrafie orizontală*, Studii şi Cercetări de Istorie Veche şi Arheologie, t. 48, pp. 87 – 137.

Zoller D.
1965 *Gräberfelder und Bestattungsbräuche der jüngeren Bronzess und älteren Eisenzeit im Oldenburg Geestgebiet*, Neue Ausgrabungen und Forschungen in Niedersachsen, 2, pp. 102 – 131.

Żychliński D.
2004 *Osada z młodszego okresu przedrzymskiego w Otorowie, pow. Szamotuły, stan. 66*, [In:] Kultura jastorfska na Nizinie Wielkopolsko – Kujawskiej, ed. H. Machajewski, Poznań, pp. 245 – 258.
2008 *Osada ludności kultury jastorfskiej z Paromierza, pow. wolsztyński, woj. wielkopolskie, stan. 19*, Archeologia Środkowego Nadodrza, t. 6, pp. 187 – 198.

Żychliński D., Przybytek M.
2008 *Grób ciałopalny ludności kultury jastorfskiej z Grodziszcza, pow. świebodziński, woj. lubuskie, stan. 12*, Archeologia Środkowego Nadodrza, t. 6, pp. 199 – 213.

Żygadło L.
2002 *Narzędzia żelazne związane z obróbką metali w kulturze przeworskiej*, [In:] Hutnictwo świętokrzyskie oraz centra i ośrodki starożytnej metalurgii żelaza na ziemiach polskich, ed. S. Orzechowski, Kielce, pp. 167 – 176.

www.ingramcontent.com/pod-product-compliance
Lightning Source LLC
Chambersburg PA
CBHW041708290426
44108CB00027B/2896